30 DAYS TO THE TOEFL® CBT

DAVID DANNENBAUM

*TOEFL is a registered trademark of Educational Testing Service (ETS). This book is not endorsed or appoved by ETS.

THOMSON

ARCO

Australia • Canada • Mexico • Singapore • Spain • United Kingdom • United States

An ARCO Book

ARCO is a registered trademark of Thomson Learning, Inc. and is used herein under license by Peterson's.

About The Thomson Corporation and Peterson's

With revenues of US$7.2 billion, The Thomson Corporation (www.thomson.com) is a leading global provider of integrated information solutions for business, education, and professional customers. Its Learning businesses and brands (www.thomsonlearning.com) serve the needs of individuals, learning institutions, and corporations with products and services for both traditional and distributed learning.

Peterson's, part of The Thomson Corporation, is one of the nation's most respected providers of lifelong learning online resources, software, reference guides, and books. The Education Supersite℠ at www.petersons.com—the internet's most heavily traveled education resources—has searchable databases and interactive tools for contacting U.S.-accredited institutions and programs. In addition, Peterson's serves more that 105 million education consumers annually.

For more information, contact Peterson's, 2000 Lenox Drive, Lawrenceville, NJ 08648; 800-338-3282; or find us on the World Wide Web at: www.petersons.com/about

ISBN: 0-7689-1096-X

Printed in Canada

10 9 8 7 6 5 4 3 2 1 04 03 02

About This Book

30 Days to the TOEFL CBT is designed to help you practice the skills you need to perform well on the TOEFL test. The book is divided into 30 one-a-day lessons for your convenience.

The audio CD that accompanies this book contains audio to accompany Days 16, 25, 27, 28, and 29. You should play the CD along with the questions you see in those sections.

For Days 10 through 15, you will practice listening in a "linear" fashion. This means that you will read, instead of hear, the conversations and lectures that accompany the questions. The scripts can be torn out of the book for this purpose; you can also have a friend read the scripts to you while you answer the questions to better simulate the testing experience.

Best of luck on the TOEFL exam!

About The Author

David Dannenbaum has been teaching ESL and TOEFL preparation for more than twenty years. He currently teaches at the Program for American Language Studies at Rutgers University-Newark.

THE 30-DAY PROGRAM

Acknowledgments

The support and patience of Farah Pedley, Mandie Rosenberg, and Bernadette Webster.

My ESL colleagues, from whom I continue to learn, particularly the late George Miller.

For showing me the ropes in test preparation, I want to tip my hat to Brooke Bridges, Atsushi Ohkatsu, and Rob Tallia.

And for more than can be written here, my wife, Lucille.

Day 1

Get to Know the TOEFL Test

Today's Assignment

- Learn the structure of the TOEFL test.
- Learn how the TOEFL test is scored.
- Contact the schools to which you want to apply.
- Take a personal inventory of what you know.

THE STRUCTURE OF THE TOEFL

The TOEFL test has four sections, and you must answer questions in all of them. In most cases, you will use a computer to take the test and answer the questions, and we will provide you with more detailed instructions about the use of computers when you do other days' activities. If you are taking the paper-based test, you will find that the items tested are identical and only the testing interface is different.

The Listening Section

The Listening section tests your ability to understand English as it is spoken in North America. That is, it tests comprehension of main ideas, supporting ideas, important details, and inferences. You will listen to three types of speech: short conversations, long conversations, and lectures. There are between 30 and 49 questions in this section (the number of questions you see on the computer-based test varies).

The Structure Section

The Structure section tests your ability to recognize language that is appropriate for standard written English. You will answer two types of questions in the Structure section: questions that require you to complete a sentence from one of four answer choices and questions that require you to identify an error in a sentence. The language used in both kinds of questions is formal, rather than conversational, English. In this section, you will be presented with anywhere from 20 to 25 questions.

The Reading Section

In the Reading section, you will read short passages similar in topic and style to academic texts used in North American colleges and universities. After each passage, you will answer several multiple-choice questions. This section contains 44 to 55 questions.

The Writing Section

In the Writing section, you will be assigned a topic and will be required to compose an essay about that topic. You must compose an essay in order to receive a total score.

How the TOEFL Test Is Scored

On the computer-based test, you will not use a #2 pencil to fill in answer sheets as you would with a paper-based test. You will use a computer to answer all questions. The Educational Testing Service (ETS) categorizes a large pool of questions according to content and difficulty level. The first question you receive in a computer-adaptive section will be of average difficulty. The next question you get depends on how well you did on the previous question. So, if you answer that first question incorrectly, the next question you receive will be an easier question. If you answer the first question correctly, you will get a more difficult question next. This is how the computer calibrates your "ability level."

However, keep in mind that the difficulty level of your questions affects your total score. For each test level (easy, medium, difficult), there is a maximum score you can obtain. So, a person who receives easy questions based on their performance cannot score as high as a person who receives difficult questions. And, since the computer "decides" your "ability level" within the first five questions, it's imperative to get them right, so you have a chance at a higher score. You cannot return to a question in the computer-adaptive sections once you have confirmed your answer. (The Structure and Listening sections are computer adaptive.)

Now, not every section of the TOEFL CBT test is computer-adaptive. The reading questions are not computer adaptive, but rather are *computer-based,* which means that you can go back and answer questions in the Reading section, but you will still use the computer to read and answer the questions in the section. Your score for the first three sections of the test (Listening, Structure, and Reading) will be available to you as soon as you finish the test. On your computer monitor, you will see a range of scores from the lowest possible score to the highest possible score. These numbers include your scores on the first three sections plus your possible score on the essay. Note that your score becomes final only when your essay is graded, which is done at a later date, so the score you see on screen is approximate.

After viewing your scores on the monitor, you may report your scores to up to four schools you choose on the day you take the test. You also have the option of canceling the scores so that no one receives them.

For more information on the scoring of the TOEFL test, as well as scheduling and application procedures, you must read the current *TOEFL Bulletin,* which you order from the Educational Testing Service at the following address:

TOEFL Services
Educational Testing Service
P.O. Box 6151
Princeton, NJ 08541-6151, USA
Telephone: 609-771-7100
(Princeton, NJ)
Monday – Friday
8:00 a.m. – 8:00 p.m. **Eastern** time
(Phones are busiest all day on Monday.)
Internet: www.toefl.org

Call the Schools to Which You Want to Apply

You should have chosen several schools that you want to apply to. Take the time to contact the registrar's office of each of those institutions. Ask them what score you must achieve on the TOEFL test in order to be admitted. This will help you set your own personal TOEFL goals.

Take a Personal Inventory of What You Know

If you're like many test takers, you have a lot of anxiety about the test. But you need to remind yourself that you know a lot, and here is the place to do it.

Remember: You are an experienced test taker.

Most likely, this is not the first test you have taken. You have taken important tests in your own country: high school examinations, university entrance examinations, occupational license and driver's license exams, etc. You understand the rules of test taking and you know the pressures that you experience during any test. You know that scoring high on any test involves more than answering questions correctly. It also involves the mental stamina needed to concentrate on a subject for a long period of time. It involves knowing what to expect on the test and having strategies for answering questions correctly. This valuable experience will help you prepare for this particular test.

You also know that every test is different in subject matter and structure, and you know this particular test evaluates the English proficiency of people whose native language is not English.

Activity: You should now take a sheet of paper and write down what test-taking strategies you know. You should write the kinds of questions you encountered on other tests you took. You should try to think of the kinds of questions that were difficult for you, and write them down, too.

Remember: You can communicate complicated ideas to others in spoken and written English, and you can understand others when they speak and write in the English language.

You have studied English in a variety of places—in your high school, in your university, or in a school specializing in Teaching English to Speakers of Other Languages (TESOL). Some schools call it English as a Second Language (ESL). You know tenses, parts of speech, clauses, phrases, infinitives, gerunds, conditionals, and many grammar rules. You used these rules as you spoke with teachers and fellow students, with family, friends, and bosses.

You can function in most personal and academic situations. You can use American idiomatic expressions and slang, and you know when to use formal English and when not to. You can ask for, understand, and give directions to a place. You can tell someone how to go through a process, and you can give and follow written and oral instructions. You know how to acquire new vocabulary using an English language dictionary. You know how to write clear, well-constructed, grammatically correct English-language sentences, paragraphs, and essays. You are able to learn and retain information about a variety of topics from English-language books, magazines, brochures, newspapers, etc.

Activity: Write down as many English grammar rules as you can remember. The order and topic of the rules is not important. Write as many as you can in the order that you remember them. Also, write as many tenses as you can for the verbs *to make, to carry*, and *to walk.*

Write down the name of two English-language books that you remember. Write what you remember about the books, including their general subject matter and a few specific facts that you remember learning from them.

Remember: You have learned much and will be able to use your knowledge when you take this test.

If you find yourself lacking in any of the things listed previously, work on them by reading English magazines and newspapers, having conversations in English with anyone you can, and watch English language TV shows, if you can. And read on, we'll make sure you have all the basics covered to take the TOEFL test.

Day 2

Grammar Review—Part I

Today's Assignment

- Review English-language grammar.

The Test of English as a Foreign Language (TOEFL) covers the linguistic skills of listening, reading, and writing, and you must apply all the rules of English language grammar that you have learned. You will not be asked to identify tenses, parts of speech, or kinds of clauses and phrases, but you will have to answer the questions using correct grammar.

Although you should use correct grammar all the time, you need to review only the grammar and tenses that you will probably deal with on the test. Prepositions, phrasal verbs, and idiomatic expressions will be reviewed tomorrow. Today, you will review:

- Present and present progressive tenses
- Present perfect tense
- Past, past progressive, and past perfect tenses
- Future tenses and time clauses
- Present unreal conditionals
- Past unreal conditionals
- Gerunds and infinitives
- Present and past participles as adjectives
- Comparative and superlative adjectives

On the TOEFL test, the perfect progressive tenses (present, past, and future) are not used in questions.

Verb Tenses in General

Your knowledge of tenses will be tested in all sections of the TOEFL test. *Tenses* indicate time and are formed by combining the verb forms with the various time periods that we experience in our lives, such as past, present, and future. Sometimes, we name the time period in our sentences, but more often we don't. We usually indicate the time period using the verb tense.

Periods of time can be called by name or by activity. Events that occupy time, such as "this class," are also considered to be periods of time. Some examples are:

- The *last* meeting (The meeting occurred in the past.)
- The *next* football game (The football game will be in the future.)
- *This* vacation (The vacation is in the present.)

- The *last* election (The election occurred in the past.)

Some tenses need what are called *auxiliary verbs* (or helping verbs) to *help* them indicate time. These auxiliary verbs are:

- To be
- To have
- To do
- Will

PRESENT AND PRESENT PROGRESSIVE TENSES

Present and present progressive tenses deal with the present period of time. Normally, we call an unfinished time period "now," "today," or "the present." Other names for unfinished time are "this week," "this month," and "this year." Unfinished time can last a microsecond or it can last a lifetime.

- Phyllis *washes* the dishes after every meal. (*Simple present tense* indicates repeated action.)

  Phyllis *is washing* the dishes now. (*Present progressive tense* always indicates *now*.)

- John *writes* the advertising for his company. (*Simple present tense*. John does this for a living.)

  John *is writing* an advertisement in his office. (*Present progressive tense* always indicates now.)

The simple present tense has one complication. All persons but one use the same verb form. Let's look at the verb "to write":

- (first person, singular) *I write* advertising for my company.
- (second person, singular) *You write* advertising for your company.
- (first person, plural) *We write* advertising copy for our company.
- (second person, plural) *You write* advertising for your company.
- (third person, plural) *They write* advertising copy for your company.

Notice that for third person above, we only listed the plural form of the verb. That's because the exception is the third person, singular. In this form, the letter *s* is always found at the end of the verb. For example:

- (third person, singular) John *writes* advertising for his company.

PRESENT PERFECT TENSE

The *present perfect* tense is used to indicate actions that are complete in an unfinished period of time, such as:

- This week
- This month
- This year
- This term

All of these periods of time are happening now but will also continue into the future. The present perfect tense is formed by using the simple present tense of the auxiliary verb *to have* plus the past participle of the verb. For example:

- John *has written* twenty-three advertisements this week. (*Present perfect tense*. This week is unfinished.)
- John *has written* more than 200 advertisements since October 1. (The time period began in finished time but continues and is not finished.)

The present perfect tense is also used to indicate an action that occurred in one's lifetime. Some examples are:

- Craig Phillips *has traveled* to Europe many times. (The period of time implied in this sentence is Craig's lifetime.)
- Bill and Mary *have been* married for eight years. (The period of time that Bill and Mary have been married is eight years *now,* but will continue into the future.)

- The airplane for London hasn't taken off yet. (The airplane *will* take off, but hasn't yet.)
- Has John written the advertisement yet? (John will write the advertisement, but hasn't finished yet.)
- What have they taken with them? (*They* are on a trip now that will continue into the future.)

SIMPLE PAST, PAST PROGRESSIVE, AND PAST PERFECT TENSES

The *simple past, past progressive,* and *past perfect* tenses deal with the past. We normally call a finished period of time "then," "yesterday," "last week," "last year," "the past," etc. Finished time can also last a microsecond or a million years. Some examples are:

- John *wrote* four advertisements yesterday. (*Simple past tense.* The action took place in finished time, in the past.)
- John *was writing* an ad at 4:13 p.m. (*Past progressive tense.* In finished time, the action was continuing at a point in time.)
- John *had written* twelve ads by the time I called him. (*Past perfect tense.* Two things happened in finished time. The action of writing took place before the action of calling him.)
- Bill and Mary *were getting married* at this time eight years ago. (The event of Bill and Mary's marriage took place in the past—specifically, eight years ago.)
- The airplane for London *hadn't taken off* when I got to the airport. (This also occurred in the past—the plane *hadn't* taken off, but it eventually did.)
- Had John *written* the advertisement when you saw him? (This asks if John is finished with the advertisement, which means it was completed in the past.)
- What *had they taken* with them? (They have already gone, the action of "taking" things with them occurred in the past.)

FUTURE TENSES AND TIME CLAUSES

Future tenses and *time clauses* are used to indicate action in a period of time that has not started yet. We normally call this period of time "the future," "tomorrow," "next week," "next year," "the next conference," etc. We also refer to the future as "then." Verbs indicating unfinished time use the auxiliary verb "will." For example:

- John *will write* four advertisements tomorrow (*Simple future tense.* The action takes place in a period of time that has not started yet.)
- John *will be writing* an ad at 4:13 p.m. next Wednesday. (*Future progressive tense.* The action continues at a point in a period of time not yet started.)
- John *will have written* twelve ads by the time he goes home tomorrow. (*Future perfect tense.* Two things will happen in time not yet started. The action of writing will take place before the action of leaving the office.)
- Bill and Mary *will get married* at this time tomorrow. (Bill and Mary are not married yet; they will be married in the future.)
- The airplane for London *won't have taken off* at 6:00 p.m. (At 6:00 p.m., the plane will not have taken off yet; it will take off in the future.)
- Will John write the advertisement when you see him tomorrow? (The person being addressed has not yet seen John; the person will see John tomorrow, in the future.)
- What *will* they *be taking* when they go on vacation? (They have not gone on vacation yet.)

Sometimes, a sentence contains a main clause and a clause beginning with "if" or "when." In this case, the verb in the main clause is always in the simple future tense. The clause beginning with "if" or "when" uses the simple present tense. For example:

- I *will visit* Ipanema, when I *travel* to Rio de Janeiro.
- If Robert *studies* Spanish, he *will be able to speak* two languages.

- The teacher *will punish* her students, if they *misbehave*.
- When Felicia *returns* from her trip, she *will take* us to dinner.

Present Unreal Conditionals

Present unreal conditionals describe a situation that does not exist. They have two clauses: a main clause and a clause beginning with *if*. The "if" clause describes the condition, and the main clause describes the effect of the condition. The verbs in the "if" clause use the simple past tense. In the main clause, the verbs use the auxiliary verb *would*, or *could*. Some examples are:

- John *could make* the best grades in his class, if he studied everyday.
- If the airplane for London didn't leave until 6:00 p.m., I *could get* to the airport in time.
- If John wrote ten advertisements every day, he *would be* a very productive employee.
- If Bill and Mary had a wedding reception, they *would get* many wedding presents.

Past Unreal Conditionals

Past unreal conditionals describe a situation that did not exist in finished time. They have two clauses: a main clause and an "if" clause. The "if" clause describes the condition, and the main clause describes the effect of the condition. The verbs in the "if" clause use the past perfect tense. In the main clause, the verbs use the auxiliary verbs *would have*, or *could have*.

- John *could have made* the best grades in his class, if he had studied everyday.
- If the airplane for London hadn't left until 6:00 p.m., I *could have gotten* to the airport in time.
- If John had written ten advertisements everyday, he *would have been* a very productive employee.
- If Bill and Mary had had a wedding reception, they *would have gotten* many wedding presents.

Gerunds

Gerunds are the present participle form (*-ing* form) of a verb that can also be used a noun. Like nouns, gerunds can be subjects, objects, or complements:

- *Running* is my favorite form of exercise. (The gerund *running* functions as subject of the sentence.)
- She hates *skiing*. (The gerund *skiing* functions as the object of the sentence.)
- My favorite pastime is *hiking*. (The gerund *hiking* functions as the complement here.)

Like verbs, gerunds can take objects (in italics) as well:

- I love eating *chocolate* more than anything!
- Reading a good mystery *novel* relaxes many people.
- Running a *marathon* is an accomplishment!

Possessive adjectives are often used with gerunds on the TOEFL test. Some examples are:

- *Tom's* writing is not as effective as *his* speaking.
- *Her* driving was too fast and careless.
- *Our* showing up late to parties always annoys our friends.

Infinitives

Infinitives are formed by combining the particle *to* with the simple form of the verb. They may also act as nouns, and they can function in the same way as nouns and gerunds.

- *To live* with roommates requires patience. (Infinitive as a subject)
- She does not like *to study*. (Infinitive as an object)
- My greatest wish is *to travel* to China. (Infinitive as a complement)

Like gerunds, infinitive nouns can take objects or predicate adjectives.

- To run *a marathon* is an accomplishment!

PRESENT AND PAST PARTICIPLE AS ADJECTIVES

The *present participle* and the *past participle* sometimes function as adjectives. Some examples are:

- The TV journalist reported some *breaking* news. (The present participle *breaking* acts as an adjective.)
- The *broken* window made the house look shabby. (The past participle *broken* acts as an adjective.)
- The *melting* ice cream ran down the side of the cone. (The present participle *melting* acts as an adjective.)
- The *melted* chocolate ice cream left a brown stain on my coat. (The past participle *melted* acts as an adjective.)

The present and past participles, when used as modifiers, often have different meanings. For example, let's look at the verb *to interest*, which means "to cause a person to feel curious about someone or something, or to give one's attention to."

- Dr. Martinez is an *interesting* professor. (Dr. Martinez causes her students to listen to her lectures with interest.)
- Dr. Martinez is an *interested* professor. (She pays attention to her students and to their problems.)

Here are some other examples:

- The *boiling* water will cook the egg. (The water is boiling now.)
- The *boiled* egg is in the refrigerator. (Someone cooked the egg and put it in the refrigerator.)

COMPARATIVES AND SUPERLATIVES

Comparatives and *Superlatives* are adjectives that compare things. The comparative of an adjective is formed by adding an *-er* to the end of the adjective. Usually, the adjective is followed by *than*. For example:

- Bill is quiet.
- Josh is *quieter than* Bill.

Superlative adjectives are formed by adding *-est*. The word *the* always precedes the adjective. If the adjective has three syllables or more, the superlative is formed by adding *the most* or *the least* in front of the adjective. Let's look at these sentences:

- John is *the tallest* boy in this class.
- Her father is *the most generous* person I know.
- I think the pine tree *is prettier than* the oak.
- Marsha was *the prettiest* bride I have ever seen.

Note: This review did not cover every grammar rule for the English language. Today's assignment covered specific rules that are likely to be covered on the TOEFL test.

Day 3

Grammar Review—Part II

Today's Assignment

- Review prepositions, phrasal verbs, and idiomatic expressions.

PREPOSITIONS—WHAT THEY DO IN A SENTENCE

Prepositions demonstrate a relationship between their objects, which may be either nouns or pronouns, and another word in the sentence. The prepositions are in bold in the following sentences:

- I used to play guitar **in** a band.
- Phyllis shopped **for** a new dress.
- The cat was **next to** the window.

Prepositional phrases are made of a preposition and its object, plus any articles or adjectives that modify the object. They act as modifiers themselves, and they may function as either adjectives or adverbs. Look at the following examples (the prepositional phrases are in bold):

> The book **on the table** is mine. (Adjective modifying *book*)

> The cat jumped **on the table**. (Adverb modifying *jump*)

Useful Rules about Prepositional Phrases

The object of the preposition is never **I, she, he, we,** or **they**. If a prepositional phrase ends with a pronoun, that pronoun must be one of the following: **me, you, her, him, it, us, them, mine, yours, his, hers, ours,** or **theirs**. For example:

> The bird was **above** ***me*** in the sky.

> The Harrisons are close friends **of** ***ours***.

> The dog sat **between** ***you*** **and** ***me*** on the floor.

The last example is worth a second look. Many people say "The dog sat by you and I." This is incorrect. A good way to figure this out is to say the sentence to yourself removing the word "you." It would be incorrect to say "The dog sat by **I**," you would say "The dog sat by **me**." So, you know that *me* would be correct—"The dog sat by you and **me**."

When the prepositional phrase ends with a gerund, which is the *-ing* form of the verb acting as a noun, the gerund may or may not take an object. For example:

She gave the child a piece of candy **for** ***answering***
preposition *gerund*

the question correctly.
object of the gerund

Before **exercising,** you should always warm up.
preposition *gerund*

Many articles and modifiers may occur between prepositions and their objects.Modifiers also may follow the object. For example:

Amy told us **about the** ***new, recently released***
preposition *modifiers*

video, ***now being rented.***
object *modifiers*

Common Prepositions

You frequently will encounter the following prepositions on the TOEFL test:

above	before	during	onto	to
about	behind	for	opposite	under
across	below	from	out	until
after	beneath	in	over	up
along	between	into	past	within
alongside	beside	near	round	
among	by	off	since	
at	down	on	through	

Phrasal Prepositions

On occasion, you will come across a preposition that is formed from two or more words, called *phrasal prepositions*. These prepositions are used in all three sections of the TOEFL test, but seldom will you be required to deal with them in a question.

because of	in on
due to	off of
down from	out from under
from. . .to	out of
in front of	up from

Common Mistakes

There are some common mistakes people make with English grammar, with prepositions in particular, and you can anticipate that the TOEFL test will contain questions with the following problems:

The prepositions **between** and **among** have different meanings. **Between** indicates the relationship of one thing to another. **Among** is used with three or more nouns. For example:

The President stood **between** Senator Brown and Senator Jackson.

The professor walked **among** her 30 students.

Another common mistake is to confuse the object of a prepositional phrase with the subject of a sentence. For example, in the following sentence which verb form is correct?

That group of friends **go** to the restaurant together every Friday.

or

That group of friends **goes** to the restaurant together every Friday.

The correct answer is **goes.** In the sentences, the object of the preposition **of** is *friends*, which is plural. You may, under the pressure of test taking, decide that **go** should agree with the plural *friends* that is closer to the verb but that is incorrect. Remember that the verb must agree with the subject of the sentence, which in the above sentences is **group**, a singular noun.

Note: Sometimes prepositions are used as part of verbs.

- How do you tell the difference between prepositions that are used in phrasal verbs and prepositions that are not?

Look at these sentences:

1. Are you going to stop or walk on?
2. Do not walk on the freshly painted floor.

1. In the first sentence, the verb is **to walk on**, which means "to continue walking." The preposition **on** is part of the phrasal verb, **to walk on**. The phrasal verb means to continue. The phrasal verb, in this case, has no object. That is, it is not followed by a noun or pronoun.
2. In the second sentence, the preposition **on** is not part of the verb **walk**. It begins a prepositional phrase that tells us where not to walk.

PHRASAL VERBS AND IDIOMATIC EXPRESSIONS

The following phrasal verbs are often found on the TOEFL exam, and you should *look them up* in the dictionary if necessary, which will help you to learn them better.

as a matter of fact

ask for

be a flop

be head and shoulders above someone

be late in the day for something

be out of circulation

be saddled with something

be up in the air

come from

come into

come over

come to

cram for an exam

cross that bridge when one comes to it

count someone in

do business with

do homework, exercises, etc.

do someone a favor

do something for someone

do well

draw a blank

find out

get along with

get a word in edgewise

get a running start

get better

get down

get dressed

get in touch with

get into

get on

get out of

get over

get something done

get through to

get through with

get together with

get up

give away

give credit to someone

go by a means of transportation

go over to

go through

have an appointment with someone

have breakfast, lunch, etc.

have in mind

have nothing to do with

have one's own problems

have someone do something

have too much on one's mind
have trouble with
in fact
I wouldn't miss it!
It's about time!
know something like the back of one's hand
look into
Looks can be deceiving.
look out for
look over something
look something over
look up something
make a living
make a mistake
make a mountain out of a molehill
make plans
make something from scratch
paddle one's own canoe
pass out
pursue a career
raise a lot of eyebrows
read one the riot act
rub salt into a wound
same here
school of hard knocks
slip one's mind
spreads oneself too thin
surf the Internet
sweep something under the carpet
something is over one's head
something is beyond someone
take a break
take an exam
take a vacation
take care of
take into account
take off
take over
take the time to do something
take the words right out of one's mouth
turn down
white elephant

Day 4

Test-taking Strategies for Listening Comprehension

Part A, Short Conversations

Today's Assignment

- Learn what to look for in Part A of the Listening Comprehension section.

LISTENING COMPREHENSION PARTS A & B

The TOEFL Listening Comprehension section has two parts. In Part A, which you are about to study, you will listen to short conversations between a man and a woman. After each conversation, you will answer questions about what you heard. In Part B, which you will study tomorrow, you will listen to long conversations and lectures, and you will answer questions after each conversation or lecture.

To complete both Part A and Part B, you will be given 15 to 25 minutes. The time you spend listening to the conversations and lectures is not counted. Your time begins when the question is asked.

TIME PRESSURE

At this point, many students experience anxiety and worry that they won't be able to finish the questions in the allotted time. This is what we call *time pressure*. You overcome this pressure by using what you know of the English language and the people who speak it. You also reduce your test anxiety by knowing what to expect from the test.

LISTEN TO PEOPLE, NOT TO A LANGUAGE

When you have a conversation, you don't listen to a language. You listen to people who have a reason for speaking. They do not plan their words according to rules in a book; they speak their thoughts spontaneously. To emphasize ideas, people use gestures—they shrug their shoulders and point their fingers. They use their face—they raise their eyebrows in surprise or wink as they share a secret with you. These facial expressions and gestures help you understand what people want to communicate.

EMPHASIZED WORDS

In the Listening Comprehension section of the TOEFL test, there will be a photo to accompany what you hear, but you can't see the speaker actually speak, so you have to depend totally on what you hear. To prepare for this, you need to practice listening to English language conversations without seeing the speaker's face or body. To do this, have English-language conversations on the telephone and listen to talk shows and news programs on the radio. When you do, you will notice that people emphasize words in their sentences and phrases.

For example, read the following sentence silently. Notice that every word receives equal emphasis:

Maria's brother is an English professor.

However, if you read the sentence *aloud*, you can change the meaning of the sentence by putting stress on different words. For example, read the same sentence aloud, stressing the word in **boldface**.

Maria's brother is an English professor.

If you speak the words this way, you are telling your listeners that it is important for them to understand that *Maria's* brother, not Tina's brother or anybody else's bother, is an English professor. Now, read the next sentence with the following emphasis:

Maria's **brother** is an English professor.

In this sentence, you are telling your listeners that it is important for them to understand that you are speaking about Maria's *brother*, not her sister, cousin, or any other relative. Now, read the next sentence with a new emphasis:

Maria's brother **is** an English professor.

By speaking the sentence that way, you are implying that someone believes that Maria's brother is not an English professor and you are correcting the misinformation. Now, read the sentence so that it communicates a completely different idea:

Maria's brother is an **English** professor.

Now you are telling your listeners that he is a professor, not of physics, or history, or Spanish, but of *English*. The final example again demonstrates another new meaning:

Maria's brother is an English **professor**.

Now you are making it clear that Maria's brother is not an English politician or banker. He is a professor and teaches in an English department of a university.

Emphasis is an important part of the conversations you will hear during the Listening section of the TOEFL.

COMMUNICATING THROUGH CONTEXT

When you have a conversation in English, you do not follow all the rules of grammar that you learned in ESL or English language classes. Sometimes, you answer in incomplete sentences and phrases that would be incorrect if you used them in a written classroom assignment. You and your conversation partners understand each other because you use the context of the conversation you are having.

If you hear the following incomplete sentences, you might not understand what they are talking about.

(Speaker A): As a gorilla.

(Speaker B): Where?

(Speaker A): At the ball.

(Speaker B): When?

(Speaker A): Last night.

However, you would have understood those phrases if you had heard the first two sentences of the conversation.

(Speaker A): You should have seen the costume that the president of the college wore to the ball last night.

(Speaker B): How was she dressed?

(Speaker A): As a gorilla.

(Speaker B): Where?

(Speaker A): At the ball.

(Speaker B): When?

(Speaker A): Last night.

In many TOEFL conversations, you will hear incomplete sentences. You will not be confused by them, because you will always hear the conversations from the start.

THE TYPES OF QUESTIONS IN PART A

Part A of the TOEFL consists of 10–20 questions. For each question, you will hear a short conversation between a man and a woman. The conversation, no longer than three or four sentences, is followed by a question from a third person who is called the "narrator."

While the people are speaking, there will be a picture on your screen. During Part A, you do not have to study the picture. Give all your attention to what the speakers are saying, because the questions in Part A are never about what you see. They are always about what you hear the speakers say.

After the conversation, the narrator will ask a question, and only then will you see the question on the screen. Unlike the TOEFL PBT, the TOEFL CBT does not allow you to read the questions while you are listening to the conversation.

After you hear the narrator ask the question, there is a slight pause of about three seconds, and then you will see four (4) possible answers on the monitor screen. With your computer mouse, click the oval on the left side of your answer choice.

You may change your answer, if you want. After you have made your final choice, click on the "NEXT" box in the lower right hand corner of the screen. To go to the next question, click on the "ANSWER CONFIRM" box.

Please note that you cannot return to the answer choices once you have clicked "ANSWER CONFIRM."

Meaning Questions and Distracters

In *meaning* type questions, you will hear the conversation, and after the conversation, the narrator will ask, "What does the man (or woman) mean?"

The answers to meaning questions will be easy for you to find because they are always in the second speaker's speech. Usually, the second speaker uses an idiomatic expression, and the incorrect answer choices have words that are part of that expression. Read the following example carefully:

(Woman): The recreation room in the dorm is open at night, isn't it?

(Man): It's easy enough to find out.

(Narrator): What does the man mean?

(A) He doesn't know whether the recreation room is open.
(B) He will help the woman find the recreation room.
(C) He doesn't want to go out tonight.
(D) He can't read well enough to help the woman.

The man does not answer the question directly with a yes or no. He says, "It's easy enough to find out." When we talk about "finding out" something, it means we do not know the answer and want to get the necessary information. So, what does the man mean?

The correct answer is (A), "He doesn't know whether the recreation room is open." The other answer choices use distracters.

Distracters take your attention away from the correct answer. They often use words found in the idiomatic expression used by the second speaker. But the words are not used with the whole phrase, so they have a meaning that differs from that of the correct answer. Choice (B) uses the verb "find," which means "to locate." The man and the woman know where the recreation hall is, so they don't have to locate it.

Choice (C) uses "go out," but the man and woman do not talk about leaving the dorm. Choice

(D) uses the word "enough" from the expression "easy enough." These distracters are similar to ones you will find in the TOEFL.

Infer/Imply Questions

When you *imply* something, you express an idea without saying it directly. For example:

(Woman): How did you like the Rembrandt exhibit?

(Man): I was in the hospital the whole time it was at the museum.

(Narrator): What did the man imply?

(A) The man is a physician.

(B) The man doesn't like museums.

(C) The man didn't see the Rembrandt exhibit.

(D) The man will go to the museum tomorrow.

The man answers the woman's question, but not directly. He was in the hospital while the Rembrandt exhibit was at the museum, so he could not have seen it. Therefore, choice (C) is correct.

Did you spot the distracters? Choice (A) implies that the man is a doctor. But the conversation is not about the man's profession. It's about whether he saw the exhibit. The second answer choice implies that the man prefers hospitals to museums, but his preferences are not the subject of the conversation. The fourth answer choice is a distracter that is incorrect, even though it uses the word "hospital" from the man's answer. The man said nothing about going to the museum.

Look at the man's answer again: "I was in the hospital the whole time *it was at the museum*." The words in italics tell us that the exhibit is no longer at the museum. Which bring us to infer questions.

When we *infer*, we come to a conclusion based on the information we gain from what others write or say. On the TOEFL test, infer questions are usually about the entire conversation. Let's look at the following example:

(Man): Wow, I feel like I was run over by a ten-ton truck! I'll be glad when finals are over!

(Woman): I know what you mean. I didn't get to bed until 2:00 a.m. last night.

(Narrator): What can be inferred about the conversation?

(A) The man and the woman have been travelling all night.

(B) The man and the woman are tired from studying for exams.

(C) The man and the woman were in an accident.

(D) The man and the woman stay up late every night.

Choice (B) is correct. The idiomatic expression, "feel like I was run over by a ten-ton truck," means that the person is very tired. He also mentions "finals," which means final examinations. The woman's reply, "I know what you mean," is a statement of agreement. She too is exhausted and will be glad when finals are over.

Did you catch the distracters? Choices (A) and (C) try to distract you with words about driving. Choice (D) is something neither said nor implied.

Action Questions

Some questions on the TOEFL test ask questions about actions. Some typical action questions are as follows:

What will the man (or the woman) probably do?

What does the woman (or the man) suggest the man (or woman) do?

What will the man and woman probably do next?

Now, look at an example of an action question:

(Woman): I couldn't find anything on our research topic in the library.

(Man): Same here. Hey! What about the Internet?

(Narrator): What will the man and woman probably do next?

(A) Look for information at a Web site.
(B) Find another topic that is more interesting.
(C) Go to another library.
(D) Get a book about tropical rainforests.

Note that the man speaks only in incomplete sentences and idiomatic expressions. "Same here" means that the man can't find anything at the library either. When he says, "What about the Internet?" he means, "We should look up our research topic on the Internet."

The first answer choice is correct. The others are distracters using parts of the conversations and sound-alike words, such as "tropical" for "topic" and "interesting" for Internet.

An Answer in Three Seconds

After the narrator asks the questions, it takes about three seconds for the answer choices to appear on the screen. Sometimes, you can use that three seconds to think of the answer in your own words. If you can do that, then all you have to do is look for the answer choice that is closest in meaning to your answer.

Practice, Practice, Practice

To *know* the strategies means to *practice* them. In Days 11 and 12 of this book, there are short conversations and questions that will help you use the strategies that you have learned today.

Summary of Strategies for Listening Comprehension, Part A

1. You will hear conversations between two people, a man and a woman.
2. You will also hear another person, the narrator, ask the question that you must answer.
3. You will see the question about the conversation on the screen when the narrator asks it.
4. You will hear the narrator ask one of three kinds of questions: Meaning, Infer/Imply, and Action.
5. You will read four possible answers to the question. Only one of the four will be correct.
6. You will recognize the distracters that the test maker has used in the answers.
7. You will select the one correct answer by clicking the oval to the left of the correct answer.
8. You will change your answer by clicking another oval, if you want.
9. You will click with the computer mouse the "NEXT" box in the lower-right corner of the screen.
10. You will go to the next question by clicking the "ANSWER CONFIRM" box.

Remember:

- When you click "ANSWER CONFIRM," you cannot go back to the question that you just answered.
- Knowing what kinds of questions to expect on a test will help you increase your score.

Day 5

Test-taking Strategies for Listening Comprehension

Part B. Long Conversations and Lectures

Today's Assignment

- Learn what to look for in Part B of the Listening Comprehension section.

General Information

In Part B of the listening section, there will be 11–30 questions about long conversations and lectures.

You will listen to long conversations between two students or between a student and a school official, usually a counselor or a professor. During these conversations, students may go over lecture notes before a test, a professor may help a student with choosing a major, or a counselor may talk to a student about getting a scholarship. As in Part A, one of the speakers will be a woman, and the other will be a man.

Sometimes the conversations will take place in a classroom, where a professor will lead a discussion. In this case, you will hear two or three students and the teacher.

The conversations will last anywhere from 2–4 minutes. At the end of the conversation, you will answer 2–4 questions asked by the narrator.

You will also listen to lectures by professors on topics that you would expect to study in a university. The lectures last 2–3 minutes. At the end of a lecture, you will answer 4–6 questions.

What to Listen For

You cannot take notes during the long conversations or lectures, so you must retain a lot of information in your memory. The information must be based on what you hear and see.

In Part A, it was unnecessary for you to pay attention to the pictures on the screen. However, in Part B, you will have to. Before you hear a long conversation or lecture, you will read on the screen the topic of the conversation or lecture. For example, on the screen you might read the words "Summer School." And you will hear the narrator say the following:

(Narrator): Listen to two students discuss a study trip abroad that they are about to make.

Make sure you pay attention to what the narrator says in his introduction. It will contain clues about the main idea. It will also give you clues about what the students will be saying. They will probably name the country they will visit and the subject they are going to study. Also, they will probably mention how they will travel and how long the trip will last. It is logical that that information will be the subject of the questions you will be asked. Anticipating the information and the questions will help you listen for information you will need to answer the questions.

The same techniques should be used for lectures. For example, on the screen you read "History of Printing," and you hear the narrator say, "Listen to a lecture about the development of printing in Imperial China." What clues do the screen and the narrator's words give you?

The lecture will not be about modern printing machines and processes such as computer layout software and digital photo reproduction. However, the narrator's words give you hints that the lecturer will name and describe processes first developed in China during the times of the emperors. The lecturer will probably mention dates and define in two or three words a particularly important process. Because you listened for this kind of information, you will be able to answer the questions about these topics.

Exercise: Anticipating the Questions

Here are three subjects followed by the narrator's descriptions. Write down 3 possible questions that you will have to answer. At the end of this chapter, you will find some sample questions that look like the questions that might be asked on the test.

1. On the screen, you read "History of Philosophy." You hear the narrator say, "Listen to a lecture about the American philosopher and teacher, William James."

2. On the screen, you read "Meeting with an Adviser." You hear the narrator say, "Listen to a conversation about a student's plan for her senior year."

3. On the screen, you read "Chemistry." You hear the narrator say, "Listen to a lecture to beginning students in a chemistry laboratory."

Rhetorical Questions and Questions That Professors Ask Students

People ask *rhetorical* questions not to get information but to emphasize a point. The answer to a rhetorical question is always obvious. During a conversation about grades, a student might ask something like the following:

(Student): Who wants to get a failing grade?

The answer to the question is obvious, and the question is an emphatic way of saying "No one wants to get a failing grade." Pay close attention to rhetorical questions, because they contain a topic that you will be asked about.

Sometimes, during a long conversation, the professor will ask a student for information about the assignment, a question that is *not* rhetorical. Pay close attention to the student's answer, because it is likely to be an answer to one of the questions about the conversation.

Question Types

Knowing the kinds of questions you will be asked will reduce your test-taking anxiety. On the TOEFL exam, there are some questions for which you will have to choose only *one* correct answer (single-answer questions). For other questions, you will have to choose *two* correct answers (multiple-answer questions). And some questions ask you to match items or put items in order; we'll call those *interactive* questions.

Single-answer Questions

There are four kinds of single-answer questions:

1. Main Idea
2. Detail
3. One of Four Letters
4. One of Four Pictures

Main Idea Questions

Many times the first question you will be asked is about the main idea of the lecture. These questions are usually like the following:

- What is the main purpose of the lecture?
- What is the main topic of the professor's talk?
- What is the professor mainly discussing?

You will be able to answer these questions because you paid attention, not only to the lecture itself, but also to the words on the screen and the narrator's description before the lecture began.

Detail Questions

These questions ask for specific information you heard in conversations and lectures. They are usually like the following:

Where did William James teach?

How many credits does the student need for graduation?

According to the speaker, where are all chemicals and other supplies stored?

You will be able to answer the detail questions because you anticipated them and listened for the information that contained the answers. The answers contain no idiomatic expressions that might confuse you. Three of the four answer choices were probably not mentioned in the lecture or they were mentioned in connection with another subject, that was not asked about.

One of Four Letters Questions

At least once during the test, you may see a picture, map, or a diagram that the lecturer uses to communicate ideas. If you do, be aware that you will *definitely* be asked questions about it.

On the screen you will see a picture or diagram, which may or may not be the same as the one used in the lecture. Parts of the diagram or picture are labeled (A), (B), (C), and (D). At the top of the computer screen, you will read a question that will also be asked by the narrator. The question will be similar to the following:

- Click on the letter that indicates the metatarsal bones.
- Click on the letter next to the Arial Sea.
- Click on the letter that indicates the Silk Road.

Using your mouse, move the cursor to the correct letter, then point and click the letter that best answers the question. As with the other questions, click on the "NEXT" icon and then the "ANSWER CONFIRM" icon.

One of Four Pictures Questions

For this type of question, you will see four pictures instead of one, and under each picture is a box with a letter (A), (B), (C), or (D). The questions are always about specific information that the lecturer gave during the talk. You will be asked to choose the picture that best answers the question. To do so, point and click the correct letter.

Multiple-answer Questions

On occasion, you will be asked to choose *two* correct answers from the four choices. It is not as difficult as you might think. Most of the time the two incorrect answers are not mentioned in the conversation or the lecture. Sometimes they relate to another subject that was talked about during the conversation or lecture. The following question shows how the question will be phrased:

According to the speaker, which two twentieth-century painters were associated with the abstract expressionist movement?

(A) Jackson Pollock

(B) Georgia O'Keefe

(C) Andrew Wyeth

(D) Mark Rothko

Interactive Questions

Matching Questions

When a speaker discusses classifications and examples, you should anticipate a matching question. In this kind of question, you will be asked to match items, usually three, with names of categories. For example:

> Based on the discussion, classify the following types of poetry.
>
> Click on the title of the poem. Then, click on the space where it belongs. Use each title only once.
>
> *Beowulf*
>
> *My Last Duchess*
>
> *The Tyger*
>
> | Quatrain | Epic | Dramatic Lyric |
> |---|---|---|

Order Questions

Sometimes, you will hear the speaker discuss a process, or you might hear them discuss things that occur in a chronological order. The speaker will stress the order and tell you that it is important. The order might involve a process, such as the stages of development of a butterfly, or a series of events in history. Order questions will be similar to the following:

> The professor explains the process of printing a lithograph.
>
> Click on a sentence. Then, click on the space where it belongs.
>
> Use each sentence only once.
>
> *The paper is pressed to the plate.*
>
> *Ink sticks to the lacquer but not to the wet plate.*
>
> *The plate is wetted and the lacquer rejects the water.*
>
> *The image to be printed is put on the plate and lacquered.*
>
> 1. [ ] 2. [ ]
>
> 3. [ ] 4. [ ]

To answer order questions, follow this procedure:

1. Read all of the sentences.
2. Choose the sentence that is the first one in the chronological order (the box marked Number 1).
3. Choose the sentence that is last (the box marked Number 4).
4. This will make choosing the middle sentences easier.

Note the order of the boxes. The boxes for Number 1 and Number 2 are next to one another. Make sure you do not put sentence Number 2 in the box for sentence Number 3.

ANTICIPATING THE QUESTIONS

Here are possible questions that you might anticipate while listening to long conversations and lectures. It's okay if you think of questions other than those listed below. What's important is your getting the habit of anticipating the questions so you will not be surprised when questions appear on the screen.

1. On the screen, you read "History of Philosophy." You hear the narrator say, "Listen to a lecture about the American philosopher and teacher, William James."

   Possible Questions:

   Where did William James teach? What was the name of his philosophy? What famous scientists and philosophers did he work with? When did he live?

2. On the screen, you read "Meeting with an Adviser." You hear the narrator say, "Listen to a conversation about a student's plan for her senior year."

   Possible Questions:

   How many credits does the student need to graduate? What is her major? What is she planning to do after she graduates? What does the adviser tell the student to do?

3. On the screen, you read "Chemistry." You hear the narrator say, "Listen to a lecture to beginning students in a chemistry laboratory."

   Possible Questions:

   According to the speaker, where are all chemicals and other supplies stored? What is the job title of the speaker? How long is a typical laboratory session? How often does a student go the chemistry laboratory.

PRACTICE EXERCISES

Directions: Read the script and then answer the questions that follow. You may have someone read the script to you, if you wish. The answers are listed at the end of this chapter.

Exercise 1

On the screen, you will see the words "Roman History" and a picture of two gladiators in the arena of the Coliseum in Rome.

(Narrator): Listen to a professor lecture about Roman gladiators.

(Professor): We get the word "gladiator" from the Latin word gladius, which means "sword." Gladiators were professional fighters in ancient Rome who originally performed at Etruscan funerals, to the death. The Etruscans believed that dead gladiator would become an armed attendant in the next world to the honoree of the funeral.

At shows in Rome, gladiatorial contests became extremely popular and increased from three pairs at the first known exhibition in 264 B.C.E. to 300 pairs by 44 B.C.E. The contests lasted for as many as 100 days. The triumphal shows honoring the emperor Trajan had 5,000 pairs of gladiators.

There were many different kinds of gladiators, classed by their weapons or modes of fighting. The Samnites fought with the national weapons—a large oblong shield, a visor, a plumed helmet, and a short sword. Thracians used a small round shield and a dagger curved like a scythe. Mirmillones, who usually fought Thracians, wore a helmet, and carried a sword and shield.

The retiarius, or "net man" always fought with a net in his right hand and a trident in his left. His method of killing was to tangle his opponent in the net and stab him with the trident. Some gladiators fought from chariots, and others protected themselves by wearing suits of armor. Yet another group, called the laquearii, or "lasso men," who tried to lasso their antagonists like cowboys did to cattle in the American West.

As Christianity grew in influence in the Roman Empire, gladiatorial shows became unpopular, and the emperor Constantine I formally abolished these contests in C.E. 325, but without much effect. They were abolished again by the emperor Honorius (393–423), but may have continued for a century after that.

1. What is the main idea of the lecture?

   (A) Gladiators were brave fighters.

   (B) There were many classes of gladiators.

   (C) Gladiators fought to honor the dead.

   (D) There were gladiators in many different countries.

2. According to the professor, what weapons did the "net man" fight with?

   Choose two answers.

   (A) A net

   (B) A small round shield

   (C) A dagger

   (D) A trident

3. How did Christianity influence gladiatorial contests?

   (A) Christianity increased the popularity of the games.

   (B) Christianity gave power to the "lasso men."

   (C) Christianity became more and more popular.

   (D) Christianity led to the abolishment of the games.

Exercise 2

On the screen, you will see the words "Architecture and Building Construction" and a picture of Bamboo scaffolding outside a building in Hong Kong.

(Narrator): Listen to a seminar of students discussing bamboo as building material.

(Professor): Marsha and Brad are going to speak to us today about unusual building materials and methods.

(Marsha): What we found was unusual in Europe and the Western Hemisphere, but not in Asia. In Hong Kong, which is filled with skyscrapers, they have kept practicing an ancient Chinese construction technique. While erecting buildings, they surround their buildings with a scaffolding of bamboo poles. This scaffolding is no different from what was used by builders in China 1,000 years ago, and it is used most commonly to give bricklayers and tile workers a platform on which to do exterior work.

(Professor): I thought the Chinese government had banned the use of such scaffolds, particularly on buildings taller than six stories.

(Brad): The government on the mainland is afraid that the quality of bamboo has deteriorated in recent years. There are rumors that Beijing may soon ban them altogether. Nevertheless, bamboo is legal in Hong Kong, and it is still used for a lot of construction projects. Bamboo scaffolds often rise fifty or sixty stories.

(Professor): Is that safe?

(Marsha): Well, the experienced construction workers believe that bamboo is as strong as steel, and it bends in high winds. That is an important quality in Hong Kong, where typhoon winds often hit half-finished skyscrapers. The bamboo survives the storm, but steel scaffolding is usually destroyed.

(Brad): And there's an aesthetic element to consider. Bamboo scaffolds have slender, hollow rods arranged in a graceful crosshatch pattern. They are, in fact, elegant and though they support the construction of thirty- to sixty-story buildings, the poles are usually no thicker than a man's clenched fist. And there is a serious training program for workers who assemble the bamboo scaffolding. Marsha, tell them what you found.

(Marsha): Young workers serve as apprentices to bamboo masters for three years, washing their clothes and carrying their lunch pails while learning the art of lashing poles. Apparently, an experienced bamboo worker knows exactly how thick a bamboo pole must be to support a multistory framework above it.

1. What kind of class did this discussion take place in?
   (A) A Chinese History class
   (B) An environmental safety class
   (C) An architecture class
   (D) A personnel management class
2. When does the Chinese government allow construction companies to use bamboo for scaffolding?
   (A) When the building is no taller than six stories
   (B) When there is a typhoon
   (C) When apprentices are being trained
   (D) When steel scaffolding is not available
3. How long do apprentices study the skills of lashing bamboo poles?
   (A) One year
   (B) Three years
   (C) Five years
   (D) Seven years

ANSWER KEY

Exercise 1

1. B
2. A and D
3. D

Exercise 2

1. A
2. D
3. B

Day 6

Test-taking Strategies for Structure

Sentence Completion

Today's Assignment

- Learn about sentence completion questions.

Section two of the TOEFL test is called the Structure section and will last from 15 to 20 minutes. You will be asked to answer two kinds of questions: sentence completion and error identification. The paper-based test separates these two types of questions into two sections, collectively called Structure and Written Expression. But on the CBT, both kinds of questions are mixed together into the Structure section. Today, you will learn about the sentence completion questions.

THE FORMAT OF THE SENTENCE COMPLETION QUESTION

On the computer monitor, you will see an incomplete sentence that has four answer choices underneath it. You are to choose the answer that would be grammatically correct when placed in the blank. Each answer choice on the CBT is preceded by a blank oval that looks like this: ❍. To mark your choice, you move your mouse to the oval next to your answer choice and click it. When you click the oval, it becomes black, and will look like this: ●.

Please note: *For ease of study, we have used (A), (B), (C), and (D) in place of ❍ in this book, as in the example below.*

Look at the following example of a sentence completion question:

1. ________ must have great skill and concentration.
   - (A) With race car drivers
   - (B) While race car drivers
   - (C) Race car drivers
   - (D) They are race car drivers

The correct answer is (C).

WHAT'S TESTED IN SENTENCE COMPLETIONS

Sentences That Begin With "There is..." and "There are..."

In addition to the grammatical forms that you reviewed in Days 4 and 5, there is another grammatical structure that appears in this section of the test, and that is the use of the phrases "There is" and "There are" at the beginning of a sentence. Examine the following sentences:

- *There is* a supermarket next to the library.
- *There are* 700 children in this school.

When you encounter this type of sentence on the test, you will always see the blank at the *beginning* of the sentence. Look at the following example:

Example

_______ a supermarket next to the library.

(A) They are

(B) There is

(C) The

(D) Is there

The correct answer is (B). *There* is a singular pronoun that refers to the singular noun, *supermarket*. The other answers are incorrect. The word *they* is a plural pronoun, which cannot refer to a singular noun such as supermarket. The word *the* is an article that, by itself, cannot be the subject of a sentence. Choice (D), *Is there,* contains the word order of a question, and since the example sentence does not end with a question mark (?), the sentence is a statement, not a question.

Proper Use of Tenses

Sentence completions will also present questions with answer choices that have contrasting tenses. In such a case, you must look at the sentence and determine whether the sentence takes place in unfinished time (the present), finished time (the past), or time not yet started (the future). Look at the following questions, determine the correct time period for each one, and write you decision next to the sentence:

1. William Jones _______ on his next birthday.
2. During every class meeting, students _______ only in the laboratory.
3. In the last election, _______ in large numbers.

Now, let's look at each of these sentences more in-depth:

1. Sentence 1 is in time not yet started (future). You should notice the clue "next birthday," since terms that include the word *next*, such as *next class, next week,* etc., tell you that the time is not yet started. So, this tells you that the answer must be a verb in one of the future tenses. Below is an example of a correct answer to this sentence:

   William Jones <u>will be 18</u> on his next birthday.

2. Sentence 2 is in unfinished time (present). You see the clue "during every class meeting," and terms that include the word *every,* such as *every day, every week,* and *every baseball game,* indicate repeated events or activities in unfinished time. Therefore, the correct answer has to contain a verb in the simple present tense. Look at an example of a correct answer to sentence 2:

   During every class meeting, students <u>use chemicals</u> only in the laboratory.

3. In sentence 3, the clue is "last election," since terms that include the word *last,* such as *last week, last semester,* and the *last party,* indicate finished time (past). The correct answer, then, must contain a verb in the simple past. Look at an example of a correct answer:

   In the last election, <u>voters turned out</u> in large numbers.

Simple Present and Present Progressive Tenses

In the Structure section, you will encounter questions that seek to confuse you with the simple present and present progressive tenses. Choose the answer with the correct tense in the following question:

The sciences and the humanities _______ each other in good educational programs.

(A) complement

(B) are complementing

(C) complemented

(D) will complement

The correct answer is (A). The time period is unfinished time, because there are no clues to indicate finished time, or time not yet started. Choice (C) is incorrect because it is in the simple past tense. Choice (D) is also incorrect because it is in the simple future tense, and we have already decided that the answer calls for a verb that indicates unfinished time. Choice (B) is in the present continuous tense, which is incorrect because the sentence is about a *general situation*, not an activity currently in progress.

Let's look at another example. Choose the correct tense in the following question:

> The volcano's lava ________, which is a danger to the villages on the mountainside.
>
> (A) flowed at a fast rate
>
> (B) will flow at a fast rate
>
> (C) is flowing at a fast rate
>
> (D) had flowed at a fast rate

The correct answer is (C). The clue about the time period comes from the simple present tense of the verb "is" in the clause "which *is* a danger to the villages on the mountainside." The present continuous tense *is flowing*, in choice (C), is correct, because the lava *is* flowing *now*. The other answers contain verbs in incorrect time periods.

The Present Perfect and Simple Past Tenses

In conversation, you may hear someone say, "I went to the supermarket today," which is correct in colloquial, informal conversational speech. But it is incorrect for the kind of English that you will encounter during the test. Verbs in the simple past tense, such as *went*, always indicate finished time, and the word *today* indicates unfinished time. Therefore, the correct way to say the sentence is to use the present perfect tense, "I *have gone* to the supermarket today."

Incorrect or informal English will *never* appear in the Structure section. However, you will often see questions that try to trick you into making incorrect choices between the present perfect and the simple past tenses in formal, written English. Choose the correct verb tense in the following example:

> Although he was an avid hunter, Ernest Hemingway ________ after tigers in India.
>
> (A) was going
>
> (B) has never gone
>
> (C) never went
>
> (D) never goes

The correct answer is (C). The clue to the time period is in the clause, "although he *was* an avid hunter." The verb is in the simple past tense, which places the sentence in finished time. The tenses used in choices (B) and (D) indicates unfinished time. The verb in choice (A) contradicts the clause "although he was an avid hunter."

Choose the correct verb tense in the following example:

> Astronomers at the Hansen Observatory ________ no fewer than 12 meteor showers since May.
>
> (A) record
>
> (B) have recorded
>
> (C) recorded
>
> (D) are recording

The correct answer is (B). The action has thus far been "completed" *since May*—a period of time that began in May but is not yet finished. Choices (A) and (D) are in unfinished time, but are not completed actions. Choice (C) takes place in finished time.

Simple Past and Past Perfect Tenses

The questions involving these tenses seek to confuse you about finished time. You learned on Day 2 that the past perfect tense is always involved in two actions in finished time. The first action is expressed in the past perfect, and the second action is expressed in the simple past. Look at the example:

> When Lincoln arrived in Washington for his inauguration in 1861, many Southern sympathizers had threatened his life.

In this sentence, there are two actions: (1) Southern sympathizers threatened Lincoln's life, and (2) Lincoln arrived in Washington. The Southern sympathizers threatened Lincoln *before* he arrived in Washington, so the verb is in the past perfect tense, *had threatened.* Complete the following sentence with a verb in the correct tense:

In the eighteenth century, science was separated from philosophy, and intellectuals __________ smaller and smaller subdivisions of knowledge.

(A) was beginning to study

(B) had begun to study

(C) was begun studies of

(D) began to study

The correct answer is (D). The verbs in the sentence do not involve a before-and-after situation, so the simple past tense, *began*, is used. Choice (A) is incorrect because in this sentence the action *begin* is not continuous. Also, the verb *was beginning* is used with singular subjects, and *intellectuals* is a plural noun.

Complete the following sentence with the verb in the correct tense:

Robespierre ordered the execution of André Chénier, because Chénier __________ in the legal defense of Louis XVI, who was guillotined a year earlier.

(A) was assisting

(B) had assisted

(C) assisted

(D) has assisted

The correct answer is (B). Chénier assisted in the legal defense of Louis XVI *before* Robespierre ordered his execution.

Present Unreal Conditional Tense

You can identify sentences that use the *present unreal conditional* tense easily. There are two clauses, a main clause and a clause that begins with *if.* The verbs in the main clause use auxiliary verbs *could* or *would* with the simple form of the verb. Read the example below:

If the Hubbell Telescope *stopped* operating, science *would lose* a source of valuable scientific information about the universe.

The questions involving this kind of sentence will offer answers with incorrect tenses and incorrect auxiliary verbs. Identify the correct answer of the following:

If the President of the United States became ill, the Vice President ________ the position temporarily.

(A) might have taken

(B) will take

(C) has taken

(D) would take

The correct answer is (D). The other answer choices do not fulfill the requirements of the present unreal conditional. Choose the correct answer of the following:

The earth would freeze if the sun _______ all its fuel.

(A) burned up

(B) had burned up

(C) would burn up

(D) burns up

The correct answer is (A). It is the only answer in the *simple past tense.*

Past Unreal Conditional Tense Sentences

You can recognize sentences that use the *past unreal conditional* tense by the past perfect tense in the *if clause*, and the auxiliary verbs *would have* and *could have.*

If fifteenth-century superstition *had been* correct, Columbus *would have sailed* off the edge of the earth.

World literature *would have lost* a great deal if Shakespeare *had stayed* in Stratford and *become* a teacher.

The questions will have answers in various tenses and with incorrect auxiliary verbs. Choose the correct answer of the following question:

If General Lee had not taken the Confederate army to Gettysburg, the Civil War ________ longer.

(A) did not last

(B) might last

(C) could have lasted

(D) has lasted

The correct answer is (C). It is the only answer that uses the auxiliary verbs *could have*. Choose the correct answer of the following:

James Whistler would have painted the Roman forum, if he ________ to Italy.

(A) traveled

(B) had traveled

(C) was traveling

(D) has traveled

The correct answer is (B). It is the only answer in the *past perfect* tense.

Day 7

Test-taking Strategies for Structure

Error Identification

Today's Assignment

- Learn about Error Identification questions.

WHAT ARE ERROR IDENTIFICATION QUESTIONS?

Error identification questions appear in the Structure section of the TOEFL test. On the screen, you will see a sentence with several words and phrases underlined. One of the underlined parts contains an error in grammar or usage. Your job is to correctly identify the part of the sentence that contains the error. On the computer screen, you will see a sentence like the following:

One of the two South American countries not bordering Brazil is Ecuador, and the another one is Chile.

During the CBT, you will move the arrow and click on the underlined part of the sentence that contains the error. In the above sentence, you would click on the underlined phrase **the another.**

For the error identification exercises in this book, you will read sentences like the following:

One of (A) the two South American countries (B) not bordering (C) Brazil is Ecuador, and the another (D) one is Chile.

In this format, you will select the letter under the part with the error, in this case the letter **D**.

TIME—USE IT WELL!

In the nineteenth century, immigrants brought to America a proverb that far too many modern Americans ignore. The proverb is "Slow and careful is fast."

In those seemingly contradictory words is a truth that helped lots of immigrant factory workers finish complicated tasks efficiently with few, if any, mistakes. They knew that each task required a different amount of time, and if they rushed through one task, they would do the job badly and have to repeat it until they got it right. However, if they took the time necessary to do the job well the first time, they actually finished before those who hurried through their work.

During the Structure section of the test, many test takers make the mistake of answering questions too quickly. They think that choices are easy to make, because mistakes are easy to spot. They are wrong.

Writers of the test create questions that will deceive you if you do not read each sentence carefully. This does not mean that you must read questions *slowly*; it means that you should read each question *carefully* before you make your choice.

The Structure section lasts between 15 and 20 minutes, and you will be asked 20 to 25 sentence completion and error identification questions. That gives you about 48 seconds per question to examine the question, make your choice, and move on to the next question. It may not sound like a lot of time, but you should do the following task to find out exactly how long 48 seconds lasts.

Look at your watch as your second hand moves around the face for 48 seconds. Do nothing but look at the watch with the same concentration you use to find the answer. *You will be surprised to learn how long 48 seconds really lasts.*

Since you have plenty of time to find the error in the sentence, you should be able to relax and examine each question with a clear mind.

TYPES OF ERRORS YOU WILL ENCOUNTER

Errors in Subject-Verb Agreement

A common type of error that will appear in this section is an error in subject-verb agreement. Remember that a singular subject always takes a singular verb form. A common error of this type is one involving a singular subject and a verb that is used with plurals. You should be able to easily spot the error in the following:

John and I is going to the movies.

In the above sentence, the subject, "John and I," is *plural*, but the verb "is going," is used only with *singular* subjects. The correct form of the verb is "are going." This type of error can be easy to spot because when a subject and verb don't agree, the sentence "sounds" odd. However, not all of these types of errors will be that easy to spot.

Many sentences contain "hidden" errors involving subject/verb agreement. In error identification questions, you should look for prepositional phrases between subjects and verbs, because they may be used to conceal errors, particularly if you rush. For example:

All three species (A) of the African hyena has (B) shoulders higher than their (C) hind quarters, massive heads, and powerful jaws (D).

The error that you should have identified is **B**. The noun in the subject is "species," a plural noun. The verb is "has," which is used with singular nouns. Many people do not recognize the error because the prepositional phrase "of the African hyena" is between the subject and the verb. If you rush through this question, you might relate the verb to the nearest singular noun, "hyena," instead of with the subject of the sentence.

Errors in Verb Tense

If you rush, you will also miss errors in tenses. Often, during an informal conversation, speakers of English use incorrect tenses, but still communicate their ideas because they also use vocal inflections, gestures, and facial expressions to send their messages. If your read the following sentence aloud, you may not identify the error, because it *sounds* correct. Nevertheless, it contains an error that you would have to identify on the test.

The Roberts Corporation already finished the
A B

experiments by the time National Chemicals, Inc.
C

made the discovery in its own laboratory.
D

The error is **B**. The verb should be "had finished," (the past perfect tense), which indicates the action that took place before "made."

Another common error found in the test involves the simple past and past progressive tenses. Be ready for this kind of error:

The Japanese artist, Katsushika Hokusai, was using
A

more than 50 different names while he
B C

was creating landscapes and book illustrations
D

during his 60-year career.

The error is **A**. The verb should be in the simple past tense. Hokusai *was never using* over 50 names at the same time. He *used* more than 50 different names (one at a time) during the period of time that he *was creating landscapes*.

Another common error is using the simple past tense instead of the present perfect tense. For example:

The crocodile, a distant relative of the dinosaurs,
A B

was on Earth for centuries.
C D

The error is **C**. The crocodile is found in many rivers throughout the world. It is not extinct. The crocodile has been on Earth for a period of time that began in the past but is *unfinished.*

Time Clauses with Main Clauses Using the Simple Future Tense

There are two errors in this category that you may encounter on the test, and they involve sentences like the following:

When I go to Paris, I will see the Eiffel Tower.

This is a correct sentence. The verb in the main clause is in the simple future tense, and the verb in the modifying, or "when," clause is in the simple present tense. Look at the following sentence:

When mankind will colonize the Moon, more than
A B C

one nation will participate.
D

This sentence is incorrect. The error is found in **B**. The simple future tense is not used in "when" clauses; the correct form of the verb is *colonizes,* in the simple present tense. Now, look at the following sentence:

Several students in this chemistry class study
A B

abroad on scholarships, when they receive the
C D

grade of "A."

You should have noticed two things. First, the "when" clause can be placed at the beginning *or* at the end of the sentence. Second, no matter its location, the "when" clause always uses the simple present, so the verb should be in the simple future tense. Therefore, the error is **B**, which should be "will study."

Conditionals

On the test, you will encounter error identification questions that involve conditional sentences.

Look at the following explanations and examples of the conditional tense errors:

Future possible conditional sentences describe possible situations that depend on conditions described in the "if" clause.

> If I go to Paris, I will/may/can/might see the Eiffel Tower.

The verb in the "if" clause is in the simple present tense, and the main clause uses auxiliary verbs, such as *will, may, can,* and *might*.

Present unreal conditional sentences describe situations that do not exist, but the writer or speaker speculates about them.

> If I went to Paris, I would/might/could see the Eiffel Tower.

The verb in the "if"clause is in the simple past tense, and the main clause uses auxiliary verbs, such as *would, might,* and *could*.

Past unreal conditional sentences describe situations that did not happen in the past, but the speaker or writer still speculates about them.

> If I had gone to Paris, I could have/would have/might have seen the Eiffel Tower.

The verb in the "if" clause is in the past perfect tense, and the verb in the main clause uses the auxiliary verbs *could have, would have*, and *might have* with the past participle form of the verb.

Look at the following sentences. Before you look for the errors, decide which kind of conditional each sentence is.

1. The library would burn (A) down if the fire department (B) hadn't answered (C) the alarm so quickly (D).

2. If Rozelle signs (A) the contract with (B) the university, she would have to teach three classes a week (C) each term. (D)

3. Professor Rubens won't teach next term (A) if (B) the university approved (C) his going on (D) sabbatical.

The first sentence is a past unreal conditional. The second sentence is a present unreal conditional. The third is a future possible conditional. The correct answers are 1. **A**, 2. **A**, and 3.**C**.

Now, you have a better idea of what kinds of errors you will encounter in error-identification questions. Later in the book, you will practice what you have learned in a series of drills.

Day 8

Test-taking Strategies for Reading

Today's Assignment

- Learn the format of questions in the reading section and acquire the strategies for answering them.

WHAT DOES THE READING SECTION CONTAIN AND HOW LONG DOES IT LAST?

The Reading section contains passages on a variety of subjects. Following each passage are several questions about the passage. You will answer from 44 to 55 questions in this section, and you will have 70 to 90 minutes to read the passages and answer the questions. Before you begin this section, you will be shown how to answer the questions with the computer screen and mouse.

The reading passages are similar to the ones you will probably read and study in North American universities and colleges. There are three important differences between the Reading section and the other sections of the exam:

- The Reading section is not computer adaptive. When you answer question number 1, the computer does not select a more difficult (or less difficult) question for number 2.
- In the Reading section, you are allowed to return to questions you have already answered and can change your answers. You are also permitted to skip a question and return to it later, which you can't do in the other sections of the exam.
- You will see the Reading passage and the question on the monitor screen at the same time. The Reading passage will appear on the left side of your screen, and the questions will appear on the right side of the screen.

TO READ OR NOT TO READ

You will not be scored on whether you read the entire passage. You will be scored on whether you answer the question correctly. It is not only probable that you can answer all questions correctly without reading the entire passage; it is imperative that you read only what is necessary to answer the questions.

So that you do not underestimate the importance of this advice, it will be repeated:

DO NOT READ THE ENTIRE PASSAGE BEFORE YOU START ANSWERING THE QUESTIONS!

Most questions will indicate which part of the reading passage is being asked about. Work through each passage answering the questions, using the process we describe in the following pages.

Read the First Sentences of Each Paragraph and the Last Sentence in the Passage

In the following passage, read only the sentences in boldface.

The American composer, George Gershwin, was born in 1898 in Brooklyn, New York, the son of Russian-Jewish immigrants. He began his musical education at age 11, when his family bought a second-hand piano. The piano was not bought for him, but for his older brother, Ira. However, George surprised everyone when he played a popular song, which he had taught himself by following the keys on a neighbor's player piano, and his parents decided that George should receive lessons. He studied piano with a famous music teacher at the time, Charles Hambitzer. He was so impressed with Gershwin's talent that he gave him lessons for free.

Gershwin dropped out of school at age 15 and earned a living by making piano rolls for player pianos and by playing in New York nightclubs. His most important job in this period was his work as a song plugger, who promoted interest in the sheet music of popular songs by playing and singing those songs in stores. At that time, sheet-music sales were the measure of a song's popularity, and song pluggers had to work long hours for the music publishers who employed them. As a result of his hard work, Gershwin's piano technique improved greatly, so much so that, while still in his teens, Gershwin became known as one of the most talented pianists in New York City. As a result, he worked as an accompanist for popular singers and as a rehearsal pianist for Broadway musicals.

His knowledge of jazz and popular music grew quickly, and one of his songs was included in the Broadway musical *The Passing Show of 1916*. George became friends to many prominent Broadway composers. He particularly admired the music of Irving Berlin whom Gershwin called "America's Franz Schubert." Jerome Kern, another Broadway composer, demonstrated to George how popular music was inferior to material in Broadway shows. In 1919, entertainer Al Jolson performed Gershwin's song *Swanee* in the musical *Sinbad*.

The song became a hit, and Gershwin became an overnight celebrity when his song sold more than 2 million recordings and a million copies of sheet music.

Questions about the Main Idea of the Passage

After you have read the sentences in boldface type, answer the following question:

Which of the following statements best expresses the main idea of the passage?

(A) Russian immigrants in America were all musical and creative.

(B) The Gershwins were school dropouts who became successes in show business.

(C) George Gershwin became a famous composer before he was 30.

(D) Musical training on Broadway did not prepare the Gershwins for success.

The correct answer is (C). By reading those four sentences in bold type, you have not only saved yourself time, you have also learned what the passage is about. In addition, you have gotten the information necessary to answer the question.

Main idea questions are usually asked first.

Vocabulary Questions

Vocabulary questions are found in the parts of the reading passage that will be highlighted to correspond with a question. This is another reason why it is unnecessary for you to read the entire passage. See the following examples:

Highlighted Words

You will answer three kinds of vocabulary questions. In the first kind, you will see a word or phrase highlighted in the text on the screen. This highlights the word or phrase that is the subject of the question. Look at the example. You will see the passage and the question on the monitor screen arranged this way:

> Gershwin dropped out of school at age 15 and earned a living by making piano rolls for player pianos and by playing in New York nightclubs. His most important job in this period was his work as a song plugger, who promoted interest in the sheet music of popular songs by playing and singing those songs in stores. At that time, sheet-music . . .

Look at the word highlighted in the text. Click on the answer choice that is closest in meaning to the words dropped out of.

(A) Graduated from college

(B) Stopped attending secondary school

(C) Scattered sheet music on the street

(D) Visited his school frequently

"Dropped out of" is an idiomatic expression, and if you are not acquainted with it, you can still figure out the correct answer by looking at the other words in the sentence. You can do this by mentally removing the words "dropped out or" from the sentence and reading the sentence this way:

> Gershwin _______ ___ __ school at age 15 and earned a living by making piano rolls for player pianos and by playing in New York nightclubs.

Then, you fill in the blank with a verb that completes the sentence so that it is logical and grammatically correct. The other words in the sentences contain clues. Look at the words:

> school at age 15 and earned a living by making piano rolls for player pianos and by playing in New York nightclubs.

A 15-year-old person who earns a living by playing in New York nightclubs is not likely to stay in high school at the same time. So, you choose a word or words that will finish the sentence correctly. It's not important what the words are; they can even be words in your native language. The word or phrase you came up with is probably "quit" or "withdrew from."

Then, you compare your word to the answer choices:

(A) Graduated from college

(B) Stopped attending secondary school

(C) Scattered sheet music on the street

(D) Visited his school frequently

The answer closest in meaning to "quit" or "withdrew from" is choice (B). Choice (A) is incorrect, because college is not mentioned in the sentence. Choice (C) is incorrect, because the sentence is not about sheet music. Choice (D) is incorrect and a tricky one, because "dropped out" it is close in sound to "dropped by," which means visited.

Highlighted Sentences

Another type of vocabulary question asks you to read a boldface sentence, and choose the correct definition of the highlighted word or phrase in that sentence.

> Gershwin dropped out of school at age 15 and earned a living by making piano rolls for player pianos and by playing in New York nightclubs. **His most important job in this period was his work as a song plugger, who promoted interest in the sheet music of popular songs by playing and singing those songs in stores. At that time, sheet-music sales were the measure of a song's popularity, and song pluggers had to work long hours for the music publishers who employed them.**

Look at the words promoted interest in the sheet music in the passage. Click on the word or phrase in the bold text that the words refer to.

(A) Sheet music sales
(B) A song's popularity
(C) Song plugger
(D) Music publishers

On the computer screen, you will highlight those words and click them as your choice. Which words would you choose?

(A) Sheet music sales

(B) A song's popularity

(C) Song plugger

(D) Music publishers

The correct answer is (C). The highlighted words "who promoted interest in sheet music" identify what song pluggers do.

Pronouns

Another kind of Reading question deals with pronouns. You will see a sentence in boldface with a highlighted pronoun, and you will be asked to identify the noun that the highlighted pronoun refers to. Look at the example:

> However, George surprised everyone when he played a popular song, which he had taught himself by following the keys on a neighbor's player piano, and his parents decided that George should receive lessons. **He studied piano with a famous music teacher at the time, Charles Hambitzer. He was so impressed with Gershwin's talent that he gave him lessons for free.**

Look at the highlighted word. Click on the word or phrase in the bold text that the word refers to.

(A) Piano

(B) Charles Hambitzer

(C) The Time

(D) Gershwin

The correct answer is (B). The pronoun "he" refers to a person, not to a thing ("piano" and "time" are things). "He" also does not refer to Gershwin, because Gershwin did not give lessons to himself, so "he" must refer to Charles Hambitzer.

Detail Questions

You will have to answer detail questions at least twice per reading passage. In these types of questions, you are asked about specific information in the text. First, read the question to find out what information you have to find. Then, search for it in the text.

> The American composer, George Gershwin, was born in 1898 in Brooklyn, New York, the son of Russian-Jewish immigrants. He began his musical education at age 11, when his family bought a second-hand piano. The piano was not bought for him, but for his older brother, Ira. However, George surprised everyone when he played a popular song, which he had taught himself by following the keys on a neighbor's player piano, and his parents decided that George should receive lessons. He studied piano with a famous music teacher at the time, Charles Hambitzer. He was so impressed with Gershwin's talent that he gave him lessons for free.

According to the passage, who did the Gershwin parents buy the piano for?

(A) George Gershwin

(B) Charles Hambitzer

(C) Other Russian immigrants

(D) Ira Gershwin

The correct answer is (D). In lines 5–6 above, the passage states that Gershwin's parents bought the piano for George's brother Ira.

Look for the Important Words

Detail questions contain important words that will lead you to the answer. They are not words such as "George Gershwin" or "composer." They are words that specify the information that will answer the question for you.

In the question, the words "buy the piano" are the most important words to help you find the answer. Instead of reading the entire passage, scan the passage for those words. You find it at the end of the second sentence and see that the correct answer is (D).

Look at the next example:

> The American composer, George Gershwin, was born in 1898 in Brooklyn, New York, the son of Russian-Jewish immigrants. He began his musical education at age 11, when his family bought a second-hand piano. The piano was not bought for him, but for his older brother, Ira. However, George surprised everyone when he played a popular song, which he had taught himself by following the keys on a neighbor's player piano, and his parents decided that George should receive lessons. He studied piano with a famous music teacher at the time, Charles Hambitzer. He was so impressed with Gershwin's talent that he gave him lessons for free.

According to the passage, why did George's piano teacher give him lessons for free?

(A) His parents were too poor to pay for the lessons.

(B) The teacher was impressed with George's talent.

(C) Famous piano teachers never received money from their students.

(D) Popular music was more important than classical music.

The most important words in the question are "lessons for free." When you scan for those words, you will find them in the last sentence of the paragraph. And you will have found the correct answer, which is choice (B).

Once again, repeat to yourself the most important strategy of answering questions in the reading section:

DO NOT READ THE ENTIRE PASSAGE BEFORE YOU START ANSWERING THE QUESTIONS!

Questions with *Except* and *Not*

The following is an example of "Except/Not" questions:

All of the following are mentioned as members of the French Impressionist group EXCEPT

(A) Edgar Dégas.

(B) Camille Pissaro.

(C) Rembrandt van Rijn.

(D) Mary Cassat.

In this question, you look for the answer that names a painter who is NOT a French Impressionist. In this case, it is choice (C), Rembrandt van Rijn.

Whenever you see this kind of question, remember that the answer is the one that is *different* from the others. Sometimes an answer has nothing to do with the main topic. In the above example, choice (C) might have been "Honore de Balzac," who was French but not a painter.

These kinds of questions will be asked at least four times per passage. Look at the following example:

The American composer, George Gershwin, was born in 1898 in Brooklyn, New York, the son of Russian-Jewish immigrants. He began his musical education at age 11, when his family bought a second-hand piano. The piano was not bought for him, but for his older brother, Ira. However, George surprised everyone when he played a popular song, which he had taught himself by following the keys on a neighbor's player piano, and his parents decided that George should receive lessons. He studied piano with a famous music teacher at the time, Charles Hambitzer. He was so impressed with Gershwin's talent that he gave him lessons for free. Gershwin dropped out of school at age 15 and earned a living by making piano rolls for player pianos and by playing in New York nightclubs. His most important job in this period was his work as a song plugger, who promoted interest in the sheet music of popular songs by playing and singing those songs in stores. At that time, sheet-music sales were the measure of a song's popularity, and song pluggers had to work long hours for the music publishers who employed them. As a result of his hard work, Gershwin's piano technique improved greatly, so much so that, while still in his teens, Gershwin became known as one of the most talented pianists in New York City. As a result, he worked as an accompanist for popular singers and as a rehearsal pianist for Broadway musicals. His knowledge of jazz and popular music grew quickly, and one of his songs was included in the Broadway musical *The Passing Show of 1916*. George became friends to many prominent Broadway composers. He particularly admired the music of Irving Berlin whom Gershwin called "America's Franz Schubert." Jerome Kern, another Broadway composer, demonstrated to George how popular music was inferior to material in Broadway shows. In 1919, entertainer Al Jolson performed Gershwin's song *Swanee* in the musical *Sinbad*. The song became a hit, and Gershwin became an overnight celebrity when his song sold more than 2 million recordings and a million copies of sheet music.

All of the following are reasons that George Gershwin became a success while he was young EXCEPT

(A) He studied piano with a famous teacher.

(B) He learned about jazz and popular music while he worked as a song plugger.

(C) He graduated from high school when he was only 15.

(D) He worked as an accompanist for popular singers in New York.

To answer this question correctly, you have to determine the time period of each answer. In the text, in what order were the answers stated? If you scan the passage you will see that the order is (A), (C), (B), and (D).

Choices (A) and (C) appear in the first paragraph, where you read that Gershwin studied with a famous teacher, which is the statement in choice (A). You also read that Gershwin's parents bought a piano for his brother, which means that Gershwin's parents did NOT give him a piano. So, choice (C) is correct.

Choices (B) and (D) give reasons why Gershwin became a success while he was young.

Questions with "Imply" and "Infer"

To *imply* something is to "communicate an idea without stating it directly." To *infer* something is to "understand the idea that is being communicated by another person, even though the other person does not say it directly."

For example:

Mildred said to Mark, "Harry is moving to Japan permanently, but he doesn't know how to speak Japanese."

Mildred *implied* that Harry would have to learn Japanese. Mark *inferred* that Harry would have to learn Japanese.

During the Reading section, you will be asked questions that begin in the following way:

It can be inferred from the passage that . . .

The author implies that . . .

The passage suggests that . . .

Based on the information in the passage, what can be inferred about . . .

The answer to these questions is always in the form of a paraphrase. It repeats an idea found in the passage but expresses it in a different way.

To answer these questions, first eliminate as a possible correct answer anything that is ridiculous and illogical. Also, eliminate any answer choice that introduces material not discussed in the passage. Answer choices that contain words such as "always," "never," and "completely" are usually incorrect, so you can eliminate them. If an answer choice simply repeats word-for-word a lot of material from the passage, you can eliminate that answer as well. Answer choices that are longer than the other answer choices are often a trap.

Answer the following question:

> His knowledge of jazz and popular music grew quickly, and one of his songs was included in the Broadway musical *The Passing Show of 1916*. George became friends to many prominent Broadway composers. He particularly admired the music of Irving Berlin whom Gershwin called "America's Franz Schubert." Jerome Kern, another Broadway composer, demonstrated to George how popular music was inferior to material in Broadway shows. In 1919, entertainer Al Jolson performed Gershwin's song *Swanee* in the musical *Sinbad*. The song became a hit, and Gershwin became an overnight celebrity when his song sold more than 2 million recordings and a million copies of sheet music.

It can be inferred from the passage that

(A) Gershwin became a famous jazz pianist in Russia.

(B) Gershwin admired the music of Franz Shubert.

(C) Gershwin disliked music by Kern and Berlin.

(D) Gershwin never became a well-known musician.

Choices (A), (C), and (D) are not true. Choice (B) is correct. Gershwin compared the music of Jerome Kern, who was his friend, to that of Franz Shubert.

Questions with Black Squares

During the reading section of the computer-based test, you will have to answer questions with black squares. On the left side of the screen, you will see the reading passage with the following black-square mark located throughout the text: ■

On the right side of the screen, you will read a sentence followed by the question:

> Where in the passage would the sentence best fit in the passage? Click on the square ■ to add the sentence in the passage.

When you point to the square and click the mouse, the sentence in the question will appear in the passage.

This is a very difficult kind of question to answer, and you should not answer it *until you have answered all other kinds of questions!* To answer this kind of question, carefully read the sentence and determine the most important words, usually found at the end of the sentence. Then, scan the passage for the squares. Look at the sentences before the square and particularly after the square. You will find that in the sentence to be inserted, the words at the end contain information that introduces ideas in the beginning of the next sentence that is in the passage.

The American composer, George Gershwin, was born in 1898 in Brooklyn, New York, the son of Russian-Jewish immigrants. He began his musical education at age 11, when his family bought a second-hand piano. The piano was not bought for him, but for his older brother, Ira. However, George surprised everyone when he played a popular song, which he had taught himself by following the keys on a neighbor's player piano, and his parents decided that George should receive lessons. ■ He studied piano with a famous music teacher at the time, Charles Hambitzer. He was so impressed with Gershwin's talent that he gave him lessons for free. Gershwin dropped out of school at age 15 and earned a living by making piano rolls for player pianos and by playing in New York nightclubs. His most important job in this period was his work as a song plugger, who promoted interest in the sheet music of popular songs by playing and singing those songs in stores. At that time, sheet-music sales were the measure of a song's popularity, and song pluggers had to work long hours for the music publishers who employed them. ■ As a result of his hard work, Gershwin's piano technique improved greatly, so much so that, while still in his teens, Gershwin became known as one of the most talented pianists in New York City. As a result, he worked as an accompanist for popular singers and as a rehearsal pianist for Broadway musicals. His knowledge of jazz and popular music grew quickly, and one of his songs was included in the Broadway musical *The Passing Show of 1916*. George became friends to many prominent Broadway composers. He particularly admired the music of Irving Berlin whom Gershwin called "America's Franz Schubert." Jerome Kern, another Broadway composer, demonstrated to George how popular music was inferior to material in Broadway shows. In 1919, entertainer Al Jolson performed Gershwin's song *Swanee* in the musical *Sinbad*. ■ The song became a hit, and Gershwin became an overnight celebrity when his song sold more than 2 million recordings and a million copies of sheet music.

The following sentence can be added to the passage:

However, Gershwin's income rose, and he worked harder and harder.

Where would it best fit in the passage? Click on the square ■ to add the sentence to the passage.

Look at the ideas at the end of the sentence:

However, Gershwin's income rose, and *he worked harder and harder.*

This sentence best fits at the place marked by the second square. With the new sentence inserted, the passage would read as follows:

At that time, sheet-music sales were the measure of a song's popularity, and song pluggers had to work long hours for the music publishers who employed them. ***However, Gershwin's income rose, and he worked harder and harder.*** As a result of his hard work, Gershwin's piano technique improved greatly, so much so that, while still in his teens, Gershwin became known as one of the most talented pianists in New York City.

SUMMING UP

Do not read the entire passage. Begin each passage by reading the first sentences in each paragraph and the last sentence of the last paragraph.

You should answer the questions not in numerical order but in the following order (as they were presented in this chapter) according to kind of question:

1. All vocabulary questions
2. All questions that ask you to identify a noun or a pronoun
3. All questions that ask for detailed information in the passage
4. All questions that ask about the main idea of the passage
5. All questions with EXCEPT and NOT
6. All questions with IMPLY and INFER
7. All questions with black squares

Day 9

Test-taking Strategies for Writing

Today's Assignment

- Learn how to structure your essay and acquaint yourself with the possible topics you may encounter on the test.

The TOEFL Essay

An *essay* is a short literary composition on a single subject that usually presents the personal view of the author—you. In the fourth and last section of the TOEFL test, you will write an essay about a topic that will be assigned to you. You will have 30 minutes to write a three- to five-paragraph essay on that topic. You must write on the topic you are assigned. An essay on any topic other than the one assigned will receive a score of "0."

Before the topic is presented, you must choose whether to type your essay on the computer or to hand write your essay on the paper essay answer sheet provided. Scratch paper will be given to you for making notes. If you choose to hand write your essay, the final version must be on the single-page, two-sided essay answer sheet. If you decide to type your essay on the computer, you will compose the final version of your essay in the "essay box" on the computer screen. The essay topic will be presented to you on the computer screen.

You will not know the topic ahead of time. Although you must write only on the topic that is assigned to you, there is a way to prepare for this section.

Your essay score will depend upon your ability to compose a well-written essay that answers the question in a relatively short period of time—in this case, 30 minutes. Your essay must be well organized and well developed; you must provide the reader with clearly appropriate details to support your thesis or illustrate your ideas. Your writing should show, throughout the essay, that you're comfortable expressing complex ideas in the English language. You should also use a variety of grammatical structures (clauses, tenses, etc.) and use a vocabulary that is appropriate to your topic.

Preparing Your First Version of the Essay

1. The Plan

Writing is a process, like a recipe for a special meal. You have a good chance of succeeding as an essayist if you follow these directions. The first step in the writing process is to have a plan.

An essay should have:

- an introduction,
- a body, and
- a conclusion.

In the *introduction*, you get the reader's attention and tell the reader what you are going to write about. You also give the reader any special information that guides the reader to the body of your essay. In the case of a TOEFL essay, the introduction should be one paragraph that contains four to five sentences.

The *body* of the essay should be made up of one to three paragraphs that contain the ideas you want to communicate to the reader.

The *conclusion*, which should be one paragraph, summarizes what you wrote in the body and reveals the conclusion you want the reader to make.

Do not write the essay without planning. Begin the process by "brainstorming."

2. Brainstorming

In all writing classes, there is an exercise called *brainstorming*, which helps you start the flow of ideas necessary for an essay. This process involves writing words and phrases that are related to your topic as they come into your head. For example, look at the following topic:

> What are some of the qualities of a good parent? Use specific details and examples to explain your answer.

Depending on your beliefs, you might write down the following words while brainstorming and any others that you would think of:

Strength of character

Love of family life

Earn a living

Spends time with children

Set an example

Help children with emotional problems in adolescence

Brainstorming should take you 3 to 5 minutes.

3. Write Sentences about What You Brainstorm

These are simple sentences that help you put ideas into complete form, but the sentences are in no way the final version that you will submit.

You might come up with sentences such as:

- A father should earn money to provide food, clothing, and shelter for his family.
- A father should not work so many hours that he ignores his family.
- Parents should show affection to their children, hugging and being affectionate with them as their culture calls for.
- Parents should encourage their children to study in school by setting the example of working hard at their jobs and at home.

Writing these sentences should take you about 5 minutes.

4. Logical Order

After you have written your sentences, put them into a logical order. That is, arrange the order of sentences so that they relate to one another in a logical sequence. Then, decide which sentences should go into the introduction, the body, and the conclusion. You will probably find that you need more sentences. If so, write them at this time, and place them in the appropriate paragraphs in the appropriate section of the essay. Do not spend too much time writing the sentences. In the margins next to the sentences, write numbers that will indicate the proper order of the sentences. This should take 3 to 5 minutes.

5. Write the Topic Sentences for All the Paragraphs in Your Essay

A topic sentence contains the controlling idea of a paragraph. These sentences tell the reader what the paragraph is about. Look at the sentences and decide which one should begin the introductory paragraph, which ones should begin the paragraphs in the body, and which one should begin the conclusion. You may have already written some topic sentences. If not, write those that are needed. This should take you about 5 minutes.

6.Write the Essay

You now have 10 minutes to put the essay into final shape. You have all the ideas, sentences, and paragraphs in the correct order, but you need to check your sentences for grammar and spelling errors. Then, following the numbers in your margin, write your sentences in the correct order in the final draft.

Write about One Choice

You have a process to write the essay, but there are rules that you should follow when looking at your assigned topic. There are 185 possible topics for the essay, but there are only four ways that the topic is stated. If you learn to recognize the kind of topic that you have been assigned, you will be able to organize your writing more efficiently.

Most essay topics ask you to make a choice. For example:

> Some people prefer to eat at food stands or restaurants. Other people prefer to prepare and eat food at home. Which do you prefer? Use specific reasons and examples to support your answer.

You probably enjoy eating in restaurants and at home, depending on your mood, your work schedule, or your diet. However, do **not** write an essay that says that sometimes you like eating in a restaurant and sometimes at home. You must choose one or the other if you want to write an essay that answers the question correctly.

Other topics ask you whether you agree or disagree with a statement. Others will ask you to tell which is better or whether you support one thing or another. These topics require you to choose *only one* thing and write about it. Do not write about both.

One kind of topic can easily deceive you. Read the following:

> Nowadays, food has become easier to prepare. Has this change improved the way people live? Use specific reasons and examples to support your answer.

This topic asks you to make a choice, but it may not be obvious. It is not about food. It's about the way food preparation affects the way people live. You have to choose between two possible opinions. Opinion one is "The change in food preparation has improved the way people live." The other is "The change has not improved the way people live." Make sure your essay covers the right topic.

Single Topics

There are some types of questions that ask you to choose the topic yourself. These topics are often referred to as "desert island questions." For example:

> If you had to live on a desert island and could have only one book to read, what would it be? Explain your answer, using specific reasons and details.

The topic question gives you the circumstances of your choice, but it leaves the choice of the details of your answer up to you. A more likely topic is as follows:

> If you could study a subject that you have never had the opportunity to study, what would you choose? Explain your choice, using specific reasons and details.

Here is the desert island question in a slightly different form. You have to write about **one** academic subject, not necessarily one that you always wanted to study, but also one that might have helped you in a particular way or one that your parents would have been pleased about. Whatever subject you write about, you must provide details about your desires or those of your parents. Or, you could write about the way the course would have helped your work.

Cause and Effect Topics

Some topics require you to identify causes, effects, and causes and effects together. Look at the following example:

> How do movies or television influence people's behavior? Use reasons and specific examples to support your answer.

In this example, the statement gives you the cause, "movies or television." It is your job to write about the effect of these media on people's behavior.

In the following example, the statement gives you the effect:

> Why do you think some people are attracted to dangerous sports or other dangerous activities? Use specific reasons and examples to support your answer.

The effect is "some people are attracted to dangerous sports or other dangerous activities." You must write about the causes of this attraction.

In the following example, you are required to write about both cause *and* effect:

> People do many different things to stay healthy. What do you do for good health? Use specific reasons and examples to support your answer.

You must write about what you do for good health, which is the *cause*. You must also write about the *effect* of what you do.

"Many Things" Topics

Topics often require you to report several facts. For example:

> Films can tell us a lot about the country where they were made. What have you learned about a country from watching its movies? Use specific examples and details to support your response.

To write this essay, you have to choose a film from a country other than your own—a film that is about the country that produced it. You have to say what you learned about that country from watching its movies. If the movies had been Francis Ford Coppola's *The Godfather, Parts 1, 2,* and 3, what would you have learned about America? About Italian immigrants in America? About Italian-American actors? About the causes of organized crime in America? About family life, religion, and divorce? About political and economic power? Let's look at the next example:

> People listen to music for different reasons and at different times. Why is music important to many people? Use specific reasons and examples to support your choice.

This topic has been the subject of magazine articles, long books, and even encyclopedias. You must write not about the kinds of music found throughout the world but about the reasons that people listen to it, e.g., relaxation, religious devotion, or artistic engagement. Before you begin writing your essay, make sure you are focusing on the correct idea.

CLASSIFYING THE TOPICS

In the *TOEFL Bulletin*, there is a list of 185 topics from which your assigned topic will be assigned. You should become familiar with this list and take extra time to practice writing essays before you take the computer-based TOEFL test.

To see a list of possible assigned topics, go to www.toefl.org and you can download the entire list. To help yourself become familiar with the topics, try to break them down into categories such as the following:

Going to College

Going to Elementary and High School

Parents and Children

Food

New Things in Your Life

The Media

Personal Preferences

Your Beliefs

Work

Spending Money

Travel and Transportation

Technology

Society

The Culture of Your Country

Ecology

Sports and Recreation

Using the steps you learned here, practice writing on a variety of these topics from each of the categories. There is no way to memorize an essay or all of the questions, but you can become more comfortable with the types of questions and the process of writing an essay under timed conditions.

Day 10

Listening Comprehension

Short Conversation Drill: Part I

Today's Assignment

- Complete Part I of the Short Conversation Drill and check your answers.

Today, you will practice listening to short conversations and answering questions about what you heard. If you need to, take a few minutes to review what you learned in Day 4. There will be 30 questions. The answers and scripts for the audio are printed at the end of this chapter. This drill is not on the CD. We have provided a script at the end of this chapter that you should tear out along the dashed line. Then, you can either read the script to yourself as you work through the questions, or you can have a friend read the script to you while you work through the questions.

Directions: In this section, you will read conversations between two people. After each conversation, you will be asked several questions, and you will see the questions printed here with four answer choices. Choose an answer and mark it either in the book or on a separate sheet of scrap paper. Remember to answer the questions based on what is stated or implied by the speakers.

1. What does the woman imply?
   (A) The professor requires students to read too many books.
   (B) The professor wants students to take only her course.
   (C) The professor thinks about students a lot.
   (D) The professor didn't assign enough work.

2. What is the man going to do tomorrow?
   (A) Get a job waiting tables.
   (B) Go to the financial aid office.
   (C) Give the woman some money.
   (D) Wait in line for 3 hours.

3. What does the man mean?
   (A) He enjoyed the film, *The Right Stuff*.
   (B) He didn't know much of the material on the exam.
   (C) He doesn't like the professor's lectures.
   (D) He isn't in the woman's class.

4. What does the woman imply?
   (A) The man doesn't have a sense of humor.
   (B) The man is lazy.
   (C) The man would be a good editor.
   (D) The man is involved in many extracurricular activities.

5. What does the man mean?
   (A) He thinks Professor Hines is an excellent teacher.
   (B) He is glad the professor was selected.
   (C) He wants the professor on his thesis committee.
   (D) He doesn't think Hines is a good professor.

6. What does the man mean?
   (A) The woman's problems are important to him.
   (B) The woman needs help with her problem.
   (C) The woman's problems are not his concern.
   (D) The woman should change roommates.

7. What does the woman imply?
   (A) The man should stay where he is.
   (B) The man is unhappy with his present school.
   (C) The man enjoys his courses at school.
   (D) The man should think about it first.

8. What is the man probably going to do?
   (A) Write a letter to the library.
   (B) Check out the book from the library.
   (C) Take a course in Italian.
   (D) Return the book to the woman.

9. What does the man imply?
   (A) He doesn't like music.
   (B) He never goes to concerts.
   (C) He won't listen to the radio.
   (D) He isn't going to the Beethoven concert.

10. What does the woman imply?
   (A) The man has never parachuted before.
   (B) The man doesn't have a parachute.
   (C) The man will have a good time.
   (D) The man didn't fly the plane.

11. What does the woman mean?
   (A) She doesn't like the professor.
   (B) She read the man's paper and liked it.
   (C) She carried the paper to class.
   (D) She doesn't want to read the paper.

12. What does the man mean?
   (A) He is going to the woods.
   (B) He doesn't like weddings.
   (C) He will go to the wedding.
   (D) He has to miss the wedding.

13. What will the man probably do?
   (A) Go to the registrar's office.
   (B) Apply for a scholarship.
   (C) Take the woman to dinner.
   (D) Mail a package at the post office.

14. What does the woman mean?
   (A) She doesn't like historical movies.
   (B) She can't go to the movies.
   (C) She doesn't like the man.
   (D) She won't let him study tonight.

15. What does the woman mean?
   (A) She knows a lot about poetry.
   (B) She doesn't want to answer the question.
   (C) She likes the work of the poet.
   (D) She doesn't remember the poet's name.

16. What does the man mean?
   (A) He knows where the building is.
   (B) He doesn't know where the building is.
   (C) He can help the woman study physics.
   (D) He is not a student.

17. What does the woman imply?
   (A) She knew about the refunds at the bookstore.
   (B) She didn't want to tell the man about the refunds.
   (C) She got a refund for her used books.
   (D) She didn't know about the refunds at the bookstore.

18. What does the man imply?
    - (A) The woman should help Professor Harris in class.
    - (B) The woman should drop the course.
    - (C) The woman should get a science dictionary.
    - (D) The woman should use the words she learns in class.

19. What does the woman mean?
    - (A) Many people are impressed with college athletes.
    - (B) Many people don't like the Impressionists.
    - (C) Man people will give scholarships to athletes.
    - (D) Many people believe athletes can't do college-level work.

20. What does the man imply?
    - (A) Pope had to have a surgery on his shoulder.
    - (B) Pope was angry because he had suffered religious persecution.
    - (C) Pope was not a religious man.
    - (D) Pope did not write pleasant poetry.

21. What does the woman mean?
    - (A) She didn't mind going to the club meeting.
    - (B) She spent the evening thinking about personal problems.
    - (C) She went to a nightclub instead.
    - (D) She is going to resign from the Science Club.

22. What does the man mean?
    - (A) He hasn't received any replies yet.
    - (B) He isn't going to medical school.
    - (C) He hasn't been rejected by any school.
    - (D) He has been admitted to one medical school.

23. What does the woman mean?
    - (A) Henry should be a chemist.
    - (B) Henry doesn't know how to play baseball.
    - (C) Henry is a very good baseball player.
    - (D) Henry will not get a job as a chemist.

24. What does the woman mean?
    - (A) She doesn't know who will teach her American history class.
    - (B) She isn't taking American history this term.
    - (C) She left the catalog in her room.
    - (D) She doesn't need to take American history.

25. What subject are the man and woman discussing?
    - (A) Mathematics
    - (B) Literature
    - (C) History
    - (D) Geography

26. What does the woman mean?
    - (A) She lives next door to Phillip's classroom.
    - (B) She doesn't like Phillip.
    - (C) She never watches television.
    - (D) She has a hearing problem.

27. What are the man and woman discussing?
    - (A) Where they are going on vacation
    - (B) What they are going to do after graduation
    - (C) Where they will hang their diplomas
    - (D) What they will look forward to doing in graduate school

28. What is the man probably going to do?
    - (A) Give Linda a book
    - (B) Take Friday off
    - (C) Tell Linda about the party
    - (D) Go to the party

29. What does the woman imply?
    - (A) The man doesn't study until the night before an exam.
    - (B) The man gets good grades all the time.
    - (C) The man shouldn't worry about getting good grades.
    - (D) The man has lots of time to study before the exam.

30. What does the woman imply?
    - (A) The exam will have information about Pluto.
    - (B) The exam will cover astrology.
    - (C) The exam will have questions about Pluto.
    - (D) The exam will take 3 hours.

Answer Key for Day 10—Short Conversation Drill: Part I

1. A
2. B
3. B
4. D
5. D
6. C
7. B
8. B
9. D
10. A
11. B
12. C
13. A
14. B
15. D
16. B
17. A
18. C
19. D
20. B
21. B
22. D
23. C
24. A
25. D
26. B
27. B
28. D
29. A
30. C

DAY 10—SCRIPT FOR SHORT CONVERSATION DRILL: PART I

(Narrator): Directions: In this section, you will hear conversations between two people. After each conversation, you will be asked several questions about what you heard, and you will see the questions printed here with four answer choices. Choose an answer and mark it either in the book or on a separate sheet of scrap paper. Remember to answer the questions based on what is stated or implied by the speakers.

1. ***(Man):*** Have you seen how many books are on the reading list for Professor Robinson's course?

   (Woman): Yes! She must think we aren't taking any courses but hers!

   (Narrator): What does the woman imply?

2. ***(Woman):*** I had to wait in line 3 hours to talk to the financial aid officer.

   (Man): Wow! I hope they have some money left tomorrow!

   (Narrator): What is the man going to do tomorrow?

3. ***(Woman):*** How many questions did you get right on the exam?

   (Man): I didn't remember any of that stuff from the lectures.

   (Narrator): What does the man mean?

4. ***(Man):*** I sure would like to edit the campus humor magazine.

   (Woman): Don't you have too much to do already?

   (Narrator): What does the woman imply?

5. ***(Woman):*** I just heard that Professor Hines won the Nobel Prize for Economics.

   (Man): He should be glad I wasn't on the selection committee.

   (Narrator): What does the man mean?

6. ***(Woman):*** I can't get my new roommate to stop playing her music so loud!

   (Man): Look, I have my own problems!

   (Narrator): What does the man mean?

7. ***(Man):*** I am going to transfer to Dartmouth College next term.

   (Woman): I thought you were so happy here.

   (Narrator): What does the woman imply?

8. ***(Man):*** I need that book on the Italian Renaissance.

   (Woman): I just returned it to the library.

   (Narrator): What is the man probably going to do?

9. ***(Woman):*** Are you going to the Beethoven concert?

   (Man): I prefer jazz, myself.

   (Narrator): What does the man imply?

10. ***(Man):*** I'm very nervous about parachuting out of the plane.

    (Woman): The first time is always the hardest.

    (Narrator): What does the woman imply?

11. ***(Man):*** I got only a "C" on my term paper.

    (Woman): I don't care what the professor thinks. It was excellent.

    (Narrator): What does the woman mean?

12. ***(Woman):*** Will I see you at Mike and Sheila's wedding?

    (Man): I wouldn't miss it!

    (Narrator): What does the man mean?

13. *(Woman):* I just heard the tower clock strike ten.
(Man): Hey! The scholarship winners have been posted at the Registrar's Office.
(Narrator): What will the man probably do?

14. *(Man):* What time do you want me to pick you up for the movie?
(Woman): I'm sorry, Bob, I have to study for a history quiz.
(Narrator): What does the woman mean?

15. *(Man):* Who wrote the poem "Stopping By Woods On A Snowy Evening?"
(Woman): Oh I should know that. He was so famous!
(Narrator): What does the woman mean?

16. *(Woman):* Excuse me, where can I find the Physics Building?
(Man): I'm new here myself.
(Narrator): What does the man mean?

17. *(Man):* I just found out that the campus bookstore doesn't give refunds on used books.
(Woman): I could have told you that.
(Narrator): What does the woman imply?

18. *(Woman):* In her lectures, Professor Harris uses a lot of words that aren't in the textbook.
(Man): I got a science dictionary that's been a lot of help.
(Narrator): What does the man imply.

19. *(Man):* Congratulations! I hear you were awarded an athletic scholarship.
(Woman): Thanks, but I hope it doesn't give people the impression that I'm just another dumb athlete.
(Narrator): What does the woman mean?

20. *(Woman):* The poet Alexander Pope was a very unpleasant man, wasn't he?
(Man): Well, if I weren't allowed to go to college because of my religion, I'd have a chip on my shoulder too.
(Narrator): What does the man imply?

21. *(Man):* I didn't see you at the Science Club meeting last night.
(Woman): I had too much on my mind to go to a club meeting.
(Narrator): What does the woman mean?

22. *(Woman):* Have you heard from any of the medical schools you applied to?
(Man): I got an acceptance letter yesterday.
(Narrator): What does the man mean?

23. *(Man):* Did you watch Henry playing baseball yesterday?
(Woman): Yes. If he can't get a job as a chemist, he can join a professional team.
(Narrator): What does the woman mean?

24. *(Man):* Who do you have for American history?
(Woman): There wasn't a professor listed in the catalog, and I haven't been to class yet.
(Narrator): What does the woman mean?

25. *(Woman):* The chinook winds are found in North America. What about the sirocco winds?
(Man): They occur in North Africa.
(Narrator): What subject are the man and woman discussing?

26. *(Man):* Phillip is going to be interviewed on national television.
(Woman): Why anyone would want to listen to him is beyond me.
(Narrator): What does the woman mean?

27. *(Woman):* After I get my diploma, I'm going to look for a job.

    (Man): I think I'm just going to hang out for a month or so.

    (Narrator): What are the man and woman discussing?

28. *(Woman):* I'm giving a birthday party for Linda on Friday night, and I hope you'll come.

    (Man): Sounds good. Should I bring a gift?

    (Narrator): What is the man probably going to do?

29. *(Man):* I don't understand how you get such good grades.

    (Woman): I study all the time so I don't have to cram the night before an exam.

    (Narrator): What does the woman imply?

30. *(Man):* Dr. Oaks has been talking a lot about the planet Pluto in class.

    (Woman): Well, that should tell us what will be on the astronomy exam tomorrow.

    (Narrator): What does the woman imply?

Day 11

Listening Comprehension

Short Conversation Drill: Part II

Today's Assignment

- Complete Part II of the Short Conversation Drill and check your answers.

Today, you will continue to practice with short conversations and questions. If you need to, take a few minutes to review what you learned in Day 4, and to review your answers from Day 10, Short Conversation Drill: Part I. There will be 30 questions in this exercise. The answers and scripts for the audio are printed at the end of this chapter. This drill is not on the CD. We have provided a script at the end of this chapter that you should tear out along the dashed line. Then, you can either read the script to yourself as you work through the questions, or you can have a friend read the script to you while you work through the questions.

Directions: In this section, you will read conversations between two people. After each conversation, you will be asked several questions, and you will see the questions printed here with four answer choices. Choose an answer and mark it either in the book or on a separate sheet of scrap paper. Remember to answer the questions based on what is stated or implied by the speakers.

1. What does the woman imply?
   (A) She has to take the course before graduation.
   (B) She hasn't taken the course.
   (C) She doesn't like westerns.
   (D) She will take it next semester.

2. What does the woman mean?
   (A) Students think basketball is hard to watch.
   (B) Students go to athletic events only during the day.
   (C) Students don't attend many athletic events.
   (D) Students enjoy all athletic events.

3. What does the man imply?
   (A) He is not going to get a DVD.
   (B) He is going to borrow his roommate's stereo.
   (C) He is not going let his roommate get a DVD.
   (D) He is going to buy his roommate's stereo.

4. What is the woman probably going to do?
   (A) Cover her windows with newspapers.
   (B) Buy a newspaper and read the ad.
   (C) Make new curtains with her sewing machine.
   (D) Go to the department store and buy new curtains.

5. What does the man mean?
   (A) He doesn't wear a watch on dates.
   (B) He was late for class yesterday.
   (C) He enjoyed his date with the woman.
   (D) He won't ask the woman for another date.

6. What did the woman imply?
   (A) She thinks the quiz was difficult.
   (B) She thinks the man was bragging.
   (C) She thinks calculus is an easy course.
   (D) She thinks studying is unnecessary.

7. What does the man mean?
   (A) A new computer will increase the speed of the download.
   (B) A model of a new computer is on display in the science building.
   (C) A new way of using the computer will help the woman.
   (D) A faster download is possible with a new modem.

8. What does the woman mean?
   (A) She didn't receive an invitation to the dance.
   (B) She looked for the man but couldn't find him.
   (C) She did not have a good time at the dance.
   (D) She stayed home on Saturday night.

9. What does the woman mean?
   (A) The man doesn't need to use currency.
   (B) The man needs proper identification.
   (C) The man doesn't need to get a new passport.
   (D) The man needs to change citizenship.

10. What does the man mean?
    (A) He's not going to Florida for spring break.
    (B) He's going to take photos at the beach.
    (C) He's getting married during spring break.
    (D) He's never going to Florida.

11. What does the man imply?
    (A) She has extra supplies in her apartment.
    (B) She can buy supplies from the paleontology department.
    (C) She has to go to the geology department for supplies.
    (D) She won't be able to take a class without supplies.

12. What does the woman mean?
    (A) It required a lot of effort to write the paper.
    (B) It was a very easy paper to write.
    (C) It was expensive to buy copies of all of the sonnets.
    (D) It took her to the library every day.

13. What does the woman mean?
    (A) She doesn't play volleyball anymore.
    (B) She can't count on the team.
    (C) She plays volleyball very well.
    (D) She was an officer of her high school class.

14. What does the man mean?
    (A) He drinks a lot of coffee.
    (B) He takes classes in the coffee shop.
    (C) He prefers to drink coffee.
    (D) He spends a lot of time in the coffee shop.

15. What does the woman mean?
    (A) The rocks weigh too much to carry.
    (B) Only a few people want to go to the concert.
    (C) The tickets are not available now.
    (D) Many people will want tickets to the rock concert.

16. What does the woman mean?
    (A) The man will do better if he studies groups.
    (B) The man should study with a group of other students.
    (C) The woman will do better on the exam than the man.
    (D) The woman doesn't want to study with the man.

17. What is the man going to do?
    (A) Give away his books.
    (B) Buy some new shirts.
    (C) Get a sweatshirt.
    (D) Find a way to lose weight.

18. What does the woman mean?
    (A) The professor will not lecture about three glaciers.
    (B) The professor will ask nothing about glaciers.
    (C) The professor will ask only three questions about glaciers.
    (D) The professor will probably ask many questions about glaciers.

19. What does the man mean?
    (A) The dorm needs to have a fire drill.
    (B) The dorm will have a fire drill on time.
    (C) The dorm needs a fire place.
    (D) The dorm will be burned down by a fire.

20. What does the man imply?
    (A) He likes fishing, but not hunting.
    (B) He likes fishing and hunting.
    (C) He likes neither fishing nor hunting.
    (D) He likes hunting, but not fishing.

21. What does the woman mean?
    (A) Many poets are really physicians.
    (B) Many poets practically write for children.
    (C) Many poets are unrealistic.
    (D) Many poets work with people as well as write.

22. What does the man mean?
    (A) He wants to join the teaching assistant's club.
    (B) He doesn't understand the teaching assistant either.
    (C) He thinks the teaching assistant speaks clearly.
    (D) He doesn't want the teaching assistant to join his club.

23. What does the man mean?
    (A) Getting elected is always harder than working.
    (B) Electing members of the student council is easy.
    (C) Being on the student council requires a lot of work.
    (D) Doing hard work always gets good results.

24. What does the woman imply?
    (A) She has an anatomy book with her.
    (B) She is looking at a skeleton.
    (C) She is wearing thick glasses.
    (D) She is not going to help the man with the answer.

25. What does the woman mean?
    (A) She has no classes on Thursday.
    (B) She has no free time on Thursdays.
    (C) She has classes only on Thursday.
    (D) She has little free time during the week.

26. What does the man mean?
    (A) Nothing happened to Roberta and Phyllis.
    (B) The man is ashamed about what happened.
    (C) Something unfortunate happened to Roberta and Phyllis.
    (D) The woman doesn't know what happened.

27. What will the man probably do?
    (A) Help the woman with her project.
    (B) Keep the woman from being hit by a car.
    (C) Bring the woman some food from the cafeteria.
    (D) Get the projector from the closet.

28. What does the man mean?
    (A) Sam looked like he was dazed.
    (B) Sam stood on a platform throughout the play.
    (C) Sam was the tallest person in the cast.
    (D) Sam was the best actor in the cast.
29. What can be inferred about the man?
    (A) He doesn't know where the notebook is.
    (B) He lost a game that he played with the woman.
    (C) He has to be at another table soon.
    (D) He wants the woman's address book.
30. What does the woman mean?
    (A) Entomology is the science of explosives.
    (B) Entomology is a subject she enjoys very much.
    (C) Entomology is a subject that can break you.
    (D) Entomology is a subject that no one likes.

ANSWER KEY FOR DAY 11—SHORT CONVERSATION DRILL: PART II

1.	B	16.	B
2.	C	17.	C
3.	A	18.	D
4.	D	19.	A
5.	C	20.	C
6.	A	21.	D
7.	D	22.	B
8.	C	23.	C
9.	B	24.	A
10.	A	25.	B
11.	B	26.	C
12.	A	27.	C
13.	C	28.	D
14.	D	29.	A
15.	D	30.	B

DAY 11—SCRIPT FOR SHORT CONVERSATION DRILL: PART II

(Narrator): Directions: In this section, you will hear conversations between two people. After each conversation, you will be asked several questions about what you heard, and you will see the questions printed here with four answer choices. Choose an answer and mark it either in the book or on a separate sheet of scrap paper. Remember to answer the questions based on what is stated or implied by the speakers.

1. *(Man):* Have you taken the Western Civilization course yet?

   (Woman): Western Civilization is not a requirement for my major.

   (Narrator): What does the woman imply?

2. *(Man):* Intercollegiate athletics aren't very popular at this university, are they?

   (Woman): Well, there was hardly anybody at the basketball game last night.

   (Narrator): What does the woman mean?

3. *(Woman):* When are you going to get a DVD player?

   (Man): My roommate's stereo and computer equipment take up all the spare space.

   (Narrator): What does the man imply?

4. *(Woman):* I need new curtains for my apartment.

   (Man): Billings Department Store ran an ad in today's paper for a special sale on curtains.

   (Narrator): What is the woman probably going to do?

5. *(Woman):* I didn't realize it was so late. I have got get home.

   (Man): Me too! Sorry, I was having such a good time, I didn't notice.

   (Narrator): What does the man mean?

6. *(Man):* That was an easy quiz, don't you think?

   (Woman): What? You must study nothing but calculus!

   (Narrator): What did the woman imply?

7. *(Woman):* My computer sometimes takes 3 minutes to download material from the Internet.

   (Man): Have you thought about getting a new modem?

   (Narrator): What does the man mean?

8. *(Man):* I saw you at the dance Saturday night. It looked like you were having a good time.

   (Woman): Well, looks can be deceiving.

   (Narrator): What does the woman mean?

9. *(Man):* Can I rent a car with a driver's license from another country?

   (Woman): I think so, as long as you have a current credit card and show your passport.

   (Narrator): What does the woman mean?

10. *(Woman):* Are you going to Florida for spring break?

    (Man): My sister is getting married, and I am going to take the wedding pictures.

    (Narrator): What does the man mean?

11. ***(Woman):*** The bookstore is all out of student supplies for paleontology.

(Man): It's okay. The department has plenty.

(Narrator): What does the man imply?

12. ***(Man):*** In your paper, you did an excellent job of explaining Shakespeare's sonnets.

(Woman): Thanks. It took me the whole term to write it.

(Narrator): What does the woman mean?

13. ***(Man):*** Do you play volleyball? My team needs one more player.

(Woman): I was captain of my high school team. Count me in.

(Narrator): What does the woman mean?

14. ***(Woman):*** They have to close the coffee shop in the student union.

(Man): Oh no! Where am I going to spend my time between my classes?

(Narrator): What does the man mean?

15. ***(Man):*** Why do we have to buy tickets to the rock concert now?

(Woman): So we don't have to wait in long lines later.

(Narrator): What does the woman mean?

16. ***(Man):*** Why don't we study together for the math final exam?

(Woman): I'll do you one better. Why don't you join our math study group?

(Narrator): What does the woman mean?

17. ***(Woman):*** How do you like this sweatshirt? They're giving them away at the bookstore.

(Man): It's great! I want one just like it.

(Narrator): What is the man going to do?

18. ***(Man):*** Will the professor ask us about glaciers?

(Woman): He spent three lectures on nothing but glaciers.

(Narrator): What does the woman mean?

19. ***(Woman):*** I saw the sign telling us that we will have a fire drill at the dorm tonight.

(Man): It's about time!

(Narrator): What does the man mean?

20. ***(Woman):*** Which do you prefer, hunting or fishing?

(Man): I'm a vegetarian.

(Narrator): What does the man imply?

21. ***(Man):*** Poets are impractical, aren't they? I mean they don't have to deal with people the way you and I have to.

(Woman): Well, the American poet, William Carlos Williams, was a pediatrician.

(Narrator): What does the woman mean?

22. ***(Woman):*** You know that new teaching assistant in biology lab? I can't understand a word he says.

(Man): Join the club!

(Narrator): What does the man mean?

23. ***(Woman):*** Well, our hard work paid off! We got elected to the student council.

(Man): I think the hard work has just begun.

(Narrator): What does the man mean?

24. ***(Man):*** Which bone is thicker, the tibia or the fibia?

(Woman): I'm going to look that up right now.

(Narrator): What does the woman imply?

25. *(Man):* What's your schedule like this semester?

(Woman): It's okay, except for Thursday, which is completely filled.

(Narrator): What does the woman mean?

26. *(Woman):* Did you hear what happened to Roberta and Phyllis.

(Man): Yes. What a shame!

(Narrator): What does the man mean?

27. *(Woman):* I'm not finished with this project, and I haven't had anything to eat all day.

(Man): Why don't I run over to the cafeteria and get you something?

(Narrator): What will the man probably do?

28. *(Woman):* How was Sam's performance in the play?

(Man): I was amazed. Sam was head and shoulders above everyone else in the cast!

(Narrator): What does the man mean?

29. *(Woman):* Wasn't my address book on the table here a few minutes ago?

(Man): Beats me.

(Narrator): What can be inferred about the man?

30. *(Man):* Hey, you have been studying entomology for 5 hours straight. I'd say it's time for a break.

(Woman): No! This stuff is a blast!

(Narrator): What does the woman mean?

Day 12

Listening Comprehension

Long Conversation Drill: Part I

Today's Assignment

- Complete Part I of the Long Conversation Drill and check your answers.

Today, you will practice with long conversations and answering questions. If you need to, take a few minutes to review what you learned on Day 5. The answers and scripts for the audio are printed at the end of this chapter. This drill is not on the CD. We have provided a script at the end of this chapter that you should tear out along the dashed line. Then, you can either read the script to yourself as you work through the questions, or you can have a friend read the script to you while you work through the questions.

Directions: In this section, you will read longer conversations. After each conversation, you will be asked several questions, and you will see the questions printed here with four answer choices. Choose an answer and mark it either in the book or on a separate sheet of scrap paper. Remember to answer the questions based on what is stated or implied by the speakers.

Questions 1–5. Listen to a conversation about improving the food in a cafeteria.

On the screen, you will see a picture of two students sitting at a table in a college cafeteria.

1. What do the man and woman want?
   (A) To protest the food in the cafeteria
   (B) To write letters to the campus newspaper
   (C) To meet with the director of food services
   (D) To get good food at reasonable prices

2. What does the man not want to do?
   (A) Write a letter
   (B) Carry a sign
   (C) Talk to his parents
   (D) Talk to food service personnel

3. What kind of letters does the woman think should be written?
   (A) Polite but firm
   (B) Threatening and rude
   (C) Boring and emotional
   (D) Filled with protest

4. Who will the man and woman get to write letters for them?
   (A) The Director of Food Services
   (B) The Dean of Students
   (C) Their parents
   (D) The editor of the campus newspaper

5. What are the man and woman going to do next?
   (A) Talk to their parents
   (B) Talk to the Director of Food Services
   (C) Talk to the editor of the campus newspaper
   (D) Talk to Dean of Students

Questions 6–10. Listen to two college students discuss their favorite high school teachers.

On the screen, you will see the words "High School Education" and then a picture of high school Yearbook photographs of faculty members.

6. Why is the woman sad?
   (A) Her mother is ill.
   (B) She won't go home for the holidays.
   (C) She didn't get a scholarship to study chemistry.
   (D) Her favorite high school teacher is ill.

7. What was the name of the woman's high school chemistry teacher?
   (A) Mr. Peterson
   (B) Miss Dickey
   (C) Mr. Payson
   (D) Miss Glass

8. How does the woman describe her chemistry teacher?
   (A) Old and tired.
   (B) Complicated and impatient.
   (C) Young and handsome.
   (D) Patient and funny.

9. Who was the man's favorite high school teacher?
   (A) His history teacher.
   (B) His English teacher.
   (C) His chemistry teacher.
   (D) His gym teacher.

10. How do the man and woman feel about their teachers?
   (A) They feel sad about them.
   (B) They feel bad about their teaching.
   (C) They feel lucky to have had them.
   (D) They feel happy that they are retired.

Questions 11–15. Listen to a conversation between a student and his adviser.

On the screen, you will see the words "Preparing a Resume" and a picture of a hand holding a student's resume.

11. How much does Robert have to revise his resume?
   (A) The entire resume
   (B) Only a couple of things
   (C) His name and address
   (D) His college degree

12. Where should the man put his name on the resume?
   (A) At the bottom of the page, to the right
   (B) After career objectives
   (C) At the center of the top of the page
   (D) Before references at the bottom

13. What is missing from his resume? Choose two answers.
   (A) His grade point average
   (B) His career objectives
   (C) His parents' names
   (D) His references

14. According to the woman, what does a company want to learn from Robert's resume?
    - (A) The kind of work Robert wants
    - (B) The kinds of magazines Robert reads
    - (C) The kinds of advisers Robert has
    - (D) The kinds of resumes Robert has written
15. According to the woman, who should Robert call?
    - (A) The advisers who helped him write his resume
    - (B) The personnel director of an accounting firm
    - (C) The managers he worked for during the summer
    - (D) The chairman of his department

Questions 16–20. Listen to a conversation between two students about their hometowns.

On the screen, you will see the words "Big city or small city" and then a picture of two students sitting on a bench on a college campus.

16. Where is the woman from?
    - (A) Ames, Iowa
    - (B) Chicago, Illinois
    - (C) Sugarland, Iowa
    - (D) Memphis, Tennessee
17. What did the man call Chicago?
    - (A) The international city
    - (B) The fun city
    - (C) The windy city
    - (D) The music city
18. Where are the Art Institute and the Field Museum?
    - (A) Near Lake Michigan
    - (B) Near Sugarland, Iowa
    - (C) Near the Tennessee River
    - (D) Near Ames, Iowa
19. What winter sport do people in Sugarland enjoy?
    - (A) Ice skating
    - (B) Going for a ride
    - (C) Sledding
    - (D) Cross-country skiing
20. Where do the man and his family go to see plays?
    - (A) At the University of Iowa
    - (B) At the University of Chicago
    - (C) At the University of Tennessee
    - (D) At the University of Illinois

Questions 21–25. Listen to a student and her professor discuss her final project.

On the screen, you will see the words "Cultural Criticism" and a picture of student in a professor's office.

21. Where did Jacques Barzun teach?
    - (A) Columbia University
    - (B) Northwestern University
    - (C) New York University
    - (D) City College of New York
22. Which philosopher was important to Jacques Barzun?
    - (A) Lionel Trilling
    - (B) Hector Berlioz
    - (C) William James
    - (D) Henry James
23. Which books did William James write? Choose two answers.
    - (A) *The Beginning of the Journey*
    - (B) *The Principles of Psychology*
    - (C) *Varieties of Religious Experience*
    - (D) *The Thought and Work of William James*
24. Whose biography did Jacques Barzun write?
    - (A) Lionel Trilling
    - (B) William James
    - (C) Francis Hodge
    - (D) Hector Berlioz

25. What did the professor tell Sandra to do with her final project?
    (A) Read at least one book by all the writers that Barzun wrote about
    (B) Write about Diana Trilling's book
    (C) Select two writers whose work Barzun and Trilling taught
    (D) Use all of Barzun's essays as resource material

Questions 26–30. Listen to a conversation between a student and his adviser.

On the screen, you will see the words "After graduation" and a picture of a male student and female professor in her office.

26. What is the conversation mainly about?
    (A) Simon's economics grades
    (B) Simon's schedule for his senior year
    (C) Simon's ability to make a decision
    (D) Simon's ability to pay for graduate school

27. What doubts does Simon have about going to graduate school? Choose two answers.
    (A) His ability to do the work
    (B) His ability to plan his senior year
    (C) His ability to pass economics
    (D) His ability to pay for school

28. What had Simon previously told his adviser that he wanted to do?
    (A) Become a poet
    (B) Go to law school
    (C) Study economics
    (D) Take history in graduate school

29. What does the woman think about Simon's ability to do graduate work?
    (A) She thinks he can do graduate work
    (B) She thinks he's spinning around a lot of choices
    (C) She thinks he will not pass economics
    (D) She thinks he is a terrible student

30. What does the woman advise Simon to do?
    (A) Put pressure on himself to make a decision
    (B) Talk to his parents and then decide
    (C) Nothing for the present
    (D) Go to law school

Answer Key for Day 12—Long Conversation Drill: Part 1

1. D
2. B
3. A
4. C
5. B
6. D
7. A
8. D
9. B
10. C
11. B
12. C
13. B and D
14. A
15. C
16. B
17. C
18. A
19. D
20. A
21. A
22. C
23. B and C
24. D
25. C
26. C
27. A and D
28. B
29. A
30. C

Day 12—Script for Long Conversation Drill: Part I

(Narrator): Directions: In this section, you will hear longer conversations. After each conversation, you will be asked several questions about what you heard, and you will see the questions printed here with four answer choices. Choose an answer and mark it either in the book or on a separate sheet of scrap paper. Remember to answer the questions based on what is stated or implied by the speakers.

(Narrator): Questions 1–5. Listen to a conversation about improving the food in a cafeteria.

(Man): The food gets worse every day. And next term, they are going to raise the price of meal tickets.

(Woman): You know, this might be a good time for a boycott of the cafeteria.

(Man): I don't think carrying signs will help us get good food.

(Woman): We don't have to do that. Look, both of us should write letters to the campus newspaper, complaining about the food. We send copies of the letters to the Dean of Student Life, and to the president of the college.

(Man): Those things never work.

(Woman): They do if the letters are well written and polite but firm in our demands. We get our friends to write letters, and they get their friends to do the same.

(Man): And they send the letters to the student newspaper with copies to the dean and president. And … and we get our parents to do the same thing.

(Woman): Good idea. Look, we aren't asking for resignations, and we aren't threatening anyone. All we want is good food at a reasonable price.

(Man): We could offer to meet with the food service personnel and talk to them about the menu and prices.

(Woman): Maybe we should offer that first, before we write the letters. If we talk personally with the director of food services, he just might agree with us.

(Man): Hey! Let's do it! We can see her now.

(Woman): Okay, but let's be polite and calm with her.

(Man): Sure! As Ben Franklin said, "You get more flies with honey than vinegar."

(Narrator):

1. What do the man and woman want?
2. What does the man not want to do?
3. What kind of letters does the woman think should be written?
4. Who will the man and woman get to write letters for them?
5. What are the man and woman going to do next?

(Narrator): Questions 6–10. Listen to two college students discuss their favorite high school teachers.

(Man): What's wrong, Ellen? You look like you just lost your best friend.

(Woman): Almost. I just got a letter from home, and my mom says that my high school chemistry teacher is in the hospital, and he's very sick!

(Man): Wow, I'm sorry. How old is he?

(Woman): Not that old, really. I saw him when I went home during the holidays. Mr. Peterson is his name, and he'd just retired, and was having a great time. No one deserved it more!

(Man): It's kind of unusual for a favorite teacher to have taught someone chemistry.

(Woman): Oh, at my high school he was everybody's favorite. He made things clear and was always so patient with students who didn't understand something the first time. And he was funny! He used jokes to ease tension. Four students in my class got scholarships to study chemistry at some of the best universities.

(Man): He reminds me of Miss Dickey.

(Woman): Who's that?

(Man): My English teacher. I hated English class until I got to be in her class.

(Woman): Did she joke like Mr. Peterson?

(Man): No, she didn't. As a matter of fact, I don't remember her smiling. She had gray hair pulled straight back from her face, and she wore wire-rimmed glasses and looked very serious. But, she made literature come alive for us. I don't know what it was with Miss Dickey, but everyone in that class worked harder for her than they did for any other teacher. Somehow, she let us know that she thought we could all do excellent work and that was what she expected from us.

(Woman): I guess we were lucky to have such good teachers.

(Man): I couldn't agree more.

(Narrator):

6. Why is the woman sad?
7. What was the name of the woman's high school chemistry teacher?
8. How does the woman describe her chemistry teacher?
9. Who was the man's favorite high school teacher?
10. How do the man and woman feel about their teachers?

(Narrator): Questions 11–15. Listen to a conversation between a student and his adviser.

(Man): Thanks for helping me with my resume, Mrs. Moore.

(Woman): Happy to help, Robert. Actually, you have done a pretty good job, and we have only a couple of things to fix.

(Man): Okay. What first?

(Woman): Well, you have your name, address, and telephone number centered at the top of the page. That's good. But the next thing should be a statement of your career objectives.

(Man): I just want a job.

(Woman): I know you're willing to work hard, but Robert, a company wants to know what kind of job you are looking for, the kind of job that you're willing to work hard doing. Understand?

(Man): Oh, I got it. Like accounting and advertising and personnel management.

(Woman): You have to choose one and put that next to the word "objective."

(Man): So, "Objective: Advertising," right?

(Woman): Well you should say something like, "Positions of increasing responsibility in personnel management." Or, "Positions in the creative department of an advertising agency."

(Man): I see now. What about "Writing copy for an advertising agency?"

(Woman): Very good! Now, then you should list the jobs you have had.

(Man): They were only summer jobs.

(Woman): Yes, but they show you wanted to work, that you didn't sit around the whole summer at the local swimming pool. And, you did work for a couple of advertising agencies, didn't you?

(Man): Yes, I did. And both department managers told me they liked my work.

(Woman): Then, you should call them and find out if you may list them as references.

(Man): Where should I list my references?

(Woman): Here at the bottom of the page. Use their names, position, name of company, address, and telephone number.

(Narrator):

11. How much does Robert have to revise his resume?
12. Where should the man put his name on the resume?
13. What is missing from his resume? Choose two answers.
14. According to the woman, what does a company want to learn from Robert's resume?
15. According to the woman, whom should Robert call?

(Narrator): Questions 16–20. Listen to a conversation between two students about their hometowns.

(Man): So, Jeannie, where are you from?

(Woman): I'm from Chicago.

(Man): The windy city, huh? I'm from Sugarland, Iowa.

(Woman): How did Sugarland get its name?

(Man): I don't know. Even my parents and their friends don't have a clue. Sugarland doesn't have anything to do with sugar. Most folks are farmers and raise corn, wheat, and dairy cattle.

(Woman): How many people live there?

(Man): About 2,000. It's a small town, but it's really a nice place to live. I like the peace and quiet, friendly neighbors. And, the good thing is it's only 3 hours from Chicago.

(Woman): I've lived in Chicago all my life, and the only time I have seen a small town like Sugarland was on a family vacation, when we drove to California.

(Man): You must like the big city life.

(Woman): I do, even though it gets noisy sometimes. But the people are very interesting. We have lots of people from different countries, because there's lots of international business there. I like the museums, particularly the Art Institute and the Field Museum. They are near Lake Michigan. And there's always good music playing at a concert hall or a club. That's what I'd miss the most, if I had to move. What do people do in Sugarland when they aren't working?

(Man): Oh, I guess what you'd expect from small towners. We visit each other, go cross-country skiing in the winter, and watch TV. My parents and I like to drive over to Ames and see the plays at the University of Iowa. They have a famous actor training and playwriting program there. Tennessee Williams went there, and so did a lot of famous actors.

(Woman): Sounds nice.

(Man): Oh, it is. We have the quiet of the small town, but we can easily drive to big cities for fun.

(Narrator):

16. Where is the woman from?
17. What did the man call Chicago?
18. Where are the Art Institute and the Field Museum?
19. What winter sport do people in Sugarland enjoy?
20. Where do the man and his family go to see plays?

(Narrator): Questions 21–25. Listen to a student and her professor discuss her final project.

(Woman): Thanks for seeing me, Professor Hodge.

(Man): What can I do for you, Sandra?

(Woman): I have here my proposal for my final project. I want to write a research paper on Jacques Barzun. I will concentrate on the great works class he taught at Columbia University with Lionel Trilling. I will also review his essays and books about the writers they discussed in the class.

(Man): Good idea. What have you found out about the class?

(Woman): Well, so far, very little. I found Barzun's brief description of the course in the introduction of a collection of his essays.

(Man): Take a look at Diana Trilling's book. It's called *The Beginning of the Journey.* Diana was Lionel Trilling's wife, and she has quite a bit to say about the friendship between Trilling and Barzun, particularly their teaching of that class you want to write about.

(Woman): Oh, thanks for the tip. I am reading Barzun's book about William James, the philosopher Barzun admired so much.

(Man): Yes, and whose work Barzun taught in his class.

(Woman): And I have read James's *Principles of Psychology* and *Varieties of Religious Experience.*

(Man): You've been busy. Sandra, there is too much to cover. Barzun was one of those critics who seemed to have read every work of Western literature ever written, and he wrote more books and essays than you can finish for this project. Narrow your research to one or two people that Barzun wrote about. James is certainly one you should include in your paper. But choose only one other, and you'll have plenty of material for your project.

(Woman): Does it have to be a writer? Barzun wrote an excellent biography about the composer Hector Berlioz.

(Man): True, but stick with your proposal. Choose from the writers of the work that he and Trilling taught.

(Woman): Okay, Dr. Hodge. Thanks a lot.

(Man): Good luck.

(Narrator):

21. Where did Jacques Barzun teach?
22. Which philosopher was important to Jacques Barzun?
23. Which books did William James write? Choose two answers.
24. Whose biography did Jacques Barzun write?
25. What did the professor tell Sandra to do with her final project?

(Narrator): Questions 26–30. Listen to a conversation between a student and his adviser.

(Woman): What can I do for you, Simon?

(Man): Well, I'm finishing my junior year, and I want to make sure I am ready and organized for next year.

(Woman): Good for you. Too many students wait until the last minute to organize things for their senior year.

(Man): I've got all the courses selected, and I have all the credits necessary for graduation.

(Woman): I remember approving your academic plan.

(Man): Well, yes you did.

(Woman): So Simon, what's the *real* problem that you want to discuss? You're ready for next year.

(Man): Well, I don't know what I want to do after I graduate.

(Woman): I thought you wanted to go to graduate school.

(Man): I did too. But I am having these doubts about whether I can do the work. I also don't know if I'll have the money. I mean, my parents want to help, but I can't keep asking them. Also, even if I could do the work and had the money, I don't know what I want to study in grad school.

(Woman): Don't you want to go to law school, become a lawyer?

(Man): I don't know. I've also been thinking of economics. I've made all A's in those courses, and the work is intriguing. Then again, I like history and poetry, too. I just can't make up my mind. I don't want to keep spinning around all these fields of study, but I just can't make up my mind. What do you think I should do?

(Woman): Nothing.

(Man): Nothing?

(Woman): For now. Simon, you are certainly capable of doing graduate work. What you should do, however, is nothing. You have a busy year ahead of you. Enjoy it. Don't think about planning your life after graduation. Don't force the decision. Eventually, you will come to find out what it is you want to do. Often, while we are under great pressure to make a decision, the best thing to do is just…

(Man): Nothing. Right, I see what you mean.

(Woman): If you want to talk again, don't hesitate to see me.

(Man): Thanks a lot.

(Narrator):

26. What is the conversation mainly about?
27. What doubts does Simon have about going to graduate school? Choose two answers.
28. What had Simon previously told his adviser that he wanted to do?
29. What does the woman think about Simon's ability to do graduate work?
30. What does the woman advise Simon to do?

Day 13

Listening Comprehension

Long Conversation Drill: Part II

Today's Assignment

- Complete Part II of the Long Conversation Drill and check your answers.

Today, you will continue to practice long conversations and answering questions. If you need to, take a few minutes to review what you learned on Day 5 and your answers from Long Conversation Drill: Part I. The answers and scripts for the audio are printed at the end of this chapter. This drill is not on the CD. We have provided a script at the end of this chapter that you should tear out along the dashed line. Then, you can either read the script to yourself as you work through the questions, or you can have a friend read the script to you while you work through the questions.

Directions: In this section, you will read longer conversations. After each conversation, you will be asked several questions, and you will see the questions printed here with four answer choices. Choose an answer and mark it either in the book or on a separate sheet of scrap paper. Remember to answer the questions based on what is stated or implied by the speakers.

Questions 1–5. Listen to two students discuss a famous archeological site.

On the screen, you will see the word "Archeology" and then a picture of the ruins of the Oracle at Delphi.

1. What did the man and woman mainly discuss?
   (A) The medical problems of the man
   (B) The religion of the Greeks
   (C) The site of the Oracle of Delphi
   (D) The Greek team of scientists
2. How far is the temple site from Athens?
   (A) About 100 miles
   (B) About 400 miles
   (C) About 700 miles
   (D) About 1,000 miles

3. What did the oracle do?
   (A) The oracle taught religion of Apollo to Greeks and Romans.
   (B) The oracle built the temple of Apollo over an underground lake.
   (C) The oracle gave advice to rulers, citizens, and philosophers.
   (D) The oracle sat in the walkway to the temple.

4. Who erected the monuments along the walkway to the temple?
   (A) Oracles to insure they would not be forgotten
   (B) States or individuals in thanks for the help they got from Apollo
   (C) A team of scientists looking for ruins
   (D) Soldiers and sailors about to go to war

5. What creates problems for the preservation of the site?
   (A) Archeology
   (B) Religion
   (C) Education
   (D) Tourism

Questions 6–10. Listen to a student talk to the president of his college.

On the screen, you will see the word "Retirement" and then a picture of a student and the president of a college sitting in the president's office.

6. Why is the man talking to the woman?
   (A) To ask her about her career and her retirement
   (B) To ask her for a recommendation to the University of Illinois
   (C) To ask her to introduce him to Barry McCarthy
   (D) To ask her about an English class

7. What organization is the man active with?
   (A) The English Department
   (B) "The Clean Slate"
   (C) The campus newspaper
   (D) The University of Illinois

8. What is the woman going to do in three weeks?
   (A) Take a trip to Ireland
   (B) Retire from the presidency of the college
   (C) Go to a poetry conference in Illinois
   (D) Become chairperson of the English Department

9. What was the woman's second job?
   (A) Writing for "The Clean Slate"
   (B) Selling educational magazines
   (C) Teaching at the University of Illinois
   (D) Recruiting students to the college

10. What are the man and woman going to talk about next?
    (A) What the man wrote about Barry McCarthy
    (B) What the woman did as president of the college
    (C) What the man did at the poetry conference
    (D) What the woman wanted to do, but couldn't

Questions 11–15. Listen to a student and professor discuss the student's paper.

On the screen, you will see the words "Computer Science" and then a picture of an abacus.

11. What is discussion mainly about?
    (A) The abacus in science
    (B) The history of the abacus
    (C) The computer in Babylon
    (D) The sand-writing in the Middle East

12. Where was the abacus probably first used?
    (A) Rome
    (B) Greece
    (C) Egypt
    (D) Babylon

13. How did the abacus get its name?
    (A) From the Babylonian word for "board"
    (B) From the Semitic word for "wipe the dust"
    (C) From the Greek word for "commerce"
    (D) From the Latin word for "string and beads"

14. When did users of the abacus string counter beads on wires?
    (A) Sometime after the fall of the Roman Empire
    (B) During the Babylonian era
    (C) In the seventeenth century
    (D) After the invention of calculators

15. What concept is the man going to look up?
    (A) The concept of arithmetic
    (B) The concept of linguistics
    (C) The concept of zero
    (D) The concept of counting

Questions 16–20. Listen to two students discuss student housing on campus.

On the screen, you will see the words "Student Housing" and then a picture of two students sitting in a student center coffee shop.

16. What are the students mainly discussing?
    (A) Physics majors
    (B) Special interest dormitories
    (C) French poetry and operas
    (D) English food and literature

17. What is the man's major?
    (A) French
    (B) Physics
    (C) English
    (D) Music

18. What is the name of the dormitory where many French majors live?
    (A) Bainbridge Hall
    (B) Ruth Jones Hall
    (C) Payson Hall
    (D) Rue de la Paix

19. What do French majors do in their dormitory?
    (A) Go to French club meetings
    (B) Attend lectures on physics
    (C) Cook French meals
    (D) Listen to opera

20. What will the man probably do next?
    (A) Ask the dorm counselor for more advice.
    (B) Ask the president of the French club for more information.
    (C) Ask the departmental secretary about the Rue de la Paix.
    (D) Ask for a book on French cooking at the library.

Questions 21–25. Listen to students discuss their volunteer work off campus.

On the screen, you will see the words "Community Service" and then a picture of two students wearing white hospital coats standing in a hospital waiting room.

21. Where do the students work?
    (A) At a kindergarten
    (B) At a hospital
    (C) At a doctor's office
    (D) At a private school

22. What kind of work are the man and the woman doing?
    (A) Professional assistance in a hospital
    (B) Interview patients for a hospital's newsletter
    (C) Make movies for children
    (D) Volunteer work for the hospital

23. According to the man, why haven't they seen each other at the hospital?
    (A) They don't like each other.
    (B) They aren't in the same sociology class.
    (C) They don't work in the same part of the hospital.
    (D) They aren't going to graduate together.

24. Why does working with children remind the woman of home?
    (A) She has six brothers and sisters.
    (B) Her mother came from a big family.
    (C) Her parents were doctors.
    (D) She wants to have a lot of children.

25. How do most of the patients feel about the man's work?
    (A) They dislike what he does.
    (B) They hope he becomes a good writer.
    (C) They are grateful for what he does.
    (D) They never want to play cards with him.

Questions 26–30. Listen to two students discuss their upcoming trips to universities in London and Tokyo.

On the screen, you will see the words "International Education" and then a picture of two senior students walking across Harvard Yard, at Harvard University in the United States.

26. Where are the man and woman from?
    (A) Cambridge, Massachusetts
    (B) London, England
    (C) Wolf Point, Montana
    (D) Tokyo, Japan

27. What did the woman do before she met the man?
    (A) She sent a telegram to the London School of Economics.
    (B) She called her teachers at Wolf Point High School.
    (C) She told her parents about being accepted at London School of Economics.
    (D) She went to class and took her final exam.

28. What is the man going to study in graduate school?
    (A) Seismology
    (B) Oceanography
    (C) Cellular Biology
    (D) Cosmic Radiation

29. According to the woman, who was one of the co-founders of the London School of Economics?
    (A) Jack London
    (B) Karl Marx
    (C) Beatrice Wolf
    (D) George Bernard Shaw

30. Why did the man and woman want to study at schools overseas?
    (A) To be in the middle of cutting-edge technology
    (B) To meet students from many different countries
    (C) To work at small schools in small cities
    (D) To get away from Wolf Point, Montana

ANSWER KEY FOR DAY 13—LONG CONVERSATION DRILL: PART II

1.	C	16.	B
2.	A	17.	A
3.	C	18.	D
4.	B	19.	C
5.	D	20.	C
6.	A	21.	B
7.	C	22.	D
8.	B	23.	C
9.	C	24.	A
10.	D	25.	C
11.	B	26.	C
12.	D	27.	C
13.	B	28.	A
14.	A	29.	D
15.	C	30.	B

DAY 13—SCRIPT FOR LONG CONVERSATION DRILL: PART II

(Narrator): Directions: In this section, you will hear longer conversations. After each conversation, you will be asked several questions about what you heard, and you will see the questions printed here with four answer choices. Choose an answer and mark it either in the book or on a separate sheet of scrap paper. Remember to answer the questions based on what is stated or implied by the speakers.

(Narrator): Questions 1–5. Listen to two students discuss a famous archeological site.

(Man): Thanks a lot for going over your notes with me.

(Woman): Oh, no problem, Mike. You had to miss class to go to the doctor. I hope everything is okay.

(Man): The doctor gave me some medication and I feel fine. So what did Professor Barnes lecture on?

(Woman): He spoke about the Oracle at Delphi.

(Man): Oh, yeah. I know a little about that, and I read about it when I studied Greek drama. It's a temple to the god Apollo about 100 miles from Athens. The Greeks called it the navel of the world. The oracle gave advice to rulers, citizens, and philosophers. They would ask the oracle to tell them what to do about a war, or a family matter, and the oracle always answered their questions in such a way that the advice might help or harm them.

(Woman): Right. Professor Barnes spoke about the ruins at Delphi, and what has been learned. First, the oracle sat in a chamber at the rear of the temple, and the chamber was built over a crack in the earth's crust. A gas leaked into the oracle chamber, and when asked a question, the oracle would inhale the gas and get a feeling of euphoria. Under the influence of this gas, the oracle would answer the questions. Recently, a team of scientists, including a geologist, found that the gas was a sweet smelling anesthetic.

(Man): What did the site look like when it was first built?

(Woman): The entire site was a large, roughly rectangular area enclosed by a wall. A walkway lined with monuments and treasuries wound up through the walled in area to the temple of Apollo itself. The monuments along the way were erected by states or individuals in thanks for the help they got from Apollo. The existing temple site includes only the foundation, some steps, and a few columns from a structure built in the fourth century B.C.E. Preservation efforts have included reburial of several lesser buildings. The site is a major tourist attraction.

(Man): That must create major problems in the effort to preserve the site.

(Woman): It does. But, you want to know what I think is most significant?

(Man): What's that?

(Woman): In a society dominated by men, the oracle was always a woman.

(Narrator):

1. What did the man and woman mainly discuss?
2. How far is the temple site from Athens?
3. What did the oracle do?
4. Who erected the monuments along the walkway to the temple?
5. What creates problems for the preservation of the site?

(Narrator): Questions 6–10. Listen to a student talk to the president of his college.

(Man): Thanks for taking time to see me, Dr. Holt. I know how busy you are.

(Woman): I always have time for the editor of the campus newspaper. Please, take a seat.

(Man): Thanks.

(Woman): What do you want to ask me?

(Man): Well, you're retiring at the end of this term, and the term ends in three weeks. So, why don't we start with whatever thoughts you have on your retirement.

(Woman): Well, of course I will miss the college, the students in particular. I have always loved being around young people, and I think students are what I will miss the most.

(Man): Well, students will miss you. You've been an extremely popular president, somebody who was always in the student's corner, so to speak.

(Woman): Thank you for that, David. Yes, I have tried to put the interests of the students first. After all, if it weren't for the students, we wouldn't have a college.

(Man): You began as an instructor right here, didn't you?

(Woman): Yes, I did. I got my first teaching job in the English Department.

(Man): Then after three years, you took a position with the University of Illinois.

(Woman): Yes. I stayed at the university for six years and came back here.

(Man): You eventually became chairman of the English Department, and you brought some nationally important professors to join the faculty. Particularly Barry McCarthy from Ireland, who started "The Clean Slate," the literary quarterly. Where did you meet Mr. McCarthy?

(Woman): At a poetry conference. I told him about the college, and invited him to visit us. He came, he saw, and he never left. I am happy to say that I sold him on our school! And "The Clean Slate" has won many literary awards. Which I think is entirely due to his work.

(Man): Most people in your position have a wish-list, things that they wanted to accomplish, but couldn't. Talk about yours.

(Narrator):

6. Why is the man talking to the woman?
7. What organization is the man active with?
8. What is the woman going to do in three weeks?
9. What was the woman's second job?
10. What are the man and woman going to talk about next.

(Narrator): Questions 11–15. Listen to a student and professor discuss the student's paper.

(Woman): I like the idea for your term paper, Howard. The abacus is a very important tool for mathematical computation. How are you doing with the research?

(Man): I have enjoyed getting the information for the paper. The abacus is a fascinating device.

(Woman): And the ancestor of our calculators and computers. What have you found out?

(Man): Well, as you know, the abacus is a board with wires that are strung with beads. The board is marked with lines and the position of the beads indicated numerical values—i.e., ones, tens, hundreds, and so on.

(Woman): Where was it first used? How did it come into being?

(Man): It was probably of Babylonian origin, and very important in commerce. The earliest abacus was a board or slab on which a Babylonian spread sand so he could trace letters for general writing purposes.

(Woman): That's how it got its name. Linguists think the word abacus comes from the Semitic word *ibeq,* which means "to wipe the dust"; and then in Greek, "abakos."

(Man): I'll look that up. The Romans cut grooves in the abacus board to keep the counter beads in the proper files. Then, sometime after the fall of the Roman Empire, the counter beads were strung on wires, and it hasn't changed much in form since then.

(Woman): Where was it used?

(Man): In that form, it was used in Europe in the Middle Ages, as well as in the Arab world and in Asia. It reached Japan in the sixteenth century. I was surprised to learn that abaci are still used throughout the Middle East, China, and Japan. An expert user can solve problems as quickly as many modern calculating machines can.

(Woman): Find out about place value and about the concept of zero. Those developments affected the use of the abacus. And that needs to be in your paper.

(Man): I sure will. Thanks a lot.

(Narrator):

11. What is the discussion mainly about?
12. Where was the abacus probably first used?
13. How did the abacus get its name?
14. When did users of the abacus string counter beads on wires?
15. What concept is the man going to look up?

(Narrator): Questions 16–20. Listen to two students discuss student housing on campus.

(Man): Martha, you're a dorm counselor, aren't you?

(Woman): Yes, I am.

(Man): Well, I need some advice about dormitory living.

(Woman): I'll be happy to help, if I can.

(Man): Well, I am majoring in French, and I need to speak it as often as possible.

(Woman): Well, you could join the French club, and meet other students who need to become fluent in French.

(Man): I already belong, and it's terrific. The president of the club told me about a dorm on campus. A dorm where only French is spoken. That's what I'm interested in. What do you know about it?

(Woman): It's one of those so-called special-interest dorms. For example, students with an interest in physics live in Jones Hall. A group of English majors are in Bainbridge. They're on the second and third floors.

(Man): Right. Where do the French-language students stay?

(Woman): The French Department has a special house called Rue de la Paix, after the famous street in Paris. The students cook French meals, read French poetry aloud, listen to French opera recordings. That sort of thing.

(Man): How do I get a residence there?

(Woman): Ask your department secretary.

(Man): You mean Mrs. Bloom?

(Woman): Yes. Mrs. Bloom has all the information about Rue de la Paix: how to get a room there, how much it costs, how many rooms are available. That sort of thing.

(Man): I didn't know that. Thanks a lot Martha.

(Woman): Happy to help.

(Narrator):

16. What are the students mainly discussing?
17. What is the man's major?
18. What is the name of the dormitory where many French majors live?
19. What do French majors do in their dormitory?
20. What will the man probably do next?

(Narrator): Questions 21–25. Listen to students discuss their volunteer work off campus.

(Woman): Hey Tim, I didn't know you were working here at the community hospital.

(Man): Oh, sure. I've been volunteering for the last six months. I come in and work with the older patients in the geriatric ward. You know, read the newspaper to them, play cards and board games. Sometimes, I wheel them to get X-rays or to physical therapy. What about you?

(Woman): I came on board two months ago at the beginning of the spring term. I volunteer in the other part of the hospital, in the children's wing of the hospital. So, I show movies in the recreation room, play games, help them in and out of their wheelchairs. I also feed them when they have broken arms or hands.

(Man): No wonder we haven't run into each other. We work in different areas. How do you like it?

(Woman): I think it's important work. Helping kids. And I have six brothers and sisters, so this reminds me of home. How did you get involved with working with the elderly?

(Man): When I started, the only job they had open was in the geriatric ward, so I took it.

(Woman): You must like it. You've stuck with it for six months.

(Man): Well, it took some getting used to. My grandparents are all healthy, so I had never dealt with the health problems of senior citizens. But, like you, I think it's very important work, and most of the patients have been so grateful for whatever I've done for them. When I finish the class in sociology, I'm going to continue here as a volunteer. It makes me feel good that I am helping other people.

(Woman): I feel the same.

(Narrator):

21. Where do the students work?
22. What kind of work are the man and the woman doing?
23. According to the man, why haven't they seen each other at the hospital?
24. Why does working with children remind the woman of home?
25. How do most of the patients feel about the man's work?

(Narrator): Questions 26–30. Listen to two students discuss their upcoming trips to universities in London and Tokyo.

(Man): I was accepted for graduate study at the University of Tokyo.

(Woman): Wow! And I'll be at the London School of Economics.

(Man): That's fabulous. Just think, two kids from Wolf Point, Montana graduating from Harvard University.

(Woman): And then going to two of the greatest educational institutions outside of the United States.

(Man): I haven't told my folks yet. What about you?

(Woman): I called them this morning. But what about Tokyo? I know you speak fluent Japanese, but why are you going there?

(Man): To study seismology. The university has one the best earthquake study centers in the world. The university also has institutes for research in molecular and cellular biology, cosmic radiation, and oceanography. So I'll be right in the middle of some cutting-edge research. What about the London School of Economics? The only thing I know about the place is that it was started by George Bernard Shaw.

(Woman): Well, he was one of the cofounders with Sidney and Beatrice Webb. But the important thing is what I'll learn there. Imagine! Five of its faculty have won Nobel Prizes. I can study courses in gender, housing, and social policy and planning in developing countries. I want to get involved with international trade in some way after I graduate.

(Man): How big is it?

(Woman): Oh, about 5,600 students. What about the University of Tokyo?

(Man): It's much larger. Twenty-five thousand students. Many of them are from countries other than Japan, and I'm looking forward to meeting students from all over the world.

(Woman): That's why I applied to the London School of Economics. Almost half the students are from overseas.

(Man): Yep, we've come a long way from Wolf Point, Montana.

(Narrator):

26. Where are the man and woman from?
27. What did the woman do before she met the man?
28. What is the man going to study in graduate school?
29. According to the woman, who was one of the cofounders of the London School of Economics?
30. Why did the man and woman want to study at schools overseas?

Day 14

Listening Comprehension

Lecture Drill: Part I

Today's Assignment

- Complete Part I of the Lecture Drill.

Today, you will practice lectures and answering questions. If you need to, take a few minutes to review what you learned on Day 5. The answers and scripts for the audio are printed at the end of this chapter. This drill is not on the CD. We have provided a script at the end of this chapter that you should tear out along the dashed line. Then, you can either read the script to yourself as you work through the questions, or you can have a friend read the script to you while you work through the questions.

Directions: In this section, you will read lectures. After each lecture, you will be asked several questions, and you will see the questions printed here with four answer choices. Choose an answer and mark it either in the book or on a separate sheet of scrap paper. Remember to answer the questions based on what is stated or implied by the speakers.

Questions 1–5. Listen to a lecture about the cultural effects of Charlemagne's rule.

On the screen, you will see the words "European History, The Reign of Charlemagne" and then a picture of Charlemagne.

1. What is the main idea of the lecture?
   (A) Charlemagne's education
   (B) Charlemagne's influence on the culture of his empire
   (C) Charlemagne's languages
   (D) Charlemagne's library

2. When did Charlemagne become Emperor of the Holy Roman Empire?
   (A) In the middle of the eighth century
   (B) In the middle of the ninth century
   (C) In the middle of the tenth century
   (D) In the middle of the eleventh century

3. What did Charlemagne's library contain?
   (A) Books and letters of the High German language
   (B) Poetry and government records
   (C) Works by Greek and Roman writers
   (D) School books for young knights

4. According to the speaker, what did Charlemagne do to raise the level of religion and justice?
   (A) He learned Latin and Greek and read many books.
   (B) He taught his family to speak High German.
   (C) He demanded that Latin be taught in all schools.
   (D) He surrounded himself with the best minds of the empire.

5. What will the lecturer probably talk about next?
   (A) How Charlemagne regarded artists and scholars
   (B) How Latin and Greek became a part of the German language
   (C) How young knights were educated
   (D) How Charlemagne's renaissance affected government

Questions 6–10. Listen to a lecture on Latin American literature.

On the screen, you will see the words "World Literature" and then a picture of a map of the Caribbean and South America.

6. What does magic realism contain?
   (A) Realistic depictions of actual events in movies
   (B) Nonfiction elements mixed with postcolonial poetry
   (C) Fantastic and mythic elements mixed with realism
   (D) Letters to conquerors of the writers country

7. When was the term "magic realism" first used?
   (A) In the 1940s
   (B) In the 1950s
   (C) In the 1980s
   (D) In the 1990s

8. According to the speaker, what was magic realism the product of?
   (A) The role of women in South America
   (B) Cuban and Brazilian politics in the 1940s
   (C) The differences between the worlds of the conqueror and the conquered
   (D) Blood diseases and mental states of patients

9. Where is Isabel Allende from?
   (A) Brazil
   (B) Chile
   (C) Colombia
   (D) Argentina

10. Which book by Allende was made into a film?
   (A) *Paula*
   (B) *Eva Luna*
   (C) *Of Love and Shadows*
   (D) *The House of the Spirits*

Questions 11–15. Listen to a lecture on alligators.

On the screen, you will see the words "Biology class" and then a picture of an alligator.

11. What do alligators use their tails for?
   (A) Laying eggs
   (B) Hibernating
   (C) Getting food
   (D) Swimming

12. How are crocodiles different from alligators?
   (A) Crocodiles have yellow and black stripes.
   (B) Crocodiles have narrower snouts.
   (C) Crocodiles are longer and heavier.
   (D) Crocodiles do not hibernate.

13. Where do alligators live?
    (A) In mud nests at the bottom of ponds
    (B) In heavily forested jungles in the tropics
    (C) In swamps, lakes, and rivers
    (D) In burrows under cypress trees

14. What do alligators mainly eat?
    (A) Fish, small animals, and birds
    (B) Deer and cattle
    (C) Humans and domesticated animals
    (D) Eggs from the nests of other alligators

15. What is the speaker going to discuss next?
    (A) Nesting habits of alligators
    (B) The Chinese Alligator
    (C) Other fascinating reptiles
    (D) The coloration of alligators

Questions 16–20. Listen to a lecture on a famous writer.

On the screen, you will see the words "American Literature" and a picture of author John Steinbeck.

16. What does the professor mainly discuss?
    (A) The literary style of John Steinbeck
    (B) The career of John Steinbeck
    (C) The manual labor of John Steinbeck
    (D) The education of John Steinbeck

17. Before becoming a successful novelist, how did Steinbeck support himself?
    (A) As a manual laborer
    (B) As a screenwriter
    (C) As a war correspondent
    (D) As a professor at Stanford University

18. Where did John Steinbeck live?
    (A) Oklahoma
    (B) Norway
    (C) Mexico
    (D) California

19. What was his most famous novel?
    (A) *Tortilla Flat*
    (B) *Of Mice and Men*
    (C) *The Grapes of Wrath*
    (D) *The Red Pony*

20. What will the speaker talk about next?
    (A) The film scripts of John Steinbeck
    (B) The writing style of John Steinbeck
    (C) The prizes awarded to John Steinbeck
    (D) The war experiences of John Steinbeck

Questions 21–25. Listen to an economics professor speak about bookkeeping.

On the screen, you will see the word "Economics" and then a picture of various balance sheets and ledgers.

21. How many types of books are used in the bookkeeping process?
    (A) 1
    (B) 2
    (C) 3
    (D) 4

22. What does a journal contain?
    (A) A record of payroll taxes paid to a company
    (B) A record of the content of computer files
    (C) A record of individual accounts
    (D) A record of a company's daily transactions

23. Where did double entry bookkeeping begin?
    (A) In Babylon, Egypt, and Greece
    (B) In London, England
    (C) In the commercial republics of Italy
    (D) In multinational corporations

24. According to the speaker, what historic event provided the stimulus to the growth of double entry bookkeeping?
    (A) The fall of Babylon
    (B) The Persian invasion of Jerusalem
    (C) The American Civil War
    (D) The Industrial Revolution

25. In the second half of the twentieth century, what information did companies have to have?
    (A) Information about various taxes
    (B) Information about sports and entertainment
    (C) Information about food costs
    (D) Information about schools and training programs

Questions 26–30. Listen to a speaker discuss the history of pyramids.

On the screen, you will see the word "Archeology" and then a picture of the pyramids in Egypt.

26. What were the Egyptian pyramids used for?
    (A) Cultivation of the fields
    (B) Storage of food and gold
    (C) Worship of the gods of Egypt
    (D) Burial of the pharaohs

27. What was usually next to a pyramid?
    (A) The Nile River
    (B) A mortuary temple
    (C) Canals and causeways
    (D) Nothing

28. How many royal pyramids have been found in Egypt?
    (A) 3
    (B) 17
    (C) 80
    (D) 102

29. How high was the Great Pyramid at Giza?
    (A) More than 1,600 feet high
    (B) More than 2,400 feet
    (C) More than 4,800 feet
    (D) More than 7,400 feet

30. What originally covered the outside surface of the pyramid?
    (A) White limestone
    (B) Granite blocks
    (C) Hieroglyphics
    (D) Fields for cultivation

ANSWER KEY FOR DAY 14—LECTURE DRILL: PART I

1.	B	16.	B
2.	A	17.	A
3.	C	18.	D
4.	C	19.	C
5.	D	20.	B
6.	C	21.	B
7.	A	22.	D
8.	C	23.	C
9.	B	24.	D
10.	D	25.	A
11.	D	26.	D
12.	B	27.	B
13.	C	28.	C
14.	A	29.	C
15.	B	30.	A

DAY 14—SCRIPT FOR LECTURE DRILL: PART I

(Narrator): Directions: In this section, you will hear lectures. After each lecture, you will be asked several questions about what you heard, and you will see the questions printed here with four answer choices. Choose an answer and mark it either in the book or on a separate sheet of scrap paper. Remember to answer the questions based on what is stated or implied by the speakers.

(Narrator): Questions 1–5. Listen to a lecture about the cultural effects of Charlemagne's rule.

(Professor): Charlemagne became emperor of the Holy Roman Empire in the middle of the eighth century. He immediately began to improve not only Europe's government, but its culture as well. He brought to his court prominent scholars from all parts of the Empire and even from abroad. With the help of these and other literary men, Charlemagne established a court library containing the writings of the founders of Christianity. The library also contained works by Greek and Roman writers. To make sure the library was used, Charlemagne founded a court academy for the education of young knights.

He surrounded himself with well-educated diplomats and administrators, and took part with his family court entertainment as much as he did instruction. His native language was Old High German, and he also learned Latin and Greek. He had historical and theological writings, including St. Augustine's *City of God*, read aloud to him, and he studied mathematics and astronomy.

His cultural interests, however, extended beyond the intellectual activities of his court. Charlemagne worked hard to raise the level of religious observance, morality, and the process of justice throughout the empire. The clearest and most famous example of this was his demand that Latin language and literature be studied extensively in all schools.

This led to the spiritual and literary movement that might be called "Charlemagne's Renaissance" that spread throughout the Empire, especially to schools in monasteries. Charlemagne found the best minds of the whole world and set them to work in the education of the clergy and, finally, of the whole people. This renaissance had an effect on the way the Holy Roman Empire was governed.

(Narrator):

1. What is the main idea of the lecture?
2. When did Charlemagne become Emperor of the Holy Roman Empire?
3. What did Charlemagne's library contain?
4. According to the speaker, what did Charlemagne do to raise the level of religion and justice?
5. What will the lecturer probably talk about next?

(Narrator): Questions 6–10. Listen to a lecture on Latin-American literature.

(Professor): Today we're going to learn about magic realism, which is a style of writing characterized by the seemingly casual and matter-of-fact inclusion of fantastic or mythical elements into what otherwise would be considered realistic fiction. Although this style is used worldwide, the term *magic realism* was first used in the 1940s by Cu-

ban novelist Alejo Carpentier, who recognized this characteristic in much Latin-American literature.

Now, I believe that magic realism is a natural product of postcolonial writing, which has to resolve differences between two separate realities—the world of the conquerors as well as that of the conquered. Prominent Latin-American magic realists are the Colombian Gabriel García Márquez, the Brazilian Jorge Amado, and Isabel Allende, who is from Chile.

Isabel Allende is a writer in the magic realist tradition, and she is considered one of the first successful women novelists in Latin America. In 1981, she began writing a letter to her terminally ill grandfather that evolved into her first novel, *The House of the Spirits*, which was made into a very successful film starring Meryl Streep and Jeremy Irons.

Allende's next novel was *Of Love and Shadows*, published in 1984, followed by *Eva Luna* (1987), and *The Infinite Plan* (1991). Allende's works use the fantasy and myth in realistic fiction and often portray South American politics. Her first four works reflect her own experiences and examine the role of women in Latin America. On the other hand, *The Infinite Plan* is set in the United States, and its main character is male. Her first nonfiction work, *Paula*, was written as a letter to her daughter, who, afflicted with a hereditary blood disease, fell into a coma and died in 1992.

(Narrator):

6. What does magic realism contain?
7. When was the term "magic realism" first used?
8. According to the speaker, what was magic realism the product of?
9. Where is Isabel Allende from?
10. Which book by Allende was made into a film?

(Narrator): Questions 11–15. Listen to a lecture on alligators.

(Professor): Alligators look like large lizards. They have powerful tails that are used for both defending themselves and for swimming. They have a long head and their eyes, ears, and nostrils are placed on top and project slightly above the water when they are at the surface of the water, as they often are.

Alligators are different from crocodiles. Crocodiles have narrower snouts and the fourth tooth in each side of the lower jaw projects outside the snout when the mouth is closed.

Alligators are carnivorous and live along the edges of lakes, swamps, and rivers. They dig burrows where they escape from danger and where they hibernate during cold weather. The Mississippi, or American, alligator is found in the southeastern United States. It is black with yellow banding when young and is generally brownish when adult. Some large specimens have reached a length of about 19 feet, but usually they are about 6–12 feet long.

The adult Mississippi alligator mainly eats fish, small mammals, and birds but may sometimes take prey as large as deer or cattle. Both male and female hiss, and the males roar loudly enough to be heard over long distances. During the breeding season, females build a nest of mud and vegetation and lay about 20 to 70 hard-shelled eggs. She guards the eggs and may at this time be dangerous. Members of this species usually avoid humans. Before leaving this fascinating animal, we should say a few words about the Chinese alligator.

(Narrator):

11. What do alligators use their tails for?
12. How are crocodiles different from alligators?
13. Where do alligators live?
14. What do alligators mainly eat?
15. What is the speaker going to discuss next?

(Narrator): Questions 16–20. Listen to a lecture on a famous writer.

(Professor): John Steinbeck received the Nobel Prize for Literature in 1962. But before we discuss his writing style, we should briefly look at his career.

Steinbeck attended Stanford University, Stanford, California, intermittently between 1920 and 1926 but did not take a degree. Before his books attained success, he supported himself as a manual laborer, and his experiences helped him write about the lives of the workers in his stories. He spent much of his life in Monterey County, California, which he used as the setting of some of his fiction.

He became popular in 1935 with *Tortilla Flat,* which was followed by *In Dubious Battle*, an account of a strike by agricultural laborers. His short novel, *Of Mice and Men,* also appeared in play and film versions and is a tragic story about the strange, complex bond between two migrant laborers.

The Grapes of Wrath, his most famous novel, won a Pulitzer Prize and a National Book Award in 1939 and was made into a film by director John Ford in 1940. The novel is about the migration of a dispossessed family from the Oklahoma Dust Bowl to California and describes their subsequent exploitation by a ruthless system of agricultural economics.

During World War II, Steinbeck wrote some effective pieces of government propaganda, among them *The Moon Is Down*, a novel of Norwegians under the Nazis, and he also served as a war correspondent. His postwar work included film scripts for his story, *The Red Pony*, and *Viva Zapata*, a retelling of the Mexican revolutionary leader Emiliano Zapata.

(Narrator):

16. What does the professor mainly discuss?
17. Before becoming a successful novelist, how did Steinbeck support himself?
18. Where did John Steinbeck live?
19. What was his most famous novel?
20. What will the speaker talk about next?

(Narrator): Questions 21–25. Listen to an economics professor speak about bookkeeping.

(Professor): Although bookkeeping procedures can be extremely complex, basically there are two types of books used in the bookkeeping process—journals and ledgers. A journal contains the daily transactions (sales, purchases, and so on), and the ledger contains the record of individual accounts.

The history of bookkeeping closely follows the history of commerce, industry, and government. Traces of financial and numerical records have been found in the archeological digs of nearly every civilization with a commercial background. In the ruins of Babylon, records of commercial contracts have been found, and farm and estate accounts were kept in ancient Greece and Rome.

The double-entry method of bookkeeping began with the development of the commercial republics of Italy, particularly the banks of Venice. Instruction manuals for bookkeeping were developed during the fifteenth century in various Italian cities, and in the late eighteenth and early nineteenth centuries, the Industrial Revolution provided an important stimulus to accounting and bookkeeping. As manufacturing, trading, and shipping grew, accurate financial records became a necessity.

For example, in the second half of the twentieth century, making business and economic decisions grew complex, and this required the sophisticated selection, classification, and presentation of information, increasingly with the aid of computers.

When taxation and government regulation became more complicated, demand for information increased; companies had to have information that supported their income tax, payroll tax, sales tax, and real estate tax reports. Governmental agencies and educational and other nonprofit institutions also grew in size, and they had to keep detailed records of the operations.

(Narrator):

21. How many types of books are used in the bookkeeping process?
22. What does a journal contain?
23. Where did double-entry bookkeeping begin?
24. According to the speaker, what historic event provided the stimulus to the growth of double-entry bookkeeping?
25. In the second half of the twentieth century, what information did companies have to have?

(Narrator): Questions 26–30. Listen to a speaker discuss the history of pyramids.

(Professor): Pyramids have been built at various times all over the world, but the best known are those of Egypt and of Central and South America. In ancient Egypt, pyramids were sites for funerals and burial. They were built over a period of 2,700 years, from about 2700 to 2345 B.C.E.

During those years, the pyramid was the typical royal tomb. It was not isolated, but rather a part of an architectural complex. The essential components were the pyramid itself, containing the grave of the king, and standing within an enclosure on high desert ground. Next to the pyramid were a mortuary temple and a causeway leading to a temple at the edge of fields developed for cultivation. They may have been connected to the Nile by a canal.

About 80 royal pyramids have been found in Egypt; many of them, however, were reduced to mere mounds of debris and long ago plundered for their treasures. Pyramid building reached its peak in 341 years, beginning about 2686 B.C.E. and ending in 2345 B.C.E. The greatest of the Egyptian pyramids are those of the pharaohs Khufu, Khafre, and Menkure at Giza. The largest pyramid of the group was built for Khufu, and it is called the Great Pyramid. The length of each side at the base is more than 7,500 feet, and its original height was more than 4,800 feet. None of the pyramids reach their original height because they have been almost entirely stripped of their outer casings of smooth white limestone.

Next, we will take a look at the Pyramid of the Sun and the Pyramid of the Moon in central Mexico.

(Narrator):

26. What were the Egyptian pyramids used for?
27. What was usually next to a pyramid?
28. How many royal pyramids have been found in Egypt?
29. How high was the Great Pyramid at Giza?
30. What originally covered the outside surface of the pyramid?

Day 15

Listening Comprehension

Lecture Drill: Part II

Today's Assignment

- Complete Part II of the Lecture Drill.

Today, you will continue to practice lectures and answering questions. If you need to, take a few minutes to review what you learned on Day 5. The answers and scripts for the audio are printed at the end of this chapter. This drill is not on the CD. We have provided a script at the end of this chapter that you should tear out along the dashed line. Then, you can either read the script to yourself as you work through the questions, or you can have a friend read the script to you while you work through the questions.

Directions: In this section, you will read lectures. After each lecture, you will be asked several questions, and you will see the questions printed here with four answer choices. Choose an answer and mark it either in the book or on a separate sheet of scrap paper. Remember to answer the questions based on what is stated or implied by the speakers.

Questions 1–5. Listen to a lecture on prehistoric art.

On the screen, you will see the words "Art History" and then a picture of paintings of animals on the walls of the Lascaux Caves.

1. Where are the Lescaux Caves?
   (A) In South Central Africa
   (B) In South Central France
   (C) In South Central Mexico
   (D) In South Central Italy

2. How old are the drawings in the cave?
   (A) 15,000 years old
   (B) 1,500 years old
   (C) 100,000 years old
   (D) 600 years old

3. What two animals are shown in the narrative composition? Click on two answers.
   (A) A bison
   (B) A bird
   (C) A stag
   (D) A rhinoceros

4. When was the cave opened to the public?
   (A) 1940
   (B) 1948
   (C) 1963
   (D) 1995

5. According to the speaker, what happened when the floor level of the cave was lowered?
   (A) Art history students were able to analyze the paintings.
   (B) Animals that lived in the cave died.
   (C) Valuable scientific information was lost.
   (D) The French government made money for scientific research.

Questions 6–10. Listen to a lecture on Eastern European History.

On the screen, you will see the words "The Steppe" and then a picture of Genghis Khan sitting on his horse, looking at the grassland.

6. What is the lecture mainly about?
   (A) How the Steppe was used for agricultural life
   (B) How the Steppe was used for the spread of people
   (C) How the Steppe was used for tribal rituals
   (D) How the Steppe was used for stabling horses

7. According to the speaker, when was the horse domesticated?
   (A) About 2000 B.C.E.
   (B) About 1700 B.C.E.
   (C) About 1400 B.C.E.
   (D) About 1100 B.C.E.

8. Why was the nomad cavalry a constant threat to the Persian Empire?
   (A) Because of their advanced knowledge of government
   (B) Because of the tribes coming under the influence of Islam
   (C) Because of their mobility and their ability to live off their animals
   (D) Because of talent for acquiring the languages of the Persian Empire

9. What happened during the period of stability, beginning in the third century B.C.E.?
   (A) The nomads converted to Christianity, then to Islam.
   (B) Trade routes carried goods and ideas between Rome and China.
   (C) Horse breeding became competitive among the nomadic tribes.
   (D) Tribal confederacies became weak and open to attack.

10. What two groups of people is the speaker going to discuss next? Click on two answers.
    (A) The Persians
    (B) The Romans
    (C) The Turks
    (D) The Mongols

Questions 11–15. Listen to a speaker talk to a group of students who are going to take a field trip into a forest.

On the screen, you will see the words "The Wolverine" and then a picture of a wolverine.

11. Why is the speaker warning students about wolverines?
    (A) Students may want to get one for a pet.
    (B) Students may encounter one during a camping trip.
    (C) Students may offer one food and drink.
    (D) Students may try to capture one.

12. What animal do wolverines resemble?
    (A) Skunks
    (B) Weasels
    (C) Deer
    (D) Bears

13. What color is a wolverine?
    (A) Yellowish-brown with a white stripe
    (B) Reddish brown with a black stripe
    (C) Blackish-brown with a light-brown stripe
    (D) Blackish-red with a light-brown stripe

14. According to the speaker, what are wolverines known for?
    (A) Strength and cunning
    (B) Cowardice and anger
    (C) Speed and stamina
    (D) Hatred and hunger

15. What have wolverines been known to destroy?
    (A) Car batteries
    (B) Tires on trucks
    (C) Rugs in apartments
    (D) Fur coats

Questions 16–20. Listen to a lecture on penicillin.

On the screen, you will see the word "Pharmacology" and then a picture of a professor in a lecture hall.

16. Who discovered penicillin?
    (A) Alexander Graham Bell
    (B) Alexander Knox
    (C) Alexander Pope
    (D) Alexander Fleming

17. What does the speaker call the contamination of a colony of the bacterium *Staphylococcus aureus*?
    (A) A sensitive observation of a petri dish
    (B) An allergic shock that is life threatening
    (C) A wonderful accident in the history of science
    (D) An observable reduction of algae in the laboratory

18. By what year were penicillin injections available?
    (A) 1931
    (B) 1941
    (C) 1951
    (D) 1961

19. What are the chief side effects of penicillin?
    (A) Skin rashes, swelling, and allergic shock
    (B) Spinal meningitis and diptheria
    (C) Acid indigestion and appendicitis
    (D) Fluid accumulation in the stomach

20. Why must penicillin be injected?
    (A) Penicillin is sensitive to light
    (B) Penicillin in pill form causes allergic shock
    (C) Penicillin is not stable in stomach acid
    (D) Penicillin is a prescription drug

Questions 21–25. Listen to a professor discuss the reign of King Richard I of England.

On the screen, you will see the words "English History" and a picture of Richard I, detail of tomb effigy in the abbey church of Fontevrault-l'Abbaye.

21. What did the speaker mainly discuss?
    (A) Richard I's popularity as king
    (B) Richard I's defeats as king
    (C) Richard I's success as king
    (D) Richard I's ability as a soldier

22. How much time did Richard I spend in England?
    (A) Six years
    (B) Six months
    (C) Ten years
    (D) Ten months

23. Who helped put down the rebellion against Richard?
    (A) Leopold of Austria
    (B) Philip of France
    (C) Eleanor of Aquitaine
    (D) The bishops of Lincoln and Salisbury

24. What activities did Richard succeed in?
    (A) Building churches and schools
    (B) Raising money and armies
    (C) Travelling and romance
    (D) Staying popular and getting elected

25. What will the speaker probably discuss next?
    (A) The Fourth Crusade
    (B) The reign of Eleanor of Aquitaine
    (C) The opposition of the Bishop of Lincoln
    (D) The problems of Richard's successor

Questions 26–30. Listen to a lecture on the construction of the Brooklyn Bridge in New York City.

On the screen, you will see the words "The Brooklyn Bridge" and a picture of the Brooklyn Bridge.

26. What river does the Brooklyn Bridge span?
    (A) The Hudson River
    (B) The Delaware River
    (C) The East River
    (D) The Potomac River

27. What are pneumatic caissons used for?
    (A) Manufacturing steel wire cable
    (B) Construction work on the bottom of rivers
    (C) Sending messages from one side of a river to another
    (D) The rescue of workers trapped at the bottom of a river

28. How did Washington Roebling send messages to the construction site?
    (A) His wife took them to the site.
    (B) His father took them to the site.
    (C) His manager took them to the site.
    (D) His workers took them to the site.

29. Which of the following statements is true?
    (A) Roebling's wife was an engineer.
    (B) Roebling was replaced by his father.
    (C) Roebling was cheated by a steel cable salesman.
    (D) Roebling visited the construction site every day.

30. What kind of traffic does the Brooklyn Bridge carry?
    (A) Bus and truck traffic
    (B) Pedestrian and subway traffic
    (C) Subway and truck traffic
    (D) Motor and pedestrian traffic

ANSWER KEY FOR DAY 15—LECTURE DRILL: PART II

1.	B	16.	D
2.	A	17.	C
3.	A and D	18.	B
4.	B	19.	A
5.	C	20.	C
6.	B	21.	A
7.	A	22.	B
8.	C	23.	C
9.	B	24.	B
10.	C and D	25.	D
11.	B	26.	C
12.	D	27.	B
13.	C	28.	A
14.	A	29.	C
15.	B	30.	D

DAY 15—SCRIPT FOR LECTURE DRILL: PART II

(Narrator): **Directions:** In this section, you will hear lectures. After each lecture, you will be asked several questions about what you heard, and you will see the questions printed here with four answer choices. Choose an answer and mark it either in the book or on a separate sheet of scrap paper. Remember to answer the questions based on what is *stated* or *implied* by the speakers.

(Narrator): Questions 1–5. Listen to a lecture on prehistoric art.

(Man): One of the most outstanding displays of prehistoric art yet discovered is in Lascaux Cave, located in South Central France. The caves were discovered by four teenage boys in September of 1940, and the cave consists of a main cavern magnificently decorated with engraved, drawn, and painted figures now known to be more than 15,000 years old.

The 600 painted and drawn animals and symbols, along with nearly 1,500 engravings, were done on a light background in various shades of yellow, red, brown, and black. Animals depicted include four huge wild oxen and an unknown two-horned animal, misleadingly nicknamed the "unicorn." Heads and necks of several stags appear to be swimming across a river.

Although there is little storytelling in these pictures, there is one composition that has some elements of a narrative. A bison appears to have been speared in the abdomen. In front of the bison's horns, and falling away from the animal, is a bird-headed man, which is the only human figure depicted in the cave. Just below the man is a spear with a bird ornament on the butt-end. To the left of the man, a rhinoceros seems to be walking away from the scene.

Archaeologists believe that the cave was used for centuries for the performance of hunting and magical rituals. The cave was in perfect condition when first discovered and was opened to the public in 1948. And we have learned some valuable lessons about preserving these treasures. Its floor level was quickly lowered to accommodate a walkway, which unfortunately destroyed information of probable scientific value in the process. Up to 100,000 tourists visit the caves each year. The heavy traffic plus the use of artificial lighting caused the colors to fade and algae and bacteria to grow over some of the paintings. Thus, in 1963 the cave was closed to the public. However, in 1983 a partial replica, "Lascaux II," was opened, and by the mid-1990s it registered some 300,000 visitors annually.

(Narrator):

1. Where are the Lascaux Caves?
2. How old are the drawings in the cave?
3. What two animals are shown in the narrative composition? Click on two answers.
4. When was the cave opened to the public?
5. According to the speaker, what happened when the floor level of the cave was lowered?

(Narrator): Questions 6–10. Listen to a lecture on Eastern European History.

(Woman): One of the most important geographical features in history is the Steppe. The Steppe is an immense band of grassland that begins in Hungary and

extends eastward across southern Russia into Central Asia and ultimately to Manchuria. It has served as an avenue for the spread of people and cultural patterns throughout recorded history. The nomads of the Eastern Steppe have throughout history sought better grazing lands either in northern China or in the Western Steppe.

In prehistoric times, the Steppe people gradually abandoned their food-gathering way of life in favor of settled farming. With the domestication of the horse about 2000 B.C.E., however, the Steppe people began raising stock on the grasslands, which was a migratory pursuit. They formed tribes and eventually tribal confederacies that chose paramount chieftains who could rapidly assemble formidable military forces.

Such forces began to sweep into the Middle East after 1700 B.C.E. Because of their mobility and their ability to live off their animals, nomad cavalry posed a constant threat to the Persian empire in the west and the Chinese empire in the east. In the third century B.C.E., these tribes occupied agricultural land and were able to defend it because they had developed an armored cavalry. A period of stability began, and caravan routes across Asia carried goods and ideas back and forth from Rome to China. But in the fourth century C.E., the Huns invaded the Roman Empire and began the dissolution of the western Roman realm.

We should now examine how the Turks and the Mongols used the Steppe to influence not only the political landscape, but also the religious and cultural life.

(Narrator):

6. What is the lecture mainly about?
7. According to the speaker, when was the horse domesticated?
8. Why was the nomad calvary a constant threat to the Persian Empire?
9. What happened during the period of stability, beginning in the third century B.C.E.?
10. What two groups of people is the speaker going to discuss next? Click on two answers.

(Narrator): Questions 11–15. Listen to a speaker talk to a group of students who are going to take a field trip into a forest.

(Woman): I am sure you've heard stories about the wolverine and how ferocious and cunning he is. Well, some may sound unbelievable, but I want to warn you that they are very dangerous, and few stories do justice to these extraordinary animals. We will be camping in the woodlands of Southern Canada, and it's likely that our campsite will be in a wolverine's territory.

Wolverines are members of the weasel family. They resemble small, squat, bears, and they are about 26–36 inches long, excluding the bushy tail. It weighs anywhere from 20 to 66 pounds. The legs are short, somewhat bowed; the soles of its paws are hairy, and it has long, sharp semi-retractable claws. The head has short ears, and its teeth are very strong.

The coat of the wolverine is blackish brown with a light-brown stripe extending from each side of the neck along the body to the base of the tail. Its anal glands secrete an unpleasant-smelling fluid; some say it's worse than the odor of a skunk.

The wolverine is noted for its strength and cunning. For example, it has been known to follow traplines to cabins and devour food stocks or carry off portable items. It has been known to deliberately destroy tires on trucks and break into cars and rip out the upholstery. The wolverine is a solitary, nocturnal hunter, eats all kinds of game, not hesitating to attack sheep, deer, or small bears. They have also attacked humans. If you see one, do not—I repeat—approach it. Do not offer it food. It may decide to attack and take the hand that is holding the food.

(Narrator):

11. Why is the speaker warning students about wolverines?
12. What animal do wolverines resemble?
13. What color is a wolverine?
14. According to the speaker, what are wolverines known for?
15. What have wolverines been known to destroy?

(Narrator): Questions 16–20. Listen to a lecture on penicillin.

(Man): Penicillin is still one of the most widely used antibiotic agents. It is derived from the Penicillium mold. It was discovered by Alexander Fleming in 1928 when one of those wonderful accidents of science occurred. In Fleming's laboratory, colonies of the bacterium *Staphylococcus aureus* had been accidentally contaminated by the green mold *Penicillium notatum*. Fleming observed that the bacterium failed to grow in those areas.

He isolated the mold, grew it in a fluid medium, and found that it produced a substance capable of killing many of the common bacteria that infect humans. Howard Florey and Ernst Boris Chain isolated and purified penicillin in the late 1930s, and by 1941 an injectable form of the drug was available.

Among the bacteria sensitive to penicillin are those that cause throat infections, pneumonia, spinal meningitis, gas gangrene, diphtheria, syphilis, and gonorrhea. The chief side effects of penicillin are skin rashes, swelling, and allergic shock. Allergic shock, which can be life threatening, may require injections of epinephrine. Milder symptoms are usually prevented by switching to alternative medications.

Penicillin is not stable in acid, which is why much of penicillin G is broken down as it passes through the stomach. This is why it must be given by intramuscular injection, which limits its usefulness.

(Narrator):

16. Who discovered penicillin?
17. What does the speaker call the contamination of a colony of the bacterium *Staphylococcus aureus*?
18. By what year were penicillin injections available?
19. What are the chief side effects of penicillin?
20. Why must penicillin G be injected?

(Narrator): Questions 21–25. Listen to a professor discuss the reign of King Richard I of England.

(Woman): Richard I was born Sept. 8, 1157, in Oxford and died April 6, 1199, in Aquitaine, France. He was called "Richard The Lion-heart," or "Lion-hearted." His bravery and leadership in the Third Crusade made him a popular king in his own time. He also became the hero of countless romantic legends. However, he has been viewed less kindly by more recent historians and scholars.

Richard spent only about six months of his ten-year reign in England. During his frequent absences he left a committee in charge of the realm. In 1193, his brother, John Lackland, tried to take the throne, and the rebellion was put down with the aid of their mother, Eleanor of Acquitaine. But when Richard returned from abroad, he forgave John and promised him the succession.

Richard's reign saw some important innovations in taxation and military organization. Warfare was expensive, and in addition Richard was captured while returning from the Crusade of Leopold V of Austria and held for a high ransom of 150,000 marks. Various methods of raising money were tried, and the ransom, although never paid in full, caused Richard's government to become highly unpopular.

Richard also had to deal with the unwillingness on the part of his English subjects to serve in France. A plan to raise an army of 300 knights was opposed by the powerful bishops of Lincoln and Salisbury. Although Richard was remarkably successful in raising money and armies in support of his wars, it can also be argued that his demands on England weakened the kingdom and that Richard left his brother John, the next king, a lot of problems to deal with.

(Narrator):

21. What did the speaker mainly discuss?
22. How much time did Richard I spend in England?
23. Who helped put down the rebellion against Richard?
24. What activities did Richard succeed in?
25. What will the speaker probably discuss next?

(Narrator): Questions 26–30. Listen to a lecture on the construction of the Brooklyn Bridge in New York City.

(Man): The Brooklyn Bridge is a suspension bridge spanning the East River from Brooklyn to Manhattan Island, New York City. The main span of the bridge is almost 1,600 feet long, and it was the longest in the world until the Firth of Forth bridge was completed in Scotland in 1890.

The Brooklyn Bridge is a brilliant feat of nineteenth-century engineering, was the first bridge to use steel for cable wire, and during its construction explosives were used inside a pneumatic caisson for the first time. A pneumatic caisson is used for construction work on the bottoms of rivers and other bodies of water. Water is kept out of the chamber by the application of enormous amounts of air pressure inside the chamber.

Its builders had to resolve many difficulties. At the beginning of the construction, the chief engineer and designer John Roebling died as a result of an accident. His son, Washington Roebling, took over as chief engineer, and he was crippled by another accident. However, Washington continued to direct the construction of the bridge from his home, watching through binoculars and sending messages to the site by his wife, Emily Warren Roebling.

There were other problems. A compressed-air blast wrecked one pneumatic caisson, and a fire burned in another caisson for several weeks. A steel cable came apart on the Manhattan side and crashed into the river. Roebling was cheated by the company that sold him the steel wire, and several tons of cable had to be replaced. Nevertheless, the bridge was completed in 1883 after thirteen years of hard work. The result is a bridge that carries motor and pedestrian traffic between Brooklyn and the island of Manhattan.

(Narrator):

26. What river does the Brooklyn Bridge span?
27. What are pneumatic caissons used for?
28. How did Washington Roebling send messages to the construction site?
29. Which of the following statements is true?
30. What kind of traffic does the Brooklyn Bridge carry?

Day 16

Listening Comprehension

Short Conversation, Long Conversation, and Lecture Drills with Audio

Today's Assignment

- Complete these Listening drills using the audio on the accompanying CD.

Today, you will continue to practice with short conversations and lectures. There will be 30 questions in this exercise. Questions 1–10 are Short Conversation questions, questions 11–20 are Long Conversation questions, and questions 21–30 are Lecture questions. Audio is provided on the CD. The answers and scripts for the audio are printed at the end of this chapter.

You may now begin listening to track 1 on the CD.

SHORT CONVERSATIONS

Directions: In this section, you will hear conversations between two people. After each conversation, you will be asked several questions about what you heard, and you will see the questions printed here with four answer choices. Choose an answer and mark it either in the book or on a separate sheet of scrap paper. Remember to answer the questions based on what is stated or implied by the speakers.

1. What does the woman mean?
   (A) She doesn't know which way to go.
   (B) She decided but doesn't want to tell the man.
   (C) She has other plans about college.
   (D) She doesn't know where she will live.

2. What does the man mean?
   (A) He doesn't know the answer to her question.
   (B) He needs more information to answer her question.
   (C) He doesn't want to answer her question.
   (D) He doesn't understand her question.

3. What does the woman mean?
   (A) In the laboratory, she nearly lost consciousness.
   (B) In the laboratory, she barely passed the exam.
   (C) In the laboratory, she liked the smell very much.
   (D) In the laboratory, she enjoyed the experiment.

4. What does the woman mean?
   (A) No one works at the lost and found department.
   (B) The watch doesn't keep good time.
   (C) The people at the lost and found department are inefficient.
   (D) She forgot where the man lost his watch.

5. What can be inferred from the man's answer?
   (A) He will take a vacation.
   (B) He will be very busy during spring break.
   (C) He will see his family.
   (D) He will not get a break on his grades.

6. What does the man mean?
   (A) Every European country has produced great artists.
   (B) The woman shouldn't take credit for Spanish art.
   (C) Other countries have also produced great artists.
   (D) The woman should study art while she's at school.

7. What does the woman mean?
   (A) The man shouldn't have waited so long to begin his research.
   (B) The man won't be able to finish his term paper.
   (C) The man shouldn't have started the fire.
   (D) The man can do research for his paper elsewhere.

8. What does the woman mean?
   (A) Verdi was active in the nineteenth century.
   (B) Verdi was not a composer.
   (C) Verdi didn't think much about the eighteenth century.
   (D) Verdi was the nineteenth composer to die in Milan.

9. What does the man mean?
   (A) He doesn't know how to find the bridge.
   (B) He has never played bridge.
   (C) He doesn't like to walk on bridges.
   (D) He has not learned where the student center is.

10. What can be inferred from the woman's statement?
   (A) Stevenson worked with children.
   (B) Stevenson specialized in the classification of literature.
   (C) Stevenson never came to class.
   (D) Stevenson wrote poems and stories for children.

LONG CONVERSATIONS

Directions: In this section, you will hear longer conversations. After each conversation, you will be asked several questions about what you heard, and you will see the questions printed here with four answer choices. Choose an answer and mark it either in the book or on a separate sheet of scrap paper. Remember to answer the questions based on what is stated or implied by the speakers.

Questions 11–15. Listen to a discussion about rules for campus organizations.

On the screen, you will see the words "Student Government" and then a picture of a man and woman looking at papers.

11. What are the man and woman discussing?
   (A) What the student government should do about computers
   (B) What the student government should do about the Dean of Students
   (C) What the student government should do about new clubs
   (D) What the student government should do about faculty members

12. At the present time, who approves new clubs?
    (A) A committee of members of the faculty and the office of the Dean
    (B) A committee appointed by the president of the college
    (C) A committee appointed by presidents of the clubs
    (D) A committee of faculty members and members of the student government
13. According to the new plan, by whom should new clubs be approved?
    (A) By a committee of club members only
    (B) By a committee of student government members only
    (C) By a committee of faculty members only
    (D) By a committee of club presidents
14. According to the woman, what is the problem with the new plan?
    (A) Unpopular students would not be allowed to form a new club.
    (B) Only popular students would be allowed to join student clubs.
    (C) Unpopular students would be expelled from college.
    (D) Only popular students would be allowed to join clubs.
15. What club does the man belong to?
    (A) The government club
    (B) The faculty club
    (C) The Greek club
    (D) The computer club

Questions 16-20. Listen to a discussion about a famous mountain.

On the screen, you will see the words "Asian culture and history" and then a photograph of Mount Fujiyama.

16. How did the man learn about Mt. Fuji?
    (A) He went to the library.
    (B) He traveled to Japan.
    (C) He asked a friend who is from Japan.
    (D) He surfed the Internet.
17. Where is Mt. Fuji?
    (A) About 16 miles east of Tokyo
    (B) About 60 miles west of Tokyo
    (C) About 600 miles from Tokyo
    (D) About 170 miles from the Meiji Shrine
18. According to the woman, what language does Fuji's name come from?
    (A) Ainu
    (B) Chinese
    (C) Japanese
    (D) Korean
19. According to the man, what does one religious group believe about Fuji?
    (A) The mountain should not be climbed by women.
    (B) The mountain has a soul.
    (C) The mountain is very old.
    (D) The mountain has a perfect shape.
20. According to the woman, what is found at the edge of the crater?
    (A) Two other volcanoes
    (B) Lava
    (C) Tourists
    (D) Shrines

LECTURES

Directions: In this section, you will hear lectures. After each lecture, you will be asked several questions about what you heard, and you will see the questions printed here with four answer choices. Choose an answer and mark it either in the book or on a separate sheet of scrap paper. Remember to answer the questions based on what is stated or implied by the speakers.

Questions 21–25. Listen to a lecture about a great Italian artist.

On the screen, you will see the words "Art History" and then a picture of Michelangelo Buonarroti.

21. According to the speaker, what showed Michelangelo's influence on Italian art in his lifetime?
    (A) His frescoes were famous throughout Europe and Asia.
    (B) Sculpture and paintings by Michelangelo are known all over the world.
    (C) His biography was published during his lifetime.
    (D) The Sistine Chapel was seen by every artist living in Rome.

22. According to the speaker, what is probably the best known of Michelangelo's works?
    (A) His sculpture of David
    (B) His paintings of Rome
    (C) The ceiling of the Sistine Chapel
    (D) His sculpture of the Piéta

23. Where is Michelangelo's statue of David?
    (A) Florence
    (B) Rome
    (C) The Vatican
    (D) Milan

24. Which art form did Michelangelo work on all during his lifetime?
    (A) Poetry
    (B) Marble sculpture
    (C) Painting
    (D) Architecture

25. What will the speaker probably discuss next?
    (A) Michelangelo's work as an architect
    (B) Michelangelo's biography by Vasari
    (C) Michelangelo's relationship with his patrons
    (D) Michelangelo's knowledge of anatomy

Questions 26–30. Listen to a lecture about the giant snake, the anaconda.

On the screen, you will see the word "Reptiles" and a picture of an anaconda.

26. According to the speaker, how do most people feel about the anaconda?
    (A) They feel that is a beautiful, gentle animal.
    (B) They feel it must be protected.
    (C) They feel it is a man-eating monster.
    (D) They feel it is an important animal.

27. Where do anacondas live?
    (A) In the rivers of the Himalayas
    (B) In the lakes and rivers east of the Andes Mountains
    (C) In the deserts of western Africa and Australia
    (D) In the Caribbean Sea

28. How long are most anacondas?
    (A) About 30 feet long
    (B) About 24 feet long
    (C) About 16 feet long
    (D) About 10 feet long

29. How do anacondas kill their prey?
    (A) By coiling
    (B) By aggression
    (C) By drowning
    (D) By constriction

30. What animals are related to anacondas?
    (A) Rattlesnakes and adders
    (B) Cobras and kingsnakes
    (C) Boas and pythons
    (D) Asps and coral snakes

DAY 16—ANSWER KEY FOR SHORT CONVERSATIONS, LONG CONVERSATIONS, AND LECTURES

1.	D	16.	D
2.	B	17.	B
3.	A	18.	A
4.	C	19.	B
5.	B	20.	D
6.	C	21.	C
7.	D	22.	C
8.	A	23.	A
9.	B	24.	B
10.	D	25.	C
11.	C	26.	C
12.	D	27.	B
13.	B	28.	C
14.	A	29.	D
15.	D	30.	C

Day 16—Script for Short Conversations, Long Conversations, and Lectures

Short Conversations

(Narrator): Directions: In this section, you will hear conversations between two people. After each conversation, you will be asked several questions about what you heard, and you will see the questions printed here with four answer choices. Choose an answer and mark it either in the book or on a separate sheet of scrap paper. Remember to answer the questions based on what is stated or implied by the speakers.

1. ***(Man):*** For next semester, are you going to stay in the dorm or move to an apartment?

   (Woman): I haven't decided one way or the other.

   (Narrator): What does the woman mean?

2. ***(Woman):*** In Mexico, will I need to get a driver's license, or will they accept an American license?

   (Man): That depends.

   (Narrator): What does the man mean?

3. ***(Man):*** The smell in the chemistry lab was so bad, I almost vomited.

   (Woman): I almost passed out, myself.

   (Narrator): What does the woman mean?

4. ***(Man):*** I misplaced my watch. Where's the lost-and-found?

   (Woman): Forget about the watch. The people who work at the lost and found are real losers.

   (Narrator): What does the woman mean?

5. ***(Woman):*** What are you going to do during the spring break?

   (Man): It's not going to be a break for me.

   (Narrator): What can be inferred from the man's answer?

6. ***(Woman):*** Why has Spain produced so many great artists?

   (Man): Well, give credit to the French and the Dutch while you're at it.

   (Narrator): What does the man mean?

7. ***(Man):*** The library is closed because of a fire, and I have to finish my research for my term paper.

   (Woman): The library isn't the only source of information.

   (Narrator): What does the woman mean?

8. ***(Man):*** Was Verdi an eighteenth-century composer?

   (Woman): Nineteenth century, I think.

   (Narrator): What does the woman mean?

9. ***(Woman):*** My afternoon class was cancelled. Why don't we head over to the student center and play some bridge?

   (Man): I don't know how.

   (Narrator): What does the man mean?

10. ***(Man):*** I really enjoyed that children's literature class.

    (Woman): Me too. Especially the works of Robert Louis Stevenson.

    (Narrator): What can be inferred from the woman's statement?

Long Conversations

(Narrator): Directions: In this section, you will hear longer conversations. After each conversation, you will be asked several questions about what you heard, and you will see the questions printed here with four answer choices. Choose an answer and mark it either in the book or on a separate sheet of scrap paper. Remember to answer the questions based on what is stated or implied by the speakers.

(Narrator): Questions 11–15. Listen to a discussion about rules for campus organizations.

(Man): Did you read my suggestions about reorganizing clubs on campus?

(Woman): Yes I did, and the suggestions are good, except for the one about starting a new club.

(Man): What's the problem with it?

(Woman): Well, new clubs are approved by a committee, faculty members, and members of the student government.

(Man): The faculty should have nothing to do with starting new clubs.

(Woman): That's where I disagree.

(Man): Why?

(Woman): If it's left up to students only, the only new clubs will be those that are popular with students.

(Man): Well, yeah. And your problem with that is…?

(Woman): Sometimes people who are not popular want to form clubs.

(Man): For example?

(Woman): Five years ago, a group of guys wanted to start a club for people interested in computers, and almost all the student members of the committee voted against them. I looked up the record of the meeting. The guys that wanted the club were called geeks and nerds, and laughed at. It was only because of the faculty that we have a computer club.

(Man): And I'm a member. Wow, I hadn't heard about that. I see your point. Well then, we could take out that part of the new plan.

(Woman): I'm glad you see it that way. Otherwise I think it's good.

(Narrator):

11. What are the man and woman discussing?
12. At the present time, who approves new clubs?
13. According to the new plan, by whom should new clubs be approved?
14. According to the woman, what is the problem with the new plan?
15. What club does the man belong to?

(Narrator): Questions 16–20. Listen to a discussion about a famous mountain.

(Woman): Okay, I read books about Mt. Fujiyama, and you surfed the Net. What did we learn?

(Man): Well, in Japan, it's sometimes called Fuji No Yama. It's the biggest mountain in Japan. It's 12,388 feet high. And it's about 60 miles from Tokyo.

(Woman): Sixty miles west of Tokyo.

(Man): Right. It's an active volcano and was formed in 286 B.C.E. by an earthquake. It looks like it's a simple cone-type volcano, but it's actually three separate volcanoes, Komitake, Ko Fuji, and Shin Fuji. Shin Fuji means "New Fuji" and has continued to smolder or erupt occasionally. The lava and ash from Shin Fuji covered over the two older volcanoes and created the current shape of the mountain. What about you? What did you learn from your books?

(Woman): The mountain's name comes from Ainu, the language of the aboriginal peoples of the Japanese Islands. In Ainu, Fuji means "everlasting life." It's considered a sacred symbol of Japan and is famous everywhere, but it's most special to the Japanese people. They all have a personal identification with the mountain, and thousands climb to the shrine on its peak every summer.

(Man): One Web site said that Fuji is a sacred mountain, and one religious group believes it has a soul.

(Woman): Right. It's surrounded by temples and shrines, and there are shrines even at the edge and at the bottom of the crater.

(Man): In fact, climbing the mountain has long been a religious practice.
More than 100,000 people climb the mountain every year.

(Woman): Yeah, but until the middle of the nineteenth century, women were not allowed to climb it.

(Man): Well, it looks like both of us learned a lot about Fuji.

(Narrator):

16. How did the man learn about Mt. Fuji?
17. Where is Mt. Fuji?
18. According to the woman, what language does Fuji's name come from?
19. According to the man, what does one religious group believe about Fuji?
20. According to the woman, what is found at the edge of the crater?

Lectures

(Narrator): Directions: In this section, you will hear lectures. After each lecture, you will be asked several questions about what you heard, and you will see the questions printed here with four answer choices. Choose an answer and mark it either in the book or on a separate sheet of scrap paper. Remember to answer the questions based on what is stated or implied by the speakers.

(Narrator): Questions 21–25. Listen to a lecture about a great Italian artist.

(Man): No discussion of Italian history is complete without mentioning Michelangelo Buonarroti, the great sculptor, painter, architect, and poet. He had such influence in his lifetime, he was the first artist to have his biography written in his lifetime.

The frescoes on the ceiling of the Sistine Chapel of the Vatican are probably the best known of his works today, but the artist thought of himself primarily as a sculptor. In fact, he signed his paintings "Michelangelo, Sculptor." His sculptures include the magnificent statue of David in Florence, Italy. His statue of Mary holding the dead body of Jesus is called the Piéta. It's in Rome and is one of the greatest works carved out of marble.

His practice of several arts, however, was not unusual in his time, when all of them were thought of as based on design, or drawing. Michelangelo worked in marble sculpture all his life and in the other arts only at certain periods. The high regard for the Sistine ceiling is partly a reflection of the greater attention paid to painting in the twentieth century and partly, too, of the fact that it was completed, unlike many of the artist's works in the other media.

Michelangelo was indeed a Renaissance man, and his relationship with his patrons is as fascinating as his works of art.

(Narrator):

21. According to the speaker, what showed Michelangelo's influence on Italian art in his lifetime?
22. According to the speaker, what is probably the best known of Michelangelo's works?
23. Where is Michelangelo's statue of David?
24. Which art form did Michelangelo work on all during his lifetime?
25. What will the speaker probably discuss next?

(Narrator): Questions 26–30. Listen to a lecture about the giant snake, the anaconda.

(Woman): The anaconda is not a destructive man killer as most movie-goers believe. Instead of a product of computer-generated animation for a popular monster movie, it is a real animal and an important part of the ecological balance wherever it is found. Giant anacondas live along tropical waters east of the Andes Mountains and on the Caribbean island of Trinidad. Their size contributes to the myth of the wicked monster, because the giant anaconda is the largest snake in the world.

Although some anacondas have reached a length of 33 feet, most do not exceed 16 feet. Giant anacondas wait in the water at night to capture caimans, which are small reptiles that resemble crocodiles. They also feed on mammals such as deer, tapirs, and wild pigs that come to drink. An anaconda seizes a large animal by the neck and almost instantly throws its coils around it, killing it by constriction. That is, it squeezes the prey to death. They also kill smaller prey, such as small turtles and diving birds, with their mouth and sharp, backward-pointing teeth.

Despite their Hollywood-made reputation of viciousness, in the wild, anacondas are not particularly aggressive. In Venezuela, they are captured easily during the day by herpetologists who, in small groups, merely walk up to the snakes and carry them off.

Related to the anaconda are boas and pythons, which are found in tropical and temperate regions from western Africa to China, Australia, and the Pacific Islands.

(Narrator):

26. According to the speaker, how do most people feel about the anaconda?
27. Where do anacondas live?
28. How long are most anacondas?
29. How do anacondas kill their prey?
30. What animals are related to anacondas?

Day 17

Structure

Error Identification Drill—Part I

Today's Assignment

- Using the strategies that you acquired on Day 7, answer correctly the following error identification questions by circling the letter under the incorrect portion of the sentence. You should give yourself only 20 minutes to do all 25 questions. Then, compare your answers with those at the end of the chapter and read the explanations carefully.

Now, begin working on the drill. The answers and explanations are printed at the end of this chapter.

1. When adrenaline is excreted by the adrenal
   A — When adrenaline; B — excreted
   glands, it increase the heart rate, energy, and
   C — increase
   resistance to fatigue.
   D — resistance to fatigue

2. François Bouchers paintings and tapestries are
   A — François Bouchers
   considered the perfect expression of the French
   B — the perfect; C — of the French
   rococo period.
   D — period

3. Geronimo's repeated escapes embarrassed the
   A — repeated; B — embarrassed
   politicians, army officer, and the non-Indian
   C — army officer,
   citizens of the Southwest.
   D — of the Southwest

4. Always an avid art collector, oilman J. Paul Getty
   A — an avid; B — oilman
   left almost their entire estate to the J. Paul Getty
   C — left; D — their entire estate
   Museum Trust.

5. By the 1850, it was no longer possible to speak of
   A — By the 1850; B — to speak of
   American literature as provincial or submissive
   C — as
   to English models.
   D — English models.

6. The mines of the Newcastle area attracted civil
   A — mines
   and mechanical engineers as well surveyors and
   B — mechanical engineers; C — as well
   managers of a very high caliber.
   D — of a very high

7. It is difficult to decide where storing radioactive
A B
waste, because the material remains radioactive for
C D
thousands to millions of years.

8. Kurt Weill used jazz-like style in his music as he
A B
stressed the corruption of European and
C
American cultures.
D

9. Most historians agree that the modern history of
A
Japan began in 1868 when the Tokugawa
B
shogunate ends and authority reverted to the
C D
young Meiji Emperor.

10. A Navy pilot during World War II, George Bush
A
shot down over the Pacific Ocean, but
B
was rescued by an American submarine.
C D

11. Castiglione's ideal Renaissance gentleman never
A B
hurt people's feelings or make them feel inferior
C
by showing off.
D

12. Oncologist study the mechanism by which cancer
A B
spreads throughout the body.
C D

13. The radio broadcasting boom started about 1922,
A
when the number of radio stations in the U.S.
B
increase from 8 to 600, and broadcasting began in
C D
England, France, and Russia.

14. Greek architecture showed strength, power, and
A
elegant that seemed to be produced without effort.
B C D

15. Gutenberg's printing press, combining technique of
A B
the Roman wine press and the goldsmith's punch,
C
used movable metal type cast in replica moulds.
D

16. William Morris Hunt brought the Barbizon style
A B
to America from France, and he painted landscapes,
C
portraits, also figure pieces.
D

17. Many of the island of Molokai retains its rural
A B
atmosphere, even though it is a popular tourist
C
resort.
D

18. The plan for Washington, D.C., was laid out by
A
the French architecture Pierre L'Enfant under the
B C
direction of Thomas Jefferson.
D

19. The automobile is a major cultural force in America,
A
providing transportation and employment, giving
B C
aesthetic pleasure to the beholder, and
causes pollution and urban blight.
D

20. Once the Industrial Revolution had taken hold,
A B
new services such as paved street and street lights
C D
began to appear in the larger cities.

21. A hurricane warning means that hurricane
A
conditions are expected within 24 hours or less,
B
but precautions should be taken.
C D

22. In engineering, fatigue is the microscopic crack
A B
of materials, after repeated applications of stress.
C D

23. Stockholm is the capital of Sweden and that
A
country's principal commercial, industrial,
B C
cultural, and finance center.
D

24. In American law, double jeopardy is the name of
A
the Constitutional principle that protects a person
B C
from being tried twice on the same charges.
D

25. It was her own disabilities that led Helen Keller to
A B
promote programs who benefited disabled people.
C D

ANSWERS AND EXPLANATIONS

Day 17—Answer Key for Error Identification Drills—Part I

1. C
2. A
3. C
4. D
5. A
6. C
7. B
8. A
9. C
10. B
11. C
12. A
13. C
14. B
15. B
16. D
17. A
18. B
19. D
20. C
21. C
22. B
23. D
24. D
25. C

Explanations

1. **The correct answer is (C).** The pronoun *it* is singular, so the verb should be *increases.*
2. **The correct answer is (A).** "François Bouchers" should be possessive, "François Boucher's."
3. **The correct answer is (C).** To achieve parallel construction, *officer* should be plural: *officers.*
4. **The correct answer is (D).** The possessive adjective should be *his.*
5. **The correct answer is (A).** The article *the* should not precede any year.
6. **The correct answer is (C).** The connecting phrase should be "as well as."
7. **The correct answer is (B).** The infinitive form, "to store," should be used instead of the gerund.
8. **The correct answer is (A).** The article *a* should precede the phrase "jazz-like."
9. **The correct answer is (C).** The verb should be in the simple past tense: *ended.*
10. **The correct answer is (B).** The passive voice should be used: "was shot down."
11. **The correct answer is (C).** The simple past tense should be used: "made them feel."
12. **The correct answer is (A).** Plural nouns indicate a classification of people, so you need the plural form: *Oncologists.*
13. **The correct answer is (C).** The simple past tense should be used: *increased.*
14. **The correct answer is (B).** The noun form is needed to achieve parallel construction: *elegance.*
15. **The correct answer is (B).** The plural form of the noun should be used: *techniques.*
16. **The correct answer is (D).** After *portraits,* the conjunction should be *and.*
17. **The correct answer is (A).** The correct modifier of *island* is the phrase "much of the."
18. **The correct answer is (B).** The correct form of the noun is *architect*, which is a person.
19. **The correct answer is (D).** To achieve parallel construction, the sentence should read "causing pollution" instead of "causes pollution."
20. **The correct answer is (C).** The plural form of the noun should be used: "paved streets."
21. **The correct answer is (C).** The coordinating conjunction should be *and.*
22. **The correct answer is (B).** The gerund form should be used: *cracking.*
23. **The correct answer is (D).** To achieve parallel construction, the noun should be changed to the adjective: *financial.*
24. **The correct answer is (D).** The phrasal verb should be "tried for."
25. **The correct answer is (C).** The relative pronoun should be *that.*

Day 18

Structure

Error Identification Drill—Part II

Today's Assignment

- Using the strategies that you acquired on Day 7, answer correctly the following error identification questions by circling the letter under the incorrect portion of the sentence. You should give yourself only 20 minutes to do all 25 questions. Then, compare your answers with those at the end of the chapter and read the explanations carefully.

Now, begin working on the drills. The answers and explanations are at the end of this chapter.

1. In *Descent of Man*, Darwin will be describing sites
   A
   used by birds during the breeding season for
   B C D
   display and courtship.

2. The cities of New York and Tokyo will be
   A
   inundated if the polar ice caps are continuing
   B C
   to melt.
   D

3. Though Alfred Nobel's family business had done
   A
   the manufacture and sale of explosives, he himself
   B
   was a man of pacifist tendencies.
   C D

4. Art historians, both American and French, disagrees
   A B
   about the work of the painter Eugene Delacroix.
   C D

5. We can't fully appreciate the silent films of
   A
   Abel Gance, because the surviving prints are
   B
   decomposed, incomplete, and
   C
   the lack of proper musical accompaniment.
   D

6. The greater the frequency of vibration in a musical
   A
   instruments, the higher the pitch that is
   B C
   experienced by the human ear.
   D

7. One tablespoon of parmesan cheese is containing about two grams of saturated fat.
(A) One (B) of (C) is containing (D) saturated

8. The handle of the Big and Little Dippers extend in opposite directions in the sky.
(A) handle (B) opposite (C) directions (D) in

9. Cuneiform, a system of writing developed from pictographs, will be used in the valley of the Tigris and Euphrates Rivers 4000 B.C.E.
(A) a (B) system (C) will be used (D) Rivers

10. By the time Spanish explorers first met the Aztecs, they already were developing the calendar.
(A) By the time (B) explorers (C) met (D) were developing

11. By reading *Back to Methuselah*, students can learn what the world is like 5,000 years from now, according to Bernard Shaw.
(A) By reading (B) can (C) what the world is like (D) according to

12. Dust inhaled during years of exposure to materials such as asbestos and coal cause the lung disease pneumoconiosis.
(A) inhaled (B) of exposure (C) such as (D) cause

13. Robert Hutchins believed on a core undergraduate curriculum built around the great books of the Western tradition.
(A) believed on (B) curriculum (C) built around (D) great books

14. The Civil War, by eliminating Southern obstructionism, is enabling farmers to win federal subsidies for agricultural and technological colleges.
(A) eliminating (B) is enabling (C) to win federal subsidies (D) colleges

15. Studies of deeds of sale during the eighteenth century shows that real value per acre of land grew 1 percent a year.
(A) during (B) shows (C) value per acre of land (D) grew

16. When Marion Michael Morrisey starred in movie *Singing Sandy*, he already had changed his professional name to John Wayne.
(A) When (B) starred (C) movie (D) had changed

17. In 1876, a group of Philadelphia civic leaders have organized an international exhibition to celebrate America's centennial.
(A) a group of (B) civic leaders (C) have organized (D) exhibition

18. The robber barons were late nineteenth-century industrialists in America, especially those who ostentatiously displayed they're wealth.
(A) were (B) in America (C) those who (D) they're wealth

19. In the United States, dialect region are distinguished mainly by differences of pronunciation and vocabulary, and only to a small extent by grammar.
(A) dialect region (B) by differences (C) only (D) by grammar

20. Henry David Thoreau disliked big government, (A) but he also wanted (B) the state to foster the arts (C) and education, building good roads (D), prevent crime and protect wildlife.

21. In the early nineteenth century, the women mill workers (A) of Lowell, Massachusetts, were paid unusual good wages (B) and lived (C) in clean, safe boarding houses provided by (D) their employers.

22. When a student goes (A) abroad to study (B), they (C) will have to speak (D) the language of the host country.

23. If John Tilson's book about Kentucky has not made (A) Daniel Boone well known (B) to Americans and Europeans, he would not have become (C) a hero in American history (D).

24. The work of the late James Baldwin continues to give (A) readers insights into (B) American racial divisions, which are among (C) the most intractable social problem (D).

25. By 1856, Cyrus McCormick's (A) factories (B) in Chicago was producing 40 reapers a day (C), and he had become (D) a millionaire.

ANSWERS AND EXPLANATIONS

Day 18—Answer Key for Error Identification Drills—Part II

1.	A	14.	B
2.	C	15.	B
3.	A	16.	C
4.	B	17.	C
5.	D	18.	D
6.	B	19.	A
7.	C	20.	D
8.	A	21.	B
9.	C	22.	C
10.	D	23.	A
11.	C	24.	D
12.	D	25.	B
13.	A		

Explanations

1. **The correct answer is (A).** The future progressive tense, "will be describing," is incorrect. The past tense *described* should be used instead.

2. **The correct answer is (C).** In the future possible conditional, the verb in the main clause must be in the simple present tense.

3. **The correct answer is (A).** The verb should be *was.*

4. **The correct answer is (B).** The subject *historians* is plural, but the verb *disagrees* is for a singular noun.

5. **The correct answer is (D).** This sentence contains a series that requires parallel construction.

6. **The correct answer is (B).** The article *a* indicates a singular noun, but the underlined word is plural.

7. **The correct answer is (C).** The verb should be in the simple present tense.

8. **The correct answer is (A).** The verb *extend* requires a plural subject, *handles.*

9. **The correct answer is (C).** The correct verb tense is the simple past in the passive voice.

10. **The correct answer is (D).** The correct verb tense is the past perfect.

11. **The correct answer is (C).** The correct verb tense is the simple future.

12. **The correct answer is (D).** The subject *dust* requires the verb *causes.*

13. **The correct answer is (A).** The phrasal verb should be "believed in."

14. **The correct answer is (B).** The verb tense should be simple past.

15. **The correct answer is (B).** The verb must be *show* in order to agree with the subject *studies.*

16. **The correct answer is (C).** The article *the* must be used with *movie.*

17. **The correct answer is (C).** The correct verb tense is the simple past.

18. **The correct answer is (D).** The possessive form *their* should be used.

19. **The correct answer is (A).** The subject should be plural, regions.

20. **The correct answer is (D).** To achieve parallel construction, the verb should be *build.*

21. **The correct answer is (B).** The correct modifier should be an adverb, *unusually.*

22. **The correct answer is (C).** The correct words to use in place of *their* are he or she.

23. **The correct answer is (A).** The verbs in if-clauses in past unreal conditionals should be the past perfect tense.

24. **The correct answer is (D).** The object of the preposition should be the plural, *problems.*

25. **The correct answer is (B).** In order to agree with the verb phrase "was producing," the subject of the sentence has to be *factory.*

Day 19

Structure

Sentence Completion Drill—Part I

Today's Assignment

- Using the strategies you acquired on Day 6, complete the following sentence completion questions. You should give yourself 20 minutes to do all 25 questions. Then, check your work with the answer sheet at the end and read the explanations carefully.

There are one or more words left out of the following sentences. Choose the correct word or phrase to complete the sentence from the four answer choices given for each question. Mark your answers on a separate sheet of scrap paper or here in the book. As stated above, you have 20 minutes for this exercise.

1. _______ excellent protection but is a fragile organ when exposed to the sun's ultraviolet rays.
   (A) The skin provides
   (B) These skins provide
   (C) No skins provides
   (D) The skins are providing

2. When it was published in 1959, Robert Frank's book, *The Americans*, _______ hostility in the United States.
   (A) is meeting the
   (B) has been met
   (C) was met with
   (D) will meet it

3. Saxophonist Coleman Hawkins developed his jazz style _______ before recording his masterpiece *Body and Soul* in 1939.
   (A) over Europe
   (B) at Europe
   (C) on Europe
   (D) in Europe

4. _______ to the Americas by European colonists and had a devastating effect on American Indians.
   (A) Smallpox introduced
   (B) Smallpox was introduced
   (C) Smallpox has introduced
   (D) Smallpox is introducing

5. American courts review the acts of all government branches and officials _______ they comply with the U.S. Constitution.
   (A) to determine if
   (B) to determine what
   (C) to determine where
   (D) to determine that

6. It is estimated that the sun _______ of the total mass of the solar system.
(A) contains 99.86 percent
(B) it contains 99.86 percent
(C) is contained by 99.86 percent
(D) is containing 99.86 percent

7. In 1913, Cecil B. DeMille directed *The Squaw Man,* _______ the first feature length film to be made in Hollywood.
(A) which will be
(B) which has been
(C) which was
(D) which can be

8. Most general readers of poetry find Ezra Pound's *Cantos* _______ poem in the English language.
(A) the difficultest
(B) a more difficult
(C) a most difficult
(D) the most difficult

9. _______ a *tachyon* is a particle that may travel faster than the speed of light.
(A) What scientists are called
(B) What scientists call
(C) What scientist calls
(D) What scientist is called

10. The Shakers, an American religious community, _______ in furniture design and herbal medicine.
(A) was a pioneer
(B) is a pioneer
(C) were pioneers
(D) are a pioneer

11. Juan Ramón Jiménez, _______ the Nobel Prize for literature, died in San Juan, Puerto Rico, in 1958.
(A) who won
(B) who is winning
(C) who has won
(D) who wins

12. Between 1889 and 1891, Mary Cassatt produced beautiful graphics _______.
(A) of exceptionally virtuosity and grace
(B) of exception virtuosity and grace
(C) of excepting virtuosity and grace
(D) of exceptional virtuosity and grace

13. Photons, _______ in electromagnetic energy, can be split into electrons and positrons.
(A) which is the fundamental particle
(B) which are fundamental particles
(C) which is the fundamental particles
(D) which are fundamental particle

14. The claw-and-ball feet on many early American chairs are adaptations of a design once found in Chinese _______.
(A) furniture
(B) a furniture
(C) furnitures
(D) the furniture

15. In 1934, the Securities and Exchange Commission _______ the commerce in stocks, bonds, and other securities.
(A) was established to regulating
(B) was established about the regulating
(C) was established to regulate
(D) was established about to regulate

16. The great masterpiece of Japanese literature, "The Tale of Genji," deals with the loves of the son of an emperor _______.
(A) in eleventh century
(B) in the eleven centuries
(C) in the eleventh century
(D) in the eleventh centuries

17. Sanitation in Roman life _______ aqueducts that supplied the city with 300 million gallons of water daily.
    (A) which was aided by
    (B) was aided by
    (C) which aided by
    (D) was aiding by

18. Alexander Pushkin grew up in a Russian family _______ was read and recited every day.
    (A) in which French poetry
    (B) of which French poetry
    (C) at which French poetry
    (D) on which French poetry

19. The changes brought about in Turkey after World War I _______ the adoption of Western-style surnames and the Latin alphabet.
    (A) were including
    (B) had been included
    (C) included
    (D) have included

20. Baseball became America's most popular sport, _______ to people in almost all social and economic classes.
    (A) while it appealed
    (B) although it appealed
    (C) but it appealed
    (D) because it appealed

21. Special areas of the brain are related to sensory discriminations, such as sense of position, _______ are involved in the use of written and spoken language.
    (A) and others
    (B) and the others
    (C) and another
    (D) and other

22. Henry James wrote great novels, and his brother William _______ the philosophy known as *pragmatism*.
    (A) has formulated
    (B) formulated
    (C) will formulate
    (D) formulates

23. The power of Caravaggio's religious paintings _______ his detailed rendering of real-world subjects.
    (A) is lying in
    (B) lays in
    (C) is laying
    (D) lies in

24. Although John Jay was the first Chief Justice of the Supreme Court, _______ as a diplomat that he exerted his greatest influence on the new government of the United States.
    (A) there was
    (B) he was
    (C) it was
    (D) his was

25. Anna Pavlova has been dead for more than seventy years, but _______, her name is virtually synonymous with ballet.
    (A) to the general public
    (B) to a general public
    (C) to general public
    (D) to her general public

ANSWERS AND EXPLANATIONS

Day 19—Answer Key for Sentence Completion Drill, Part I

1. A
2. C
3. D
4. B
5. A
6. A
7. C
8. D
9. B
10. C
11. A
12. D
13. B
14. A
15. C
16. C
17. B
18. A
19. C
20. D
21. A
22. B
23. D
24. C
25. A

Explanations

1. **The correct answer is (A).** In choices (B) and (D), the plural noun does not agree with the verb *is*. In choice (C), there is an incorrect agreement of noun and verb.

2. **The correct answer is (C).** In choice (A), the present progressive tense is incorrect for action in the past. In choice (B), the present perfect tense in the passive voice is incorrect. In choice (D), the simple future tense is incorrect for actions in the past.

3. **The correct answer is (D).** All other prepositions are incorrect.

4. **The correct answer is (B).** In choice (A), the active voice with this subject is incorrect. In choice (C), the present perfect tense is incorrect for an action in the past. In choice (D), the present progressive tense is incorrect for actions in the past.

5. **The correct answer is (A).** The other answer choices do not contain conjunctions.

6. **The correct answer is (A).** In choice (B), the pronoun *it* is used incorrectly. In choice (C), the passive voice is incorrect. In choice (D), the present progressive tense is incorrect.

7. **The correct answer is (C).** In choice (A), the simple future tense is incorrect for actions in the past. In choice (B), the present perfect tense is incorrect for an action in the past. In choice (D), there is an incorrect use of possibility (can) for and action in the past.

8. **The correct answer is (D).** In choices (A) and (C), there is an incorrect form of the superlative. In choice (B), there is an incorrect use of the comparative.

9. **The correct answer is (B).** In choice (A), there is an incorrect use of the passive voice. In choices (C) and (D), the noun needs an article or plural form.

10. **The correct answer is (C).** In choices (A) and (B), the singular verb and noun do not agree with *Shakers*. In choice (D), the plural verb *are* does not agree with the singular noun *pioneer*.

11. **The correct answer is (A).** In choice (B), the present progressive tense is incorrect for action in the past. In choice (C), the present perfect tense is incorrect for action in the past. In choice (D), the simple present tense is incorrect for action in the past.

12. **The correct answer is (D).** In choice (A), there is the incorrect use of adverb *exceptionally*. In choice (B), there is the incorrect use of the noun *exception*. In choice (C), there is the incorrect use of the present participle *excepting*.

13. **The correct answer is (B).** In choice (A), the singular verb and noun do not agree with *photons*. In choice (C), the singular verb *is* does not agree with plural noun *particles*. In choice (D), the plural verb *are* does not agree with singular noun *particle*.

14. **The correct answer is (A).** In choice (B), there is an incorrect use of article *a*. In choice (C), there is an incorrect use of a plural noun. In choice (D), there is an incorrect use of the article *the*.

15. **The correct answer is (C).** In choice (A), there is the incorrect form of the infinitive "to regulate." In choice (B), there is an incorrect use of a prepositional phrase. In choice (D), there is the incorrect use of the preposition *about*.

16. **The correct answer is (C).** In choice (A), the article *the* was omitted. In choice (B), there is an incorrect use of the adjective and noun *eleven centuries*. In choice (D), the plural noun *centuries* is incorrect.

17. **The correct answer is (B).** In choices (A) and (C), there is an incorrect use of subordinating clauses. In choice (D), the past progressive tense is incorrect.

18. **The correct answer is (A).** In the other answer choices, the prepositions are incorrect.

19. **The correct answer is (C).** In choice (A), the past progressive tense is incorrect. In choice (B), there is an incorrect use of the passive voice and the past perfect tense. In choice (D), the present perfect tense is incorrect for action in the past.

20. **The correct answer is (D).** The other answer choices use incorrect conjunctions.

21. **The correct answer is (A).** In choice (B), *the others* is incorrect because not all other areas of the brain are involved in the use of language. In choice (C), the pronoun *another* is incorrectly used. In choice (D), the adjective *other* is an adjective, not a pronoun.

22. **The correct answer is (B).** In the other answers, the verb tenses do not agree with the past tense verb *wrote*.

23. **The correct answer is (D).** In choice (A), there is an incorrect use of the progressive tense. In choices (B) and (C), the meanings of the verb choices are incorrect.

24. **The correct answer is (C).** In choice (B), an incorrect pronoun is used. In choice (D), the possessive adjective was incorrectly used.

25. **The correct answer is (A).** In choice (B), there is an incorrect use of the article *a*. In choice (C), the article *the* is incorrectly omitted. In choice (D), the possessive adjective *her* is incorrectly used.

Day 20

Structure

Sentence Completion Drill—Part II

Today's Assignment

- Today, you will practice with more sentence completion drills. Use no more than 20 minutes to complete the following sentence completion questions. Then, check your work with the answer sheet at the end.

For the following Sentence Completion questions, circle the letter next to the word or phrase that best completes the sentence.

1. Thomas Paine's *Common Sense*, ________, crystallized the growing sense that George III was a king who merited disdain, rather than allegiance.
   (A) who was published in January, 1776
   (B) was published in January, 1776
   (C) published in January, 1776
   (D) publishing in January, 1776

2. According to many musicians, ________ more difficult to play than Rachmaninoff's "Third Piano Concerto."
   (A) there is no piano composition
   (B) there are no piano composition
   (C) there is any piano composition
   (D) there are any piano composition

3. When Alexis de Toqueville wrote *Democracy in America*, he reported the lack of class distinctions but ________.
   (A) was ignoring sexual inequality and slavery
   (B) has ignored sexual inequality and slavery
   (C) had ignored sexual inequality and slavery
   (D) ignored sexual inequality and slavery

4. In *The Theory of the Leisure Class*, Thorstein Veblen presented the principle that middle-class men and women practiced "conspicuous consumption" in the way ________.
   (A) they are choosing their clothes
   (B) they chose their clothes
   (C) they chose her
   (D) they had chosen their clothes

5. When scientists predicted that plastics ________ in society, few realized how accurate they were.
   (A) will play an important role
   (B) is going to play an important role
   (C) were playing an important role
   (D) would play an important role

6. _______ Buffalo Bill's Wild West Shows that featured horses and riders in a variety of displays.
   (A) England's Queen Victoria has been a fan of
   (B) England's Queen Victoria was a fan of
   (C) England's Queen Victoria has been doing a fan of
   (D) England's Queen Victoria is a fan of

7. When rural free delivery began in the 1890s, _______ their order in the mail box and expect delivery within a few days.
   (A) farmers and small town residents will place
   (B) farmers and small town residents can place
   (C) farmers and small town residents place
   (D) farmers and small town residents could place

8. If the movie star Greta Garbo had not invested her money wisely, she _______ live comfortably in her old age.
   (A) would not have been able to
   (B) will not be able to able to
   (C) was not able to
   (D) was not going to be able to

9. Huntington's disease is a neurological disease that usually _______ in middle age.
   (A) is beginning
   (B) began
   (C) begins
   (D) has begun

10. _______ to an audience in a gallery in San Francisco, he had an immediate impact on the culture of America.
   (A) When Allen Ginsberg has read his poem *Howl*
   (B) When Allen Ginsberg is reading his poem *Howl*
   (C) When Allen Ginsberg read his poem *Howl*
   (D) When Allen Ginsberg doesn't read his poem *Howl*

11. The blue whale is the largest mammal that has ever lived, and _______.
   (A) it's weight reaches 150 tons
   (B) its weight reaches 150 tons
   (C) its' weight reaches 150 tons
   (D) its weight reaches 150 tons'

12. As secretary to the Massachusetts Board of Education, Horace Mann _______, gave lectures, and wrote articles for a biweekly journal for teachers.
   (A) visited schools
   (B) was visiting schools
   (C) had visited schools
   (D) would visit schools

13. The gigantic land tortoises _______ are now facing extinction, despite the efforts of scientists.
   (A) that is indigenous to the Galapagos Islands
   (B) that were indigenous to the Galapagos Islands
   (C) who were indigenous to the Galapagos Islands
   (D) that are indigenous to the Galapagos Islands

14. The 1913 Armory Show gave American artists and the public _______ modernist painting and sculpture produced in Europe.
   (A) its first look at
   (B) their first look at
   (C) her first look at
   (D) your first look at

15. Agriculture was _______ in America from the founding of Virginia in 1607 to about 1890.
   (A) the most important economic activity
   (B) the important economic activities
   (C) the importantest economic activity
   (D) the most important economic activities

16. Unlike the brown sparrow, the passenger pigeon ________ became extinct in 1914.
    (A) slaughtered indiscriminately and
    (B) was slaughtered indiscriminately and
    (C) did not slaughter indiscriminately and
    (D) had been slaughtered indiscriminately and
17. New England and Spanish colonies required settlements to be grouped in towns, close to a central plaza or meetinghouse square ________.
    (A) in governmental and religious structures
    (B) for governmental and religious structures
    (C) over governmental and religious structures
    (D) from governmental and religious structures
18. ________ in films, Fred Astaire turned movie dancing into a fine art.
    (A) By direction his own dance numbers
    (B) By directed his own dance numbers
    (C) By direct his own dance numbers
    (D) By directing his own dance numbers
19. Diamonds are mined by raising chunks of earth from underground tunnels, carefully crushing them, and then ________ the diamonds as pressurized water rinses away the soil.
    (A) remove
    (B) move
    (C) be removed
    (D) removing
20. In 1803, John Jacob Astor ________ that is now known as Times Square.
    (A) paid $25,000 for land
    (B) was paying $25,000 for land
    (C) will pay $25,000 for land
    (D) pays $25,000 for land
21. From the founding of America to the mid-twentieth century, ________ in domestic work than in any other occupation.
    (A) there were more woman
    (B) there was more woman
    (C) there were more women
    (D) there was more women
22. In the late eighteenth century, the textile industry transformed New England from an agricultural to an industrial area and pointed the way to the ________ and big business.
    (A) growth of corporations
    (B) grow of corporations
    (C) grows of corporations
    (D) grown of corporations
23. Approximately 20 percent of the earth's atmosphere ________, and most of the remainder is comprised of nitrogen.
    (A) is comprised of oxygen
    (B) comprised of oxygen
    (C) are comprised of oxygen
    (D) are comprising oxygen
24. By 1933, two thirds of American homes had at least one radio, twice as many ________.
    (A) as those telephones
    (B) with telephones
    (C) as those with telephones
    (D) as telephones
25. ________than during the last century due to the campaigns of white Americans against Native Americans.
    (A) There are few buffalo roaming the Great Plains today
    (B) There are fewer buffalos roaming the Great Plains today
    (C) There are little buffalo roaming the Great Plains today
    (D) There are less buffalo roaming the Great Plains today

ANSWERS AND EXPLANATIONS

Day 20—Answer Key for Sentence Completion Drill—Part II

1. C	14. B
2. A	15. A
3. D	16. B
4. B	17. B
5. D	18. D
6. B	19. D
7. D	20. A
8. A	21. C
9. C	22. A
10. C	23. A
11. B	24. C
12. A	25. B
13. D	

Explanations

1. **The correct answer is (C).** Choice (A) is a relative clause that modifies a person. Choice (B) has no subject for the relative clause. Choice (D) incorrectly uses a present participle to begin the modifying phrase.

2. **The correct answer is (A).** Choice (B) incorrectly uses the word *are*. Choices (C) and (D) use *any* without a negative in the sentence.

3. **The correct answer is (D).** Choice (A) is incorrectly in the past progressive tense, which reports continuing action in the past. Choice (B) is incorrectly in the present perfect tense, which should be used in unfinished time. Choice (C) is incorrectly in the past perfect tense, which should not be used when two actions take place simultaneously in finished time.

4. **The correct answer is (B).** The verbs in choices (A) and (D) are in the wrong tenses. Choice (C) uses an incorrect possessive adjective.

5. **The correct answer is (D).** Choice (A) is in the simple future tense, which is incorrect in a sentence that is in finished time. Choice (B), in the present progressive tense, is also incorrect in a sentence that is in finished time. Choice (C) makes no sense with the verb predicted.

6. **The correct answer is (B).** The other answer choices contain verbs that are in incorrect tenses for a sentence in finished time.

7. **The correct answer is (D).** The other answer choices use incorrect verb tenses for a sentence in finished time.

8. **The correct answer is (A).** The other answer choices do not meet the requirements of past unreal conditional sentences.

9. **The correct answer is (C).** Choice (A) is incorrect because the present progressive tense indicates "no." The verb in choice (B) is in finished time. The verb in choice (D) indicates an action completed in unfinished time.

10. **The correct answer is (C).** The verbs in the other answer choices are not correct for a sentence in finished time.

11. **The correct answer is (B).** The other answer choices use incorrect forms of the possessive.

12. **The correct answer is (A).** The other answer choices do not meet the requirements of parallel construction.

13. **The correct answer is (D).** In choice (A), the subject is plural, and the verb is used with singular subjects. In choice (B), the verb should be in the simple present tense but is in the simple past. In choice (D), the relative pronoun and the tense of the verb are incorrect.

14. **The correct answer is (B).** The other answers contain incorrect possessive adjectives.

15. **The correct answer is (A).** Choices (B) and (D) are plural but should be singular. Choice (C) contains an incorrect form of the superlative.

16. **The correct answer is (B).** Choices (A) and (C) imply that the pigeon itself did some slaughtering. Choice (D) uses the past perfect tense incorrectly.

17. **The correct answer is (B).** The other answer choices contain incorrect prepositions.

18. **The correct answer is (D).** The other answer choices do not contain a gerund as the object of the preposition *by*.

19. **The correct answer is (D).** The other answer choices do not contain the *–ing* form of the verb that is required for parallel construction.

20. **The correct answer is (A).** Choice (B) is the past progressive tense, which is incorrect for a completed, not continuous, action. The verbs in choices (C) and (D) are incorrect for actions in finished time.

21. **The correct answer is (C).** Choice (A) contains a singular noun, which is incorrect. Choice (B) contains an incorrect structure *more woman*. Choice (D) contains the singular verb, which is incorrect.

22. **The correct answer is (A).** The other answer choices are incorrect forms of the verb *grow*.

23. **The correct answer is (A).** Choice (B) is a participial phrase. Choice (C) uses a verb for a plural noun. Choice (D) uses a verb in the progressive form for plural nouns. Percent is always singular.

24. **The correct answer is (C).** Choice (A) lacks the preposition *with*. Choice (B) lacks *as those*. Choice (D) lacks *those with*.

25. **The correct answer is (B).** Choice (A) is not in the comparative form. Choice (C) contains *little*, which is used for non-countable nouns, such as *coffee, courage*, and *traffic*. Choice (D) contains *less*, which is also used for non-countable nouns.

Day 21

Reading

Reading Drill—Part I

Today's Assignment

- Use the skills you acquired on Day 8 to answer the reading section questions in this chapter. Give yourself no more than 75 minutes to complete this exercise.

Each passage is followed by a series of questions. Answer the questions based on the information you gathered from the passage. Choose the best answer to each question and answer each question based on what is *stated* or *implied* in the passage.

Questions 1–10 refer to the following passage.

Line People have been donating blood since the early twentieth century to help accident victims and patients undergoing surgical procedures. Usually a pint of whole blood is donated, and it is then (5) divided into platelets, white blood cells, and red blood cells. People can donate blood (for red blood cells) about once every two months.

Transfusing the blood from the donor to the recipient is straightforward. It involves taking the (10) blood from a donor's arm vein by means of a hypodermic syringe. The blood flows through a plastic tube to a collection bag or bottle that contains sodium citrate, which prevents the blood from clotting. (15) When the blood is given to a patient, a plastic tube and hypodermic needle are connected to the recipient's arm. The blood flows down from the container by gravity. This is a slow process and may last as long as 2 hours to complete the infu- (20) sion of blood into the recipient. The patient is protected from being infected during the transfusion. Only sterile containers, tubing, and needles are used, and this helps ensure that transfused or stored blood is not exposed to disease-causing (25) bacteria.

Negative reactions to transfusions are not unusual. The recipient may suffer an allergic reaction or be sensitive to donor leukocytes. Some may suffer from an undetected red-cell incompatibility. Un- (30) explained reactions are also fairly common. Although they are rare, other causes of such negative reactions include contaminated blood, air bubbles in the blood, overloading of the circulatory system through administration of excess (35) blood, or sensitivity to donor plasma or platelets

Today, hospitals and blood banks go to great lengths to screen all blood donors and their blood.

All donated blood is routinely and rigorously tested for diseases, such as HIV (which causes
40 AIDS), hepatitis B, and syphilis. When the recipient is a newborn or an infant, the blood is usually irradiated to eliminate harmful elements. Donated blood is washed, and the white blood cells and platelets are removed.

45 Storing the blood sometimes requires a freezing process. To freeze the red blood cells, a glycerol solution is added. To unfreeze, the glycerol is removed. The ability to store blood for long periods has been a boon to human health.

1. Which of the following words is closest in meaning to the word "donating" in line 1?
   (A) Adorning
   (B) Giving
   (C) Taking
   (D) Distributing

2. In line 4, the word "it" refers to
   (A) accident victims.
   (B) surgical procedures.
   (C) a pint of whole blood.
   (D) surgery patients.

3. According to the passage, how often can people donate blood for red blood cells?
   (A) Every four months
   (B) Every three months
   (C) Every two months
   (D) Every month

4. Where in the passage is the best place for the following sentence?

   Inserting the needle into the recipient's arm causes little pain.

   (A) After the last sentence in the first paragraph
   (B) After the word "syringe" in paragraph 2
   (C) After the word "arm" in paragraph 3
   (D) After the word "transfusion" in paragraph 3

5. Which sentence in paragraph 2 explains how clotting is prevented in the blood container?
   (A) The first sentence
   (B) The second sentence
   (C) The third sentence
   (D) None of the above

6. All of the following are mentioned as potential negative reactions to transfusions EXCEPT
   (A) allergies.
   (B) red-cell incompatibility.
   (C) air bubbles in the blood.
   (D) sensitivity to donor leukocytes.

7. What answer choice is closest in meaning to the word "undetected" in line 29?
   (A) Not wanted
   (B) Not captured
   (C) Not found
   (D) Not illustrated

8. Look at the phrase "go to great lengths to screen" in paragraph 5, lines 36–37. Choose the word that has the same meaning.
   (A) Routinely
   (B) Rigorously
   (C) Irradiated
   (D) Removed

9. Based on the information in the passage, what can be inferred about blood transfused to infants and newborns?
   (A) It is as rigorously tested as blood for adults.
   (B) It is treated with radiant energy.
   (C) It is not treated differently from adults.
   (D) It is not dangerous for children.

10. What does the author imply in the passage?
    (A) Transfusing blood is a dangerous process.
    (B) Storing blood benefits mankind.
    (C) Clotting cannot be prevented.
    (D) Freezing blood destroys platelets.

Questions 11–20 refer to the following passage.

Line Duncan Phyfe made some of the most beautiful furniture found in America. His family name was originally Fife, and he was born in Scotland in 1768. In 1784, the Fife family immigrated to Albany,
(5) where Duncan's father opened a cabinetmaking shop in Albany, New York. Duncan followed in his father's footsteps and was apprenticed to a cabinetmaker. After completing his training, Duncan moved to New York City.

(10) Duncan Fife was first mentioned in the 1792 NYC Directory as a furniture "joiner" in business at 2 Broad Street. Two years later, he moved, expanded his business, and changed his name to Phyfe. He was a quiet-living, god-fearing young man who
(15) felt his new name would probably appeal to potential customers who were definitely anti-British in this post–Revolutionary War period.

Duncan Phyfe's name distinguished him from his contemporaries. Although the new spelling helped
(20) him better compete with French émigré craftsmen, his new name had more to do with hanging it on a sign over his door stoop.

The artisans and merchants who came to America discovered a unique kind of freedom. They were
(25) no longer restricted by class and guild traditions of Europe. For the first time in history, a man learned that by working hard, he could build his business based on his own name and reputation and quality of work.

(30) Phyfe's workshop apparently took off immediately. At the peak of his success, Phyfe employed 100 craftsmen. Some economic historians point to Phyfe as having employed division of labor and an assembly line. What his workshop produced
(35) shows Phyfe's absolute dedication to quality in workmanship. Each piece of furniture was made of the best available materials. He was reported to have paid $1,000 for a single Santo Domingo mahogany log.
(40) Phyfe did not create new designs. Rather, he borrowed from a broad range of the period's classical styles, Empire, Sheraton, Regency, and French Classical among them. Nevertheless, Phyfe's high-quality craftsmanship established him as
(45) America's patriotic interpreter of European design in the late eighteenth and early nineteenth centuries.

Although the number of pieces produced by Duncan Phyfe's workshop is enormous, compara-
(50) tively few marked or labeled pieces have been found extant. In antiques shops and auctions, collectors have paid $11,000 for a card table, $24,200 for a tea table, and $93,500 for a sewing table.

11. Based on the information in the passage, what can be inferred about Duncan Phyfe?
    (A) He was an excellent businessman with a good sense of craftsmanship and design.
    (B) He regretted that Great Britain no longer governed New York City.
    (C) He built all his furniture by himself in a workshop in Santo Domingo.
    (D) He joined the cabinetmakers' guild after he moved to Scotland in 1792.

12. According to the passage, which of the following does the author imply?
    (A) Duncan Fife and his father had the same first name.
    (B) Duncan Fife worked for his father in Scotland.
    (C) Duncan Fife and his father were in the same business.
    (D) Duncan Phyfe made over 100 different kinds of tables.

13. Which sentence in paragraph 2 explains Duncan's name change?
    (A) The first sentence
    (B) The second sentence
    (C) The third sentence
    (D) None of the above

14. Which choice does the word "it" refer to in line 21?
    (A) His spelling
    (B) His chair
    (C) His French
    (D) His name

15. Which choice is closest in meaning to the word "guild" in line 25?
    (A) Verdict of a jury
    (B) Organization of craftsmen
    (C) Political party of émigrés
    (D) Immigrant's club

16. Which of the following does the word "freedom" in line 24 refer to?
    (A) No longer restricted
    (B) Restricted
    (C) By working hard
    (D) Took off

17. Where in the passage could the following sentence be added to the passage?

    Every joint was tight, and the carved elements were beautifully executed.

    (A) After the word "workmanship" in paragraph 5
    (B) After the word "cabinetmaker" in paragraph 1
    (C) After the word "stoop" in paragraph 3
    (D) After the word "table" in the last paragraph

18. In his business, Duncan Phyfe used all of the following EXCEPT
    (A) division of labor.
    (B) an assembly line.
    (C) continental designs.
    (D) the least expensive materials.

19. Based on information in the passage, what can be inferred about Duncan Phyfe's death?
    (A) He died in the eighteenth century.
    (B) He died in Albany.
    (C) He died in the nineteenth century.
    (D) He died in Scotland.

20. The author implies that
    (A) furniture from Duncan Phyfe's workshop no longer exists.
    (B) furniture from Duncan Phyfe's workshop costs a lot of money today.
    (C) furniture from Duncan Phyfe's workshop was ignored by New Yorkers.
    (D) furniture from Duncan Phyfe's workshop was made by his father.

Questions 21–30 refer to the following passage.

Line

Roman gladiators are intriguing figures in history. We get "gladiator" from the Latin word *gladius*, which means sword. Gladiators were professional combatants who originally performed, to the (5) death, at Etruscan funerals. The losers became armed attendants in the next world to the person whose funeral was being held.

In Rome, these exhibitions became very popular and increased in size from 3 pairs at the first known (10) exhibition in 264 B.C.E. to 300 pairs in the middle of the first century B.C.E. These spectacles increased to as many as 100 pairs under the emperor Titus, while the emperor Trajan in 107 C.E. had 5,000 pairs of gladiators for his triumph.

(15) There were various classes of gladiators, distinguished by their arms or modes of fighting. The Samnites fought with the national weapons—a large oblong shield, a visor, a plumed helmet, and a short sword. Thracians had a small round shield, (20) called a buckler, and a dagger curved like a scythe. They usually fought the Mirmillones, who were armed in Gallic fashion with helmet, sword, and shield. Similarly, a Retiarius, or net man, was often matched with a Secutor, or pursuer. The netman (25) wore nothing but a short tunic or apron and tried to entangle the fully armed pursuer with the cast net he carried in his right hand. If successful, the netman dispatched the pursuer with a large, three-pronged weapon called a trident, which the netman (30) carried in his left. Others fought on horseback, and some carried a short sword in each hand. There were also gladiators who fought from chariots and others who tried to lasso their antagonists.

Gladiators came from a variety of social classes.
35 Though they were usually slaves and criminals, a ruined man of high social position might hire himself out as a gladiator. Emperor Domitian had unusual gladiators, dwarfs and women, and the half-mad emperor Commodus fought in the arena,
40 where he won his bouts with the aid of his Praetorian Guard.

To a victorious gladiator was given branches of palm and sometimes money. If they survived a number of combats, they were often freed from
45 gladiatorial service. However, many gladiators reentered after discharge. Some became politically important bodyguards to controversial politicians.

21. What is the main topic of the passage?
    (A) The life of Roman gladiators
    (B) The emperors of Rome
    (C) The weapons used in the Roman arena
    (D) The social status of gladiators

22. According to the passage, where did gladiators originally perform?
    (A) In Roman arenas
    (B) At Thracian cities
    (C) At Etruscan funerals
    (D) In Trajan's triumph

23. According to the passage, when did the first known gladiatorial exhibition take place in Rome?
    (A) In 50 B.C.E.
    (B) In 264 B.C.E.
    (C) In 107 C.E.
    (D) In 157 B.C.E.

24. Which of the words below is closest in meaning to the word "spectacles" as used in line 11?
    (A) Eyeglasses
    (B) Displays
    (C) Prospects
    (D) Corpses

25. The word "they" in line 21 refers to which of the following?
    (A) Samnites
    (B) Gladiators
    (C) Thracians
    (D) Daggers

26. All of the following were used as weapons by gladiators EXCEPT
    (A) a buckler.
    (B) a cast net.
    (C) a tunic.
    (D) a trident.

27. Where would the following sentence fit best in the passage?

    In the recent film, *Gladiator*, Joaquin Phoenix played the role of Commodus and fought Maximus, the gladiator.
    (A) At the end of paragraph 1
    (B) At the end of paragraph 2
    (C) At the end of paragraph 3
    (D) At the end of paragraph 4

28. Which word is closest in meaning to the word "antagonists" as used in line 33?
    (A) Enemies
    (B) Injured soldiers
    (C) Horsemen
    (D) Fighters

29. From the passage, it can be inferred that
    (A) gladiators could become Emperor.
    (B) emperors enjoyed fighting gladiators.
    (C) gladiators sometimes gained their freedom.
    (D) emperors fought on horseback.

30. Where could the following sentence best be added to the passage?

    Some, in turn, became trainers of new gladiators.
    (A) After the word "history" in paragraph 1
    (B) After the word "shield" in paragraph 3
    (C) After the word "classes" in paragraph 4
    (D) After the word "service" in paragraph 5

Questions 31–40 refer to the following passage.

Line The Forbidden City is the former imperial palace in the center of Beijing, China. Construction began in 1406, and the emperor's court officially moved in by 1420. The Forbidden City got its name (5) because most people were barred from entering the 72-hectare site, surrounded by walls. Even government officials and the imperial family were permitted only limited access. Only the emperor could enter any section at will.

(10) The architecture of the Forbidden City conforms rigidly to traditional Chinese principles. All buildings within the walls follow a north-south line, and the most important ones face south to honor the sun. The designers arranged the other buildings, (15) and the ceremonial spaces between them, to impress all visitors with the great the power of the Emperor, while reinforcing the insignificance of the individual. This architectural concept was carried out to the smallest detail. For example, the im- (20) portance of a building was determined not only by its height or width but also by the style of its roof and the quantity of statuettes placed on the roof's ridges.

In recognition of the importance of its unparalleled (25) architecture, UNESCO added the palace to its World Heritage List in 1987. Today, visitors from all over the world do not wait for an imperial invitation to walk about this palace, now a museum of imperial art.

(30) One of the most impressive landmarks of the Forbidden City is the Meridian Gate, the formal entrance to the southern side of the Forbidden City. The gate, with its auxiliary wings on either side of the entryway, is 38 meters high at its roof ridge. (35) When you stand in front of this majestic structure, you understand how awed people felt when they stood there listening to imperial proclamations.

As you walk through the gate, you come into a large courtyard, 140 meters long and 210 meters (40) wide. Running through the courtyard is the Golden River, which is crossed by five parallel white marble bridges. These bridges lead to the Gate of Supreme Harmony, which, in turn, leads to the heart of the Forbidden City. Its three main (45) halls stand atop a three-tiered marble terrace overlooking an immense plaza. The plaza has enough space to hold tens of thousands of subjects paying homage to the emperor.

At the northernmost end of the Forbidden City is (50) the Imperial Garden, which is totally different from the rest of the compound. Instead of rigid formality, you see a seemingly spontaneous arrangement of trees, fishponds, flowerbeds, and sculpture. Here is the place of relaxation for the emperor. The (55) motion picture *The Last Emperor* (1987), which portrays the life of Hsüan-t'ung P'u-i, was filmed partly within the Forbidden City.

31. Which sentence in paragraph 1 explains who could go anywhere in the Forbidden City at any time?
    (A) Sentence 2
    (B) Sentence 3
    (C) Sentence 4
    (D) Sentence 5

32. How long did it take to build the Forbidden City?
    (A) About five years
    (B) About seven years
    (C) About ten years
    (D) About fourteen years

33. From the passage, it can inferred that
    (A) Chinese architects borrowed ideas from many different countries.
    (B) the design of the Forbidden City is dull and colorless.
    (C) the architecture of the Forbidden City exemplifies traditional Chinese values.
    (D) the garden of the Forbidden City was laid out in a strict, rectangular pattern.

34. Which phrase is closest in meaning to the word "unparalleled" as used in line 24?
    (A) At an angle from the main line
    (B) A high quality found nowhere else
    (C) Partially designed in a foreign country
    (D) Careless of small details in design

35. Which word(s) does the word "its" refer to in line 25?
    (A) UNESCO
    (B) Architecture
    (C) Palace
    (D) World Heritage List

36. From the passage, it is implied that the main entrance area to the Forbidden City
    (A) is surrounded by three tall walls.
    (B) is painted gold and green.
    (C) is decorated with statuettes.
    (D) is not very impressive.

37. Which phrase is closest in meaning to the word "proclamations" as used in line 37?
    (A) Music composed for public ceremonies
    (B) Speeches encouraging soldiers to fight
    (C) Official public announcements
    (D) Poetry written for the emperor

38. All of the following are found in the Imperial Garden EXCEPT
    (A) fishponds.
    (B) sculpture.
    (C) white marble bridges.
    (D) flowerbeds.

39. According to the passage, what do the bridges over the Golden River lead to?
    (A) The Meridian gate
    (B) The center of Beijing
    (C) The Gate of Supreme Harmony
    (D) The Imperial Gardens

40. Which phrase is closest in meaning to the word "spontaneous" as used in line 52?
    (A) Without meaning
    (B) Without thinking
    (C) Without planning
    (D) Without drawing

Questions 41–50 refer to the following passage.

Line Early mariners gradually developed ways of observing and recording in their journals their position, the distances and directions they traveled, the currents of wind and water, and the hazards and havens they encountered. The information in these (5) journals enabled them to find their way home and, for them or their successors, to repeat and extend the recorded voyages. Each new observation could be added to an ever-increasing body of reliable information. (10)

Ship captains and navigators were not concerned about running into other vessels, but as heavy traffic developed along shipping routes, avoiding such collisions became a serious matter. In all fields of navigation, keeping a safe distance between ships (15) moving in different directions at different speeds became as important as knowing how to reach one's destination.

The larger the ship, the easier it is to see, but the larger a ship, the more time it requires to change (20) its speed or direction. When many ships are in a small area, an action taken by one ship to avoid colliding with another might endanger a third. In busy seaports, such as Hamburg and New York, this problem has been solved by assigning incoming (25) and outgoing ships to separate lanes, which are clearly marked and divided by the greatest practical distance.

The speed of jet airplanes makes collision a deadly possibility. Even if two pilots see one another in (30) time to begin evasive action, their maneuvers may be useless if either pilot incorrectly predicts the other's move. Ground-based air traffic controllers assign aircraft to flight paths that keep airplanes a safe distance from one another. (35)

When steam engines began to replace sails during the first half of the nineteenth century, a ship's navigator had to compute fuel consumption as well as course and location. Today, in airplanes as well as in ships, large amounts of fuel, needed for long trips, reduce the cargo capacity, and economy requires that its consumption be kept to a minimum. *40*

In modern air and sea navigation, a schedule has to be met. A single voyage or flight is only one link in a complicated and coordinated transportation network that carries goods and people from any starting place to any chosen destination. Modern navigation selects a ship's course, avoids collision with other moving ships, minimizes fuel consumption, and follows an established timetable. *45* *50*

41. What is the main topic of the passage?
    (A) Historical records of navigation
    (B) Airplane navigation in Europe
    (C) Schedules and shipping long distances
    (D) The growing importance of navigation

42. Which of the choices is closest in meaning to the word "hazards" as used in line 4?
    (A) Dangerous obstacles
    (B) Safe seaports
    (C) Whales and large fish
    (D) Inaccurate navigation

43. Which of the following has the same meaning as the word "collisions" as used in line 14?
    (A) Other vessels
    (B) Running into
    (C) Avoiding such
    (D) Serious matter

44. Which of the following does the word "it" in line 19 refer to?
    (A) Ship
    (B) Time
    (C) Speed
    (D) Larger

45. Where can the following sentence be added to the passage?

    In fact, many harbors were burned down from fires begun as a result of ship's colliding in port.

    (A) After the word "encountered" in paragraph 1
    (B) At the end of paragraph 2
    (C) After the word "third" in paragraph 3
    (D) After the word "possibility" in paragraph 4

46. How are ships kept apart in the ports of Hamburg and New York?
    (A) The port controllers guide ship captains by Radio.
    (B) Incoming and outgoing ships are assigned to clearly marked lanes.
    (C) Ships are not allowed to change their course or their speed while in port.
    (D) Captains use their journals to determine the hazards in port.

47. What does the author imply about the speed of jet airplanes?
    (A) Air traffic is now safer than it was with planes with piston-driven engines.
    (B) Radio communication between ships and planes help schedules.
    (C) Collisions of jet airplanes almost always result in the deaths of passengers and crew.
    (D) Pilots are now able to predict evasive maneuvers that others will take.

48. What can be inferred about fuel consumption in the nineteenth century?
    (A) A ship's captain had to decide how many sails would be used on a ship.
    (B) A navigator had to determine how much fuel a ship needed for a voyage.
    (C) A large amount of fuel made room for extra cargo space.
    (D) A journal was kept about the amount of coal a steam engine used during a voyage.

49. Look at the word "timetable" in the last sentence of the passage. Which of the following words has the same meaning?
    (A) Schedule
    (B) Network
    (C) Navigation
    (D) Established

50. Which of the following statements is supported by the passage?
    (A) Information in mariners' journals is better than modern navigation techniques.
    (B) Collisions in the air are more dangerous than those at sea.
    (C) Mariners today have to compute more things than those in the past did.
    (D) Air traffic controllers use the same navigation techniques as sea captains.

ANSWERS AND EXPLANATIONS

Day 21—Answer Key for Reading Drill—Part I

1. B	26. C
2. C	27. D
3. C	28. A
4. C	29. C
5. C	30. D
6. C	31. D
7. C	32. D
8. B	33. C
9. B	34. B
10. B	35. A
11. A	36. A
12. C	37. C
13. C	38. C
14. D	39. C
15. B	40. C
16. A	41. D
17. A	42. A
18. D	43. B
19. C	44. A
20. B	45. C
21. A	46. B
22. C	47. C
23. B	48. B
24. B	49. A
25. C	50. C

Explanations

Congratulations if you remembered NOT to read the entire text before answering the questions. If you did read the entire text, go back to Day 8 and review the strategies for the Reading Section.

1. **The correct answer is (B).** *Adorning* means "making beautiful" or "adding decorations to." *Taking* is the opposite of *donating*. *Distributing* is similar to *donating* but means "giving the same amount to more than two people."

2. **The correct answer is (C).** *It* refers to "a pint of whole blood." The whole phrase is necessary for the rest of the sentence to be understood. All other answer choices are plural; *it* is singular.

3. **The correct answer is (C).** The last sentence of paragraph one is, "People can donate blood [for red blood cells] about once every two months."

4. **The correct answer is (C).** The sentence fits best in the third paragraph, after the first sentence. The paragraph is about what happens to the person who receives the blood. That person is a recipient or a patient.

5. **The correct answer is (C).** The sentence is as follows:

   "The blood flows through a plastic tube to a collection bag or bottle that contains sodium citrate, which prevents the blood from clotting."

6. **The correct answer is (C).** "Air bubbles in the blood" is not a reaction to a transfusion. It is a *cause* of a negative reaction.

7. **The correct answer is (C).** *Undetected* means "not discovered" or "not realized." In the sentence, the other answer choices are incorrect.

8. **The correct answer is (B).** The correct word is *rigorously*.

9. **The correct answer is (B).** In the fifth paragraph, it is stated that blood is irradiated when the recipient is a newborn or an infant. To radiate means to treat with radiant energy.

10. **The correct answer is (B).** None of the other answer choices are stated or implied in the passage.

11. **The correct answer is (A).** The other answer choices use countries and dates mentioned in the passage but in an incorrect way.

12. **The correct answer is (C).** The first name of Duncan's father is neither mentioned nor implied. Duncan did not work in Scotland. He worked after he came to America. Duncan Phyfe employed 100 craftsmen, but the passage does not say how many kinds of tables his workshop made.

13. **The correct answer is (C).** "He was a quiet-living, god-fearing young man who felt his new name would probably appeal to potential customers who were definitely anti-British in this post Revolutionary War period."

    In paragraph 2, this is the only sentence about his name change.

14. **The correct answer is (D).** Phyfe did not put *his spelling, his chair,* or *his French* on a sign over his door stoop.

15. **The correct answer is (B).** As the word was used in the fourth paragraph, it refers to the organizations that trained craftsmen for a variety of work. Guilds also controlled who could work in a particular craft and stood for high standards. As the word was used in the fourth paragraph, trials are not mentioned. The verdict of a jury may be "Guilty" but never "guild." As the word was used in the fourth paragraph, it does not refer to émigrés, political parties, or clubs.

16. **The correct answer is (A).** *No longer restricted* is the correct phrase.

17. **The correct answer is (A).** The sentence best fits in the fifth paragraph after the following sentence: "What his workshop produced shows Phyfe's absolute dedication to quality in workmanship." The inserted sentence tells the reader about the results of Phyfe's dedication to quality in workmanship.

18. **The correct answer is (D).** In paragraph 5, the last sentence reports that Phyfe spent a lot of money on materials.

19. **The correct answer is (C).** Paragraph 2 tells the reader that Phyfe began his work as a joiner in 1792, in the late eighteenth century. Paragraph 6 tells us he interpreted European design in the late eighteenth and early nineteenth centuries.

20. **The correct answer is (B).** The last paragraph says that few pieces of Phyfe's work have been found, but they do exist ("are extant"). His furniture was not ignored; it was popular. His father did not work for him.

21. **The correct answer is (A).** The emperors, weapons, and social status are mentioned in the passage, but they are only part of the main topic, not the main topic itself.

22. **The correct answer is (C).** See the third sentence of the first paragraph.

23. **The correct answer is (B).** See paragraph 2, first sentence.

24. **The correct answer is (B).** *Spectacles* sometimes means the same thing as eyeglasses but not in this passage. The other two words are distractors that have no connection to the meaning of the word *spectacle.*

25. **The correct answer is (C).** *They* is a plural pronoun, which has to refer to a plural noun. The plural noun in the preceding sentence is *Thracians.*

26. **The correct answer is (C).** A *tunic* is an article of clothing, not a weapon.

27. **The correct answer is (D).** This sentence would best fit the passage at the end of paragraph 4. It adds information about the previous sentence that mentions the emperor Commodus.

28. **The correct answer is (A).** The other answer choices are not related to the meaning of the word as it is used in the last sentence of paragraph 3.

29. **The correct answer is (C).** See the second sentence of paragraph 5. Gladiators could not become emperors. Although Commodus fought gladiators, no other emperor did so. The passage does not mention whether emperors fought on horseback.

30. **The correct answer is (D).** The sentence best fits in paragraph 5, after the second sentence. *Some* refers to gladiators who had been freed from gladiatorial service.

31. **The correct answer is (D).** Only the emperor could enter any section at will. See the last sentence of paragraph 1.

32. **The correct answer is (D).** See sentence 2 in paragraph 1.

33. **The correct answer is (C).** The first sentence of the second paragraph tells the reader that Chinese architects did not borrow ideas from any other country. The first sentence of the third paragraph tells the reader how important the design was. Paragraph 4 tells the reader to enter through the Meridian Gate.

34. **The correct answer is (B).** *Unparalleled* is not related in meaning to *parallel.* The last two answer choices are distractors that contain words, but incorrect ideas, from the passage.

35. **The correct answer is (A).** *Its* refers to UNESCO.

36. **The correct answer is (A).** The fourth paragraph tells the reader about the gate and its two auxiliary walls.

37. **The correct answer is (C).** All other choices are distracters that incorrectly define the word *proclamations.*

38. **The correct answer is (C).** White marble bridges are found in the courtyard behind the Meridian gate. See the second sentence of paragraph 5.

39. **The correct answer is (C).** See the fifth paragraph of the passage.

40. **The correct answer is (C).** The other three choices are distracters that are not related in meaning to the correct answer.

41. **The correct answer is (D).** The three other choices are mentioned or implied in the passage, but the main topic includes these ideas.

42. **The correct answer is (A).** *Safe seaports* are not hazards. *Whales and large fish* could be a hazard but are not as close in meaning to *hazards* as *dangerous obstacles. Inaccurate* is a distractor that is not related to the meaning of the word in context.

43. **The correct answer is (B).** The correct phrase is *running into other vessels.*

44. **The correct answer is (A).** The correct word is *ship.*

45. **The correct answer is (C).** The sentence best fits in paragraph 3, after the second sentence. This sentence reports the results of two ships colliding in a harbor.

46. **The correct answer is (B).** See the third sentence in paragraph 3.

47. **The correct answer is (C).** See the first sentence of paragraph 4.

48. **The correct answer is (B).** See the first sentence of paragraph 5.

49. **The correct answer is (A).**

50. **The correct answer is (C).** The passage reports how navigation became more complex over time.

Day 22

Reading

Reading Drill—Part II

Today's Assignment

- Use the skills you acquired on Day 8 to answer the reading section questions in this chapter. Give yourself no more than 75 minutes to complete this exercise.

Each passage is followed by a series of questions. Answer the questions based on the information you gathered from the passage. Choose the best answer to each question and answer each question based on what is *stated* or *implied* in the passage.

Questions 1–10 refer to the following passage.

Line Jonas Salk is the American physician and medical researcher who developed the first safe and effective vaccine for poliomyelitis. Salk received his M.D. in 1939 from New York University College
5 of Medicine, where he worked with Thomas Francis Jr., who was studying how to develop vaccines from killed viruses. Salk joined Francis in 1942 at the University of Michigan School of Public Health and became part of a group that was
10 working to develop a vaccine against influenza.

In 1947, Salk became associate professor of bacteriology and head of the Virus Research Laboratory at the University of Pittsburgh School of Medicine, where he began research on poliomyelitis.
15 Working with scientists from other universities in a program to classify the various strains of the polio virus, Salk corroborated other studies in identifying three separate strains. He then demonstrated that killed virus of each of the three, al-
20 though incapable of producing the disease, could induce antibody formation in monkeys.

In 1952, he conducted field tests of his killed-virus vaccine, first on children who had recovered from polio and then on subjects who had not had the
25 disease. The results of both tests showed that the children's antibody levels rose significantly and no subjects contracted polio from the vaccine. His findings were published the following year in the Journal of the American Medical Association. In
30 1954, a mass field trial was held, and the vaccine, injected by needle, was found to safely reduce the incidence of polio. On April 12, 1955, the vaccine was released for use in the United States.

Salk served successively as professor of bacteriol-
35 ogy, preventive medicine, and experimental medicine at Pittsburgh, and in 1963, he became fellow and director of the Institute for Biological Studies in San Diego, California, later called the Salk Institute. Among many other honors, he was awarded
40 the Presidential Medal of Freedom in 1977.

1. What is the main idea of the passage?
   (A) How Jonas Salk trained to be a physician and medical researcher
   (B) How the medical research of Jonas Salk led to the development of the polio vaccine
   (C) How Salk and his colleagues learned to kill viruses
   (D) How Salk was promoted to important positions at the University of Pennsylvania

2. Which of the following is the closest in meaning to the word "vaccine" as used in line 3 of the passage?
   (A) Medicine designed to cure a disease temporarily
   (B) Medicine that cures a disease after the patient gets sick
   (C) Medicine designed to kill viruses that are fatal to children
   (D) Medicine that creates immunity against a disease

3. In the first paragraph, what was Thomas Francis Jr. studying?
   (A) How to prevent the spread of influenza in Michigan
   (B) How to work with physicians from Manhattan
   (C) How to develop vaccines from killed viruses
   (D) How to get a degree in medicine from New York University

4. Which sentence in the second paragraph describes Salk's first work at the University of Pittsburgh?
   (A) The first sentence
   (B) The second sentence
   (C) The third sentence
   (D) None of the above

5. Which word is closest in meaning to the word "collaborated" as used in line 17 of the passage?
   (A) Rejected
   (B) Published
   (C) Examined
   (D) Confirmed

6. All of the following statements about the killed-virus vaccine are true EXCEPT
   (A) it did not induce antibody formation in monkeys.
   (B) it had three strains that scientists worked with.
   (C) it was incapable of producing the disease.
   (D) it helped monkeys form antibodies.

7. Look at the word "findings" in line 28. Which of the following words or phrases from the previous sentence does the word "findings" refer to?
   (A) Results
   (B) Antibody levels
   (C) Vaccine
   (D) Polio

8. From the passage, it can be inferred that the experimental polio vaccine was given to people by
   (A) pill.
   (B) injection.
   (C) surgery.
   (D) liquid.

9. In the passage, it is implied that the Salk Institute was
   (A) originally called the Institute for Biological Studies.
   (B) originally the University of Michigan School of Public Health.
   (C) originally the Virus Research Laboratory at the University of Pittsburgh.
   (D) originally the medical school at New York University.

10. Where in the passage could the following sentence best fit?

    Thousands of children and adults were free from the fears of contracting this terrible disease.

    (A) At the end of paragraph 1
    (B) At the end of paragraph 2
    (C) At the end of paragraph 3
    (D) At the end of paragraph 4

Questions 11–20 refer to the following passage.

Line The word *synthesize* means to produce by combining separate elements. Thus, synthesized sound is sound that a musician builds from component elements. A synthesized sound may resemble a traditional acoustic musical timbre, or it may be completely novel and original. One characteristic is common to all synthesized music, however. The sound qualities themselves, as well as the relationships among the sounds, have been "designed," or "composed," by a musician.

Many people believe that synthesized music imitates traditional musical instruments and ensembles. They believe that synthesized music is created mechanically without control by a musician. These ideas are not true.

A builder of a traditional musical instrument assembles a collection of acoustic elements whose interrelationships cannot change. For example, a violin has four strings positioned over a fingerboard and coupled through the bridge to the violin's body. Violinists bring the strings into contact with the fingerboard and a bow to cause the strings to vibrate. The resultant sound is resonated by the hollow body of the violin. However, violinists do not change the relationship of the strings to the bridge, nor that of the bridge to the body. Nor, do they reconfigure its slightly hour-glass shape.

Synthesists, on the other hand, view their instrument as a collection of parts that they configure to produce the sounds they want. They call this "programming," or "patching," and they may do this before or during performance. The parts that synthesists work with depend on the design of the instruments that they are using. In general, synthesizers include elements that generate and combine waveforms and that shape loudness of the sounds. Other sound-producing and -processing elements, which can exist as electronic circuits or as built-in computer programs, may also be available. To control these elements, a synthesist may use a combination of a conventional keyboard and other manual control devices, such as wheels, sliders, and joysticks.

11. Which answer choice is closest in meaning to the word "resemble" as used in line 4?
    (A) Recreate
    (B) Put together
    (C) Sound like
    (D) Take apart

12. According to the passage, what do component elements of synthesizers include?
    (A) Computer programs and hollow bodies
    (B) Bridges and electronic circuits
    (C) Fingerboards and patchers
    (D) Computers and electronic keyboards

13. It can be inferred from the passage that many people
    (A) dislike synthesized music because it lacks harmony and beauty.
    (B) enjoy imitating the sounds of musical instruments.
    (C) build musical instruments in their home.
    (D) believe that synthesized music is created by a machine, not by a musician.

14. According to the passage, the interrelationships of acoustical elements in traditional musical instruments
    (A) comprise wood and horsehair.
    (B) cannot be changed.
    (C) resonate musical notes.
    (D) resemble an hour glass.

15. Which answer choice is the closest in meaning to the word "coupled" as used in line 20?
    (A) Connected
    (B) Performed
    (C) Folded
    (D) Vibrated

16. All of the following contribute to the sound of a violin EXCEPT
    (A) a bridge.
    (B) a fingerboard.
    (C) a keyboard.
    (D) a bow.

17. Where in the passage would the following sentence best fit?

    This, in turn, vibrates the air and sends the sound to the listener's ears.

    (A) After the word "original" in the first paragraph
    (B) After the word "ensembles" in the second paragraph
    (C) After the phrase "hollow body of a violin" in the third paragraph
    (D) At the end of the fourth paragraph

18. The word "its" as used in line 27 refers to which of the following words or phrases from the preceding sentence?

    (A) Violinists
    (B) Strings
    (C) The body
    (D) The bridge

19. What is the main idea of the passage?

    (A) Synthesized music is loved by everyone who enjoys rock and popular music.
    (B) Synthesized music is used mostly in film and TV.
    (C) Synthesized music combines separate elements and changes the relationships of those elements.
    (D) Synthesized music cannot resemble traditional musical instruments.

20. According to the passage, what are wheels, sliders, and joysticks?

    (A) Relationships among elements
    (B) Parts of computer game boards
    (C) Manual control devices on sound synthesizers
    (D) Sound qualities designed by a synthesist

Questions 21–30 refer to the following passage.

Line The *New York Times* is a daily newspaper published in New York City. For a long time, it has been the newspaper of record in the United States and one of the world's great newspapers. Its strength is in (5) its editorial excellence; it has never been the largest newspaper in terms of circulation.

The *Times* was established in 1851 as a penny paper whose editors wanted to report the news in a restrained and objective fashion. It enjoyed early (10) success as its editors set a pattern for the future by appealing to a cultured, intellectual readership instead of a mass audience. However, in the late nineteenth century, it came into competition with more popular, colorful, if not lurid, newspapers in New (15) York City. Despite price increases, the *Times* was losing $1,000 a week when Adolph Simon Ochs bought it in 1896.

Ochs built the *Times* into an internationally respected daily. He hired Carr Van Anda as editor. Van Anda (20) placed greater stress than ever on full reporting of the news of the day, and his reporters maintained and emphasized existing good coverage of international news. The management of the paper decided to eliminate fiction from the paper, added a Sunday (25) magazine section, and reduced the paper's price back to a penny. In April 1912, the paper took many risks to report every aspect of the sinking of the Titanic. This greatly enhanced its prestige, and in its coverage of two world wars, the Times continued to en- (30) hance its reputation for excellence in world news.

In 1971, the *Times* was given a copy of the so-called "Pentagon Papers," a secret government study of U.S. involvement in the Vietnam War. When it published the report, it became involved in sev- (35) eral lawsuits. The U.S. Supreme Court found that the publication was protected by the freedom-of-the-press clause in the First Amendment of the U.S. Constitution. Later in the 1970s, the paper, under Adolph Ochs's grandson, Arthur Ochs Sulzberger, (40) introduced sweeping changes in the organization of the newspaper and its staff and brought out a national edition transmitted by satellite to regional printing plants.

21. What is the main idea of the passage?
    (A) The *New York Times* publishes the best fiction by American writers.
    (B) The *New York Times* became highly respected throughout the world.
    (C) The *New York Times* broadcasts its news to TV stations via satellite.
    (D) The *New York Times* lost its prestige after the Vietnam War.

22. It can be inferred from the passage that the circulation of the *Times*
    (A) is not the largest in the world.
    (B) is not the best in the world.
    (C) is the smallest in the world.
    (D) is the worst in the world.

23. Which phrase is closest in meaning to the word "restrained" as it is used in line 9?
    (A) Put in prison
    (B) In handcuffs
    (C) Without education
    (D) With self-control

24. According to the passage, what caused the loss of money at the *Times*?
    (A) Other newspapers were more colorful.
    (B) Other newspapers had better reporters.
    (C) Other newspapers added a Sunday magazine.
    (D) Other newspapers were better managed.

25. What word or phrase does the word "his" as used in line 21 refer to?
    (A) Van Anda
    (B) Reporters
    (C) News of the day
    (D) International news

26. Where can the following sentence best be added to the passage?

    Their publishers ran sensational stories, not because they were true, but because they sold newspapers.

    (A) At the end of the first paragraph
    (B) After the word "City" in the second paragraph
    (C) At the end of the third paragraph
    (D) After the phrase "lawsuits" in the fourth paragraph

27. To improve its circulation, the management of the *Times* did all of the following EXCEPT
    (A) emphasized good coverage of international news.
    (B) added a Sunday magazine section.
    (C) increased the number of lurid stories, even if they were not true.
    (D) eliminated fiction from the paper.

28. The passage implies that the newspaper's reputation
    (A) decreased when it lowered it price to a penny.
    (B) grew because Adolph Ochs bought it in 1896.
    (C) increased because of its coverage of the Titanic's sinking.
    (D) decreased because it could not compete with other New York papers.

29. What word or phrase does the word "publication" as used in line 36 refer to?
    (A) The *Times*
    (B) "The Pentagon Papers"
    (C) The Report
    (D) The Constitution

30. According to the passage, the *Times* has a national edition that is
    (A) protected by the Supreme Court.
    (B) printed in the form of a Sunday magazine.
    (C) shipped by train and air transport daily.
    (D) transmitted by satellite to regional printing plants.

Questions 31–40 refer to the following passage.

Line Pittsburgh, Pennsylvania, is located where the Allegheny and Monongahela rivers unite to form the Ohio River. Its fascinating history began in 1758 when General John Forbes and his British and (5) colonial army captured Fort Duquesne from the French and renamed it Fort Pitt, for the British statesman William Pitt the Elder. After an agreement between the Indian tribes and William Penn's family, settlers began arriving. Pittsburgh was laid (10) out (1764) by John Campbell in the area around the fort.

Following the American Revolution, the town became an outfitting point for settlers traveling westward down the Ohio River. Pittsburgh's strategic (15) location and wealth of natural resources spurred its commercial and industrial growth in the nineteenth century. A blast furnace, erected by George Anschutz about 1792, was the forerunner of the iron and steel industry that for more than a cen- (20) tury was the city's economic power. By 1850, it was known as the "Iron City." The Pennsylvania Canal and the Portage Railroad, both completed in 1834, opened vital markets for trade and shipping.

After the American Civil War, great numbers of (25) European immigrants swelled Pittsburgh's population, and industrial magnates such as Andrew Carnegie, Henry Clay Frick, and Thomas Mellon built their steel empires there. The city became the focus of historic friction between labor and man- (30) agement, and the American Federation of Labor was organized there in 1881. By 1900, the city's population had reached 321,616. Growth continued nearly unabated through World War II, and during the war years, Pittsburgh was a boom town.

(35) During this period of economic and population growth, Pittsburgh became a grimy, polluted industrial city. After the war, however, the city undertook an extensive redevelopment program, with emphasis on smoke-pollution control, flood (40) prevention, and sewage disposal. In 1957, it became the first American city to generate electricity by nuclear power. By the late 1970s and early 80s, the steel industry had virtually disappeared, but Pittsburgh successfully diversified its economy (45) through more emphasis on light industries and on such high-technology industries as computer software, industrial automation (robotics), and biomedical and environmental technologies.

31. In the mid-eighteenth century, what two countries wanted to control the area now known as Pittsburgh?
    (A) England and the United States
    (B) England and France
    (C) England and Germany
    (D) England and Pennsylvania

32. When did settlers begin arriving in Pittsburgh?
    (A) After an agreement between the Indians and the Penn family
    (B) After the Allegheny and Monongahela rivers united
    (C) After the British captured Fort Pitt
    (D) After the American Revolution

33. Which phrase is closest in meaning to the phrase "outfitting point" as used in line 13?
    (A) A store that sells gasoline and oil
    (B) A location of food and water
    (C) A place to buy business suits and accessories
    (D) A source of equipment and supplies

34. What became the most important industry in Pittsburgh following the American Revolution?
    (A) The shipping industry
    (B) The iron and steel industry
    (C) The outfitting industry
    (D) The computer software industry

35. Which of the following phrases is closest in meaning to the phrase "vital markets" as used in line 23?
    (A) Hospitals and medical centers
    (B) Large stores for food and clothing
    (C) Places with customers for Pittsburgh's products
    (D) Indian tribes and military forts

36. According to the passage, who moved to Pittsburgh in great numbers after the Civil War?
    (A) Indian tribes
    (B) British soldiers
    (C) Confederate veterans
    (D) European immigrants

37. Which of the following phrases is closest in meaning to the phrase "focus of historic friction" as used in line 29?
    (A) Center of an important conflict
    (B) Museum for historical photographs
    (C) Famous furniture factory
    (D) City of many professional sports

38. According to the passage, what can be inferred about Pittsburgh's population during World War II?
    (A) It did not grow.
    (B) It declined.
    (C) It grew enormously.
    (D) It stayed the same.

39. Between the Civil War and World War II, all of the following happened in Pittsburgh EXCEPT
    (A) automobile factories produced most of the transportation for Americans.
    (B) Carnegie, Frick, and Mellon created their steel empires.
    (C) the American Federation of Labor was organized.
    (D) the air became seriously polluted, and buildings were dirty.

40. Where in the passage could the following sentence best fit?

    The elder Penn, who lived in Philadelphia, believed that peaceful settlements with the Indians would help his young colony prosper.

    (A) After the word "arriving" in the first paragraph
    (B) After the words "Ohio River" in the second paragraph
    (C) At the end of the third paragraph
    (D) After the words "polluted industrial city" in the fourth paragraph

Questions 41–50 refer to the following passage.

Line

The Missouri River is the longest tributary of the Mississippi River, and it begins its trip to join the Mississippi in the Rocky Mountains in Montana. The Missouri flows eastward to central North Dakota, where it turns southward across South Dakota, Nebraska, and Iowa. When it reaches Missouri, it turns eastward at Kansas City and meanders across central Missouri to join the Mississippi River, about 10 miles north of St. Louis, after traveling 2,315 miles. (5, 10)

Its drainage basin occupies about 529,400 square miles of the Great Plains. Elevations within its basin are extreme: from 14,000 feet above sea level in the Rockies near the Continental Divide to 400 feet where it joins the Mississippi. The flow of the Missouri changes frequently from 4,200 cubic feet per second to 900,000 cubic feet per second. (15)

Its mouth was discovered in 1673 by the French explorers Jacques Marquette and Louis Joliet while they were canoeing down the Mississippi River. In the early 1700s, French fur traders began to navigate upstream. The first exploration of the river from its mouth to its headwaters was made in 1804–05 by Meriwether Lewis and William Clark. For many years, the river was, except for fur traders, little used by the earliest American settlers moving west. The American Fur Company began to use steamers on the river in 1830 but began to decline in the following year with the completion of the Hannibal and St. Joseph Railway to St. Joseph, Missouri. (20, 25, 30)

For the first 150 years after settlement along the river, the Missouri was not developed as a useful waterway or as a source of irrigation and power. In 1940, a comprehensive program was started for flood control and water-resource development in the Missouri River basin. The Fort Peck Dam is one of the largest earthfill dams in the world. The entire system of dams and reservoirs has greatly reduced flooding on the Missouri and provides water to irrigate millions of acres of farmland. Electricity for many communities is generated along the river's upper course. (35, 40)

41. In which state does the Missouri begin its trip to the Mississippi?
(A) Iowa
(B) South Dakota
(C) North Dakota
(D) Montana

42. Which of the following is closest in meaning to the word "meanders" as used in lines 7–8?
(A) Is harsh to the land it is in
(B) Follows a winding and turning course
(C) Causes a lot of damage with floods
(D) Flows slowly and gently

43. The passage implies that the elevation of the Missouri River's drainage basin
(A) remains level throughout the trip from Montana through Missouri.
(B) rises almost 2,315 feet.
(C) changes frequently.
(D) drops more than 13,000 feet between the Rocky mountains and its mouth on the Mississippi.

44. Which of the following is the closest in meaning to the word "mouth" as it is used in line 18?
(A) Entrance to a harbor, valley, or cave
(B) The opening of a container
(C) Part of a river that flows into a lake or ocean
(D) Oral cavity

45. Where could the following sentence best be added to the passage?

The speed of the river's current is just as extreme.

(A) After the word "Iowa" in the first paragraph
(B) After the word "Mississippi" in the second paragraph
(C) After the word "upstream" in the third paragraph
(D) At the end of the fourth paragraph

46. Who discovered the mouth of the Missouri River?
(A) Meriwether Lewis and William Clark
(B) French fur traders
(C) Jacques Marquette and Louis Joliet
(D) American fur traders

47. When were steamers first used on the Missouri River?
(A) 1673
(B) 1700
(C) 1804
(D) 1830

48. Which word does the word "power" as used in line 34 refer to?
(A) Waterway
(B) Irrigation
(C) Development
(D) Electricity

49. When was a flood control program for the Missouri River begun?
(A) 1940
(B) 1840
(C) 1740
(D) 1640

50. In the passage, all the following topics are briefly discussed EXCEPT
(A) the geography of the Missouri River.
(B) the history of the Missouri River.
(C) tourism and recreation on the Missouri River.
(D) twentieth-century development of the Missouri River.

Answers and Explanations

Day 22—Answer Key for Reading Drill—Part II

1. B
2. D
3. C
4. B
5. D
6. A
7. A
8. B
9. A
10. C
11. C
12. D
13. D
14. B
15. A
16. C
17. C
18. C
19. C
20. C
21. B
22. A
23. D
24. A
25. A
26. B
27. C
28. C
29. A
30. D
31. B
32. A
33. D
34. B
35. C
36. D
37. A
38. C
39. A
40. A
41. D
42. B
43. D
44. C
45. B
46. C
47. D
48. D
49. A
50. C

Explanations

1. **The correct answer is (B).** Choice (A) does not contain the most important facts about the career of Jonas Salk. Choice (C) contains information that is not mentioned in the passage. Choice (C) is incorrect; Salk was at the University of Pittsburgh.
2. **The correct answer is (D).** The other answer choices are incorrect definitions.
3. **The correct answer is (C).** The other answer choices contain words and phrases from the paragraph but are all incorrect.
4. **The correct answer is (B).** The sentence reads, "Working with scientists from other universities in a program to classify the various strains of the polio virus, Salk corroborated other studies in identifying three separate strains."
5. **The correct answer is (D).** Choice (A) is incorrect because Salk did not reject the studies; he used them. Choice (B) is incorrect because the text does not mention publishing until the third paragraph. Choice (C) is incorrect because *examined* is not close in meaning to *corroborate*.
6. **The correct answer is (A).** It is NOT true. All other answers are found in the second paragraph.
7. **The correct answer is (A).** *Findings* means the "information gained from research and experimentation." The correct answer is "the results of both tests."
8. **The correct answer is (B).** In the third paragraph, the text reports that the vaccine was injected by needle.
9. **The correct answer is (A).** This information is found in the last paragraph of the passage.
10. **The correct answer is (C).** The correct answer is the square at the end of paragraph 3.
11. **The correct answer is (C).** The first two letters in choice (A) are the same as those in choice (B), but they do not make the words synonymous. Choice (B) uses a definition that might remind you of the word *assemble*. Choice (C) is the opposite of choice (B), but it is not the same as *resemble*.

12. **The correct answer is (D).** The other answer choices contain parts of synthesizers and violins.

13. **The correct answer is (D).** The other answer choices are not stated in the passage.

14. **The correct answer is (B).** The other answer choices are not stated in the passage.

15. **The correct answer is (A).** The meanings of the other answers have nothing to with the word *coupled*.

16. **The correct answer is (C).** It is NOT used with a violin.

17. **The correct answer is (C).** The placement in the third paragraph is correct.

18. **The correct answer is (C).** The word *its* refers to the *body* of the violin in this instance.

19. **The correct answer is (C).** The other answer choices are not stated anywhere in the passage.

20. **The correct answer is (C).** All other answer choices are incorrect and are misstatements of parts of the passage.

21. **The correct answer is (B).** Choice (A) is incorrect; fiction is not published in the *Times*. Choice (C) is incorrect; the *Times* does not broadcast news on TV. Choice (C) is incorrect; see paragraph 4.

22. **The correct answer is (A).** See the last sentence of the first paragraph.

23. **The correct answer is (D).** Choices (A) and (B) can be used to mean restrained but not in the context of this sentence. Choice (C) is not related to any meaning of *restrained*.

24. **The correct answer is (A).** The other answer choices were not stated in the passage.

25. **The correct answer is (A).**

26. **The correct answer is (B).** The preceding sentence mentions how other newspapers have "lurid" stories. The sentence, "Their publishers ran sensational stories, not because they were true, but because they sold newspapers," gives further detail about the other newspapers' stories.

27. **The correct answer is (C).** All of the other answer choices are not true.

28. **The correct answer is (C).** Choice (A) is incorrect because the passage does not connect the paper's reputation to its price. Choices (B) and (D) are incorrect, because the passage does not connect the paper's reputation to Ochs's or the other New York papers.

29. **The correct answer is (A).** The word *publication* refers to the *Times*.

30. **The correct answer is (D).** The other answer choices are not stated in the passage.

31. **The correct answer is (B).** Choice (A) is incorrect; the United States did not exist in the mid-eighteenth century. Choice (C) is incorrect; Germany is not mentioned in the passage. Choice (D) is incorrect because Pennsylvania is not identified as a country in the passage.

32. **The correct answer is (A).** This is stated in the first paragraph.

33. **The correct answer is (D).** The passage mentions that travelers heading west would stop at the "outfitting point," and it makes sense that travelers would need *equipment and supplies* on their journey.

34. **The correct answer is (B).** See the second paragraph.

35. **The correct answer is (C).** *Vital* in this sentence means "of high importance." *Markets* are places where people can sell their products.

36. **The correct answer is (D).** No one mentioned in the other answers moved to Pittsburgh in great numbers after the Civil War.

37. **The correct answer is (A).** The other answer choices do not make sense within the context of the paragraph.

38. **The correct answer is (C).** See paragraph 3.

39. **The correct answer is (A).** The automobile industry is not mentioned in the passage.

40. **The correct answer is (A).** The sentence makes the most sense in this part of the passage.

41. **The correct answer is (D).** This is stated in the first sentence of the passage.

42. **The correct answer is (B).** When the word *meandering* is used to describe a river, it usually means that the river is "winding and turning," so choice (B) is the correct answer.

43. **The correct answer is (D).** This information can be inferred from the second paragraph of the passage.

44. **The correct answer is (C).** Choice (A) is incorrect, because the topic is a river, not a harbor, valley, or cave. Choices (B) and (D) are incorrect meanings for the context.

45. **The correct answer is (B).** This is where the sentence best fits into the passage.

46. **The correct answer is (C).** See paragraph 3.

47. **The correct answer is (D).** See paragraph 3.

48. **The correct answer is (D).** *Electricity* can also be thought of as "electric *power*."

49. **The correct answer is (A).** This is mentioned in the last paragraph of the passage.

50. **The correct answer is (C).** The other answer choices are all mentioned in the passage.

Day 23

Writing

Writing Drill—Part I

Today's Assignment

- Use the writing strategies you acquired in Day 9 and complete this practice drill. Do not begin work on the topics until you have read all the instructions on this page. When you begin this drill, finish each step before going to the next.

Step 1 Review what you learned on Day 9.

Step 2 Read each of the topics on the next page carefully.

Step 3 For each topic, spend 5 minutes writing ideas in words and phrases (brainstorming). This should take 15 minutes.

Step 4 For each topic, write sentences about the ideas you write during the brainstorm. Spend no more than 5 minutes on each topic.

Step 5 Put these sentences into a logical order. Collect the sentences into paragraphs. Spend 3 to 5 minutes on each topic.

Step 6 Write topic sentences for all the paragraphs in your essay, if you haven't done so already.

Step 7 Write the essay and check your writing for grammar and spelling errors. Write the final version of each essay.

Step 8 Go to steps 9 through 13, but only after you have finished steps 1 through 7.

Topics

A. Your parents have given you a birthday present of money. You have wanted a new portable CD player, and now you have the money to buy it. Then, you learn that your favorite musicians are giving a concert and the gift is enough to buy tickets. Which would you buy? Use specific reasons and details to support your answer.

B. The corporation that you work for has announced its plans to give money either to a local art museum or to an organization that works to protect the environment. You have to tell the company which one they should choose. Use specific reasons and examples to support your answer.

C. The government of your country has announced that it has enough money to start one of two programs: space exploration or food and clothing for the unemployed. Which do you think the government should spend lots money on?

Step 9 Check your topics in each essay. In each topic, you were asked to choose one thing over another. Did you choose only one topic, or did you try to write about both choices? During the test, if you wrote about both choices, you would lose points. So remember:

CHOOSE ONLY ONE THING TO WRITE ABOUT!

Although the topics were about spending money, they asked you to choose *one* thing to spend the money on and tell your reasons in an essay.

How many paragraphs did you write? You should have written no fewer than three and no more than five.

Check your brainstorm notes and first sentences. Did you write about anything that was not about the topic? For example, in Topic A, did you write about your favorite musicians, or did you write about how important live concerts are? If you wrote about how important live concerts are, then you probably did a good job. It's okay to mention your favorite musicians, but remember, the topic was *why you chose going to a concert.*

Step 10 Check your logical order. Did you group sentences according to subject?

Step 11 Check the first sentences in each paragraph. These are your topic sentences. Do the topic sentences tell the reader what the paragraph is about?

Step 12 Check your writing for grammar and spelling mistakes. Remember, on the test, you cannot use a dictionary, and the computer program you will be using does not have a spell-check.

Step 13 Go to the latest *TOEFL Bulletin* and look over the list of essay topics. One of these topics will be assigned to you, and if you are prepared to write about the topic, you will get a good score.

Day 24

Writing

Writing Drill—Part II

Today's Assignment

- Use the writing strategies you acquired in Days 9 and 23, and complete this practice drill. Do not begin work on the topics until you have read all the instructions on this page. When you begin this drill, finish each step before going to the next.

Step 1 Review what you learned on Days 9 and 23.

Step 2 Read each of the topics on the next page carefully:

Step 3 For each topic, spend 5 minutes writing ideas in words and phrases (brainstorming). This should take 15 minutes.

Step 4 For each topic, write sentences about the ideas you write during the brainstorm. Spend no more than 5 minutes on each topic.

Step 5 Put these sentences into a logical order. Collect the sentences into paragraphs. Spend 3 to 5 minutes on each topic.

Step 6 Write topic sentences for all the paragraphs in your essay, if you haven't done so already.

Step 7 Write the essay and check your writing for grammar and spelling errors. Write the final version of each essay.

Step 8 Go to the next steps on the following page but only after you have finished steps 1 through 7.

Topics

A. Do you believe that boys and girls should not attend the same schools until they reach the university or technical school? Use specific reasons and examples to support your answer.

B. What one important change would you make in a school that you attended? Use reasons and specific examples to support your answer.

C. Students have difficulties when they start attending a new school. What should schools do to help these students with their problems? Use specific reasons and examples to explain your answer.

Step 9 Check your topics in each essay. In topic A, you were asked to choose one thing over another. Did you choose only one topic, or did you try to write about both choices? During the test, if you wrote about both choices, you would lose points. So remember:

CHOOSE ONLY ONE THING TO WRITE ABOUT!

The topics asked you to choose one thing as a solution and tell your reasons in an essay.

Step 10 How many paragraphs did you write? You should have written no fewer than three and no more than five.

Step 11 Check your brainstorm notes and first sentences. Did you write about anything that was *not* about the topic? For example, in Topic A, did you write about the good points of children attending separate schools? Or did you write about the good points of coeducational schools as well. If you wrote about only one side of the question, then you probably did a good job.

Topic C presents a particularly interesting problem:

Students have difficulties when they start attending a new school. What should schools do to help these students with their problems? Use specific reasons and examples to explain your answer.

The topic does not ask you to choose between alternatives. Instead, the topic implies that you should list a few of the problems that students have when they move to a new city. Then, you should write the actions that schools should take to help the students. If you did that, then you probably did a good job.

Step 10 Check your logical order. Did you group sentences according to subject?

Step 11 Check the first sentences in each paragraph. These are your topic sentences. Do the topic sentences tell the reader what the paragraph is about?

Step 12 Check your writing for grammar and spelling mistakes. Remember, on the test, you cannot use a dictionary, and the computer program you will be using does not have a spell-check.

Step 13 Go to the latest *TOEFL Bulletin* and look over the list of essay topics. One of these topics will be assigned to you, and if you are prepared to write the topic, you will get a good score.

Day 25

More Listening Comprehension Practice

Short Conversations, Long Conversations, and Lectures with Audio

Today, you will continue to practice with short conversations and lectures. There will be 30 questions in this exercise. Questions 1–10 are Short Conversation questions, questions 11–15 are Long Conversation questions, and questions 15–25 are Lecture Questions. The answers and scripts for the audio are printed at the end of this chapter.

You may now begin listening to track 2 on the CD.

SHORT CONVERSATIONS

Directions: In this section, you will hear conversations between two people. After each conversation, you will be asked several questions about what you heard, and you will see the questions printed here with four answer choices. Choose an answer and mark it either in the book or on a separate sheet of scrap paper. Remember to answer the questions based on what is stated or implied by the speakers.

1. What does the woman mean?
   (A) She had to wait in line for her copy of the book.
   (B) She thinks the man should buy his book on the Internet.
   (C) She doesn't want him to use her copy of the book.
   (D) She will find the book at another store.

2. What can be inferred from the woman's statement?
   (A) Professor Marcus has not been in class for a while.
   (B) Professor Marcus hurt his back last week.
   (C) Professor Marcus is weak and ill.
   (D) Professor Marcus is a very good teacher.

3. What does the man mean?
   (A) Wilma should lighten up.
   (B) Wilma wants to be a lab assistant.
   (C) Wilma needs to turn on the light.
   (D) Wilma wants to be the center of attention.

4. What does the man mean?
   (A) He dropped his watch in the swimming pool.
   (B) He doesn't like tall buildings.
   (C) He quit the course because it was too difficult for him.
   (D) He couldn't find the way to the class.

5. What does the woman mean?
   (A) The man needs to go on a camping trip.
   (B) The man needs to stop depending on other people's help.
   (C) The man needs to find another means of transportation.
   (D) The man needs to buy some canned fruit.

6. What does the woman mean?
   (A) The trip will take a maximum of 2 hours.
   (B) The trip will take them through a long tunnel.
   (C) The trip will take much longer than 2 hours.
   (D) The trip will be postponed.

7. What does the man mean?
   (A) They should play a game of bridge and forget about the fire.
   (B) They should deal with the fire only if it gets closer to the campus.
   (C) They shouldn't get cross at each other.
   (D) They shouldn't call the fire department until later.

8. What does the woman mean?
   (A) Professor Twining trained to be a prizefighter before he became a teacher.
   (B) Professor Twining worked his way through school by playing cards.
   (C) Professor Twining isn't a very good teacher because he doesn't have a degree.
   (D) Professor Twining's wide experience in the field qualifies him for his position.

9. What does the woman imply?
   (A) Patricia doesn't like raisins in her salad.
   (B) Patricia will not return to class.
   (C) Patricia said something shocking.
   (D) Patricia put on too much make-up.

10. What does the woman mean?
   (A) The woman is hungry.
   (B) The woman agrees with the man's opinion.
   (C) The woman does not agree with the man.
   (D) The woman has a toothache.

LONG CONVERSATIONS

Directions: In this section, you will hear longer conversations. After each conversation, you will be asked several questions about what you heard, and you will see the questions printed here with four answer choices. Choose an answer and mark it either in the book or on a separate sheet of scrap paper. Remember to answer the questions based on what is stated or implied by the speakers.

Questions 11–15. Listen to two students discuss the famous playwright, Moliere.

On the screen, you will see the words "French literature" and a picture of a portrait bust of Moliere.

11. Why did the man do extra reading on Moliere's life and career?
   (A) To find out whether he wanted to be an actor
   (B) To get information for his psychology class
   (C) To make up for not reading the plays in French
   (D) To get extra credit from his French language professor

12. What was the profession of Moliere's father?
    (A) He was a politician.
    (B) He was a member of the court.
    (C) He was an upholsterer.
    (D) He was a lawyer.
13. What did Moliere do before he became a successful playwright?
    (A) He worked with his father as a lawyer in Paris.
    (B) He toured small towns in France with his own theater company.
    (C) He worked for several prominent politicians.
    (D) He helped people solve their personal problems.
14. Who was king of France when Moliere became a success?
    (A) Louis XII
    (B) Louis XIII
    (C) Louis XIV
    (D) Louis XV
15. According to the man, what did Moliere write about?
    (A) Politicians in the royal court
    (B) People living in small towns and villages
    (C) The strength of Louis XIV
    (D) The weaknesses of humanity

LECTURES

Directions: In this section, you will hear lectures. After each lecture, you will be asked several questions about what you heard, and you will see the questions printed here with four answer choices. Choose an answer and mark it either in the book or on a separate sheet of scrap paper. Remember to answer the questions based on what is stated or implied by the speakers.

Questions 16–20. Listen to lecture on polar bears.

On the screen, you will see the word "Zoology" and a picture of a polar bear.

16. Why are polar bears scientifically called *Ursus maritimus*?
    (A) Because Eskimos like to hunt them
    (B) Because they are white and small
    (C) Because they are semi-aquatic animals
    (D) Because they are not meat-eaters
17. What do Eskimos hunt polar bears for?
    (A) For use as food for their dogs
    (B) For their hides, fat, and flesh
    (C) For their ability to swim
    (D) For traditional weapons
18. In what unexpected place have polar bears been found?
    (A) The Arctic Ocean
    (B) The Hudson Bay
    (C) The Gulf of St. Lawrence
    (D) The Bering Strait
19. What does the polar bear primarily eat?
    (A) Seals
    (B) Humans
    (C) Dogs
    (D) Fish

20. How does a polar bear's head compare to that of a grizzly bear?
    (A) A grizzly bear's head is not bigger.
    (B) A polar bear's head is not as small.
    (C) A grizzly bear's head is not as big.
    (D) A polar bear's head is much smaller.

Questions 21–25. Listen to a lecture about the ruins of Angkor Wat.

On the screen, you will see the word "Archeology" and a picture of Angkor Wat in Cambodia.

21. Where is Angkor Wat?
    (A) India
    (B) Thailand
    (C) Cambodia
    (D) Laos
22. When was Angkor Wat built?
    (A) In the ninth century
    (B) In the twelfth century
    (C) In the fifteenth century
    (D) In the eighteenth century
23. What did the temples at Angkor express?
    (A) Indian cosmological and mythical themes
    (B) Happiness in international trade
    (C) Cambodian legends
    (D) Fear of death
24. What was Angkor Wat built for?
    (A) To bury the body of the king
    (B) To provide work for the temple priests
    (C) To express beliefs found in Shinto
    (D) To shelter the citizens of Angkor
25. What stories do the wall reliefs tell?
    (A) Stories from The Koran
    (B) Stories from Cambodian legends
    (C) Stories from Indian history
    (D) Stories from Hindu holy books

DAY 25—MORE LISTENING PRACTICE ANSWER KEY

1. B
2. A
3. D
4. C
5. B
6. A
7. B
8. D
9. C
10. B
11. C
12. C
13. B
14. C
15. D
16. C
17. B
18. C
19. A
20. D
21. C
22. B
23. A
24. A
25. D

DAY 25—MORE LISTENING COMPREHENSION PRACTICE SCRIPT

Short Conversations

(Narrator): Directions: In this section, you will hear conversations between two people. After each conversation, you will be asked several questions about what you heard, and you will see the questions printed here with four answer choices. Choose an answer and mark it either in the book or on a separate sheet of scrap paper. Remember to answer the questions based on what is stated or implied by the speakers.

1. *(Man):* They are all out of the assigned textbook. I can't even find a used copy at the campus bookstore.

   (Woman): What about on line?

   (Narrator): What does the woman mean?

2. *(Man):* I don't like the way that the new student assistant is grading our papers.

   (Woman): Professor Marcus will be back next week.

   (Narrator): What can be inferred from the woman's statement?

3. *(Woman):* Every time I try to say something, Wilma interrupts me.

   (Man): She certainly tries to grab the limelight.

   (Narrator): What does the man mean?

4. *(Woman):* I haven't seen you in geology class lately.

   (Man): I dropped the course. It was way over my head.

   (Narrator): What does the man mean?

5. *(Man):* I wish you'd help me study for the calculus final.

   (Woman): I'm sorry, you're going to have to paddle your own canoe.

   (Narrator): What does the woman mean?

6. *(Man):* How long will it take us to drive to your hometown from here?

   (Woman): Two hours at the outside.

   (Narrator): What does the woman mean?

7. *(Woman):* What'll we do if the forest fire reaches the campus?

   (Man): Let's cross that bridge when we come to it.

   (Narrator): What does the man mean?

8. *(Man):* I heard that Professor Twining never graduated from college.

   (Woman): He must have learned everything in the school of hard knocks.

   (Narrator): What does the woman mean?

9. *(Man):* Did you hear what Patricia said in class today?

   (Woman): Yes. I bet it raised a lot of eyebrows.

   (Narrator): What does the woman imply?

10. *(Man):* The critics were wrong about that movie. It was the worst thing I have ever seen!

    (Woman): You took the words right out of my mouth!

    (Narrator): What does the woman mean?

Long Conversations

(Narrator): Directions: In this section, you will hear longer conversations. After each conversation, you will be asked several questions about what you heard, and you will see the questions printed here with four answer choices. Choose an answer and mark it either in the book or on a separate sheet of scrap paper. Remember to answer the questions based on what is stated or implied by the speakers.

(Narrator): Questions 11–15. Listen to two students discuss the famous playwright, Moliere.

(Man): I don't think I have enjoyed a class more than this one. What funny plays Moliere wrote!

(Woman): Have you read them in French?

(Man): No, only in translation. But to make up for that, I did a lot of extra reading on his life and career as an actor and theater manager.

(Woman): What did you find out?

(Man): Well, his real name was Jean-Baptiste Poquelin, and he was born in Paris in 1622. His father was a well-to-do upholsterer who knew many people at the French court. Moliere was very well educated, and he disappointed his father by wanting to pursue a theatrical career. He was a flop in Paris, but instead of quitting, he organized a troupe and toured all over France, for thirteen years!

(Woman): For thirteen years? He must have gotten a lot of good experience.

(Man): He did. He learned a lot from the players in small towns and villages. He picked up tricks of the trade and started writing the plays for his company. Then, he returned to Paris and performed the short play, *The Affected Young Ladies*.

(Woman): That play is a joy to read. And it could be about those rich young women we see in car advertisements on TV.

(Man): True, and the play was so successful that soon after, he had a permanent theater and wrote plays for both the popular audiences and for the royal court of Louis XIV.

(Woman): I think his plays are very funny, but at the same time, they challenge you to see yourself in the characters. And some people don't like to see their own habits and behavior on the stage.

(Man): And that was a problem for him. Powerful politicians hated his plays, because they thought he was mocking them. Of course, he wasn't. He wrote about the weaknesses of humanity in general, and made his audiences recognize them.

(Woman): And laugh at them.

(Man): Yes. They still do. You know, some critics have compared even Charlie Chaplin to Moliere.

(Narrator):

11. Why did the man do extra reading on Moliere's life and career?
12. What was the profession of Moliere's father?
13. What did Moliere do before he became a successful playwright?
14. Who was king of France when Moliere became a success?
15. According to the man, what did Moliere write about?

Lectures

(Narrator): Directions: In this section, you will hear lectures. After each lecture, you will be asked several questions about what you heard, and you will see the questions printed here with four answer choices. Choose an answer and mark it either in the book or on a separate sheet of scrap paper. Remember to answer the questions based on what is stated or implied by the speakers.

(Narrator): Questions 16–20. Listen to a lecture on polar bears.

(Woman): The scientific name for polar bears is *Ursus maritimus*. It's called that because it is a semiaquatic animal that lives throughout the Arctic regions, generally on drifting oceanic ice floes. The polar bear is sought for its trophy value and especially by Eskimos for its hide, tendons, fat, and flesh. Since 1973, the polar bear has been protected by an international agreement that allows hunting of polar bears only by local populations using traditional weapons.

Polar bears are camouflaged against ice and snow by their white fur, and they're strong and swift swimmers. In fact, they're often found in the water many miles from land or ice packs. The polar bear's primary prey is the seal, and it follows the seal as far south as the Gulf of St. Lawrence in Canada and the mouth of the Amur River in Russia.

Polar bears also eat fish, seaweed, grass, birds, caribou, and the occasional stranded whale. The male polar bear, usually larger than the female, weighs about 900 to 1,600 pounds. It grows to about 5 feet at the shoulder and about 6 feet in length. The feet are broad with hairy soles, which protect and insulate it from the cold and help it move across the ice. Polar bears have an unusually long neck and a small head compared to the grizzly bear or the giant Kodiak.

(Narrator):

16. Why are polar bears scientifically called *Ursus maritimus*?
17. What do Eskimos hunt polar bears for?
18. In what unexpected place have polar bears been found?
19. What does the polar bear primarily eat?
20. How does a polar bear's head compare to that of a grizzly bear?

(Narrator): Questions 21–25. Listen to a lecture about the ruins of *Angkor Wat*.

(Man): *Angkor Wat* is in the city of Angkor, an archaeological site in what is now northwestern Cambodia. It was the capital of the Khmer empire from the ninth to the fifteenth century C.E., a period that is considered the Classical Era of Cambodian history. *Angkor Wat* is its most imposing monument—a temple complex built in the twelfth century.

All of the great temples at Angkor expressed Indian cosmological and mythical themes, and many were built in order to provide a center for religious groups that assured kings and other members of the royal family of immortality by becoming identified with Siva or one of the other preeminent gods of the realm.

For example, *Angkor Wat*, perhaps the greatest and certainly the most famous of all the temples in the Angkor complex, was built as a vast funerary temple within which the king's body was to be buried. Inside an enclosure at *Angkor Wat* are bas-reliefs that run for hundreds of yards. These reliefs tell stories from the Hindu holy books of the Mahabharata and the Ramayana. Hundreds of statues of angelic dancers also decorate the temple.

(Narrator):

21. Where is *Angkor Wat*?
22. When was *Angkor Wat* built?
23. What did the temples at Angkor express?
24. What was *Angkor Wat* built for?
25. What stories do the wall reliefs tell?

Day 26

More Structure, Reading, and Writing Drills

Today's Assignment

- Use the strategies you have acquired for Structure, Reading, and Writing in a timed sequence. You may want to review Days 6 and 7 before you begin for Structure and Days 8 and 9 for Reading and Writing.

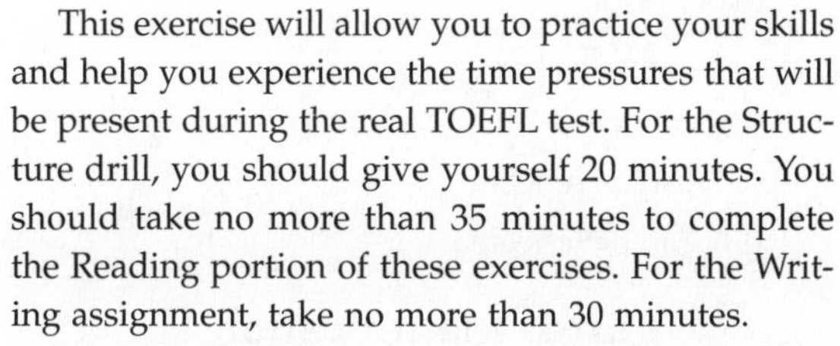

This exercise will allow you to practice your skills and help you experience the time pressures that will be present during the real TOEFL test. For the Structure drill, you should give yourself 20 minutes. You should take no more than 35 minutes to complete the Reading portion of these exercises. For the Writing assignment, take no more than 30 minutes.

You should wait until you have finished the Writing portion before you check your answers, which appear at the end of this chapter.

STRUCTURE

In this section, you will complete both sentence completion and error identification questions.

For the sentence completions, you will see 10 incomplete sentences. Beneath each sentence, there are four words or phrases. You will choose the one word or phrase that best completes the sentence. During the real TOEFL test, you will use a mouse to click on the correct answer on the screen. During this practice test, select the letter next to the answer choice you think is correct.

Sentence Completion

1. Chester Arthur taught school in Schenectady, New York, before he moved to New York City, ________ in 1854.

   (A) where he was admitted to the bar
   (B) which he admitted to the bar
   (C) who was admitted to the bar
   (D) which he was admitted to the bar

2. The Great Lakes played an important role in the European ________ of North America.

   (A) colonies and developing
   (B) colonials and developments
   (C) colonization and development
   (D) colony and develop

3. Charles Ives was awarded a Pulitzer Prize for his Third Symphony in 1947, by which time he was a 73-year-old recluse ________.
   (A) that was not a composer for more than twenty-five years
   (B) who had not composed for more than twenty-five years
   (C) that did not compose for more than twenty-five years
   (D) who was not composed for more than twenty-five years

4. ________, people in rural America did not have doctors in their areas and had to combine local folk custom with information from medical dictionaries and popular books.
   (A) Treating illnesses and injuries
   (B) Treatment of illnesses and injuries
   (C) Treat illnesses and injuries
   (D) To treat illnesses and injuries

5. Since the beginning of the eighteenth century in the United States, ________ against the sale and consumption of alcoholic beverages.
   (A) there has been a well-organized movement
   (B) there is a well-organized movement
   (C) there will be a well-organized movement
   (D) there is being a well-organized movement

6. Sculptor Frédéric Auguste Bartholdi used his mother's face ________ for the Statue of Liberty.
   (A) as a model
   (B) to a model
   (C) at a model
   (D) of a model

7. Paul Revere and his assistants turned out silver bowls, pots, and utensils, ________.
   (A) many are in museums today
   (B) many of whom are in museums today
   (C) many of which are in museums today
   (D) many that are in museums today

8. Hudson Bay is named for Henry Hudson, who, in 1610, found the large body of water ________ a Northwest Passage to Asia.
   (A) when he sought
   (B) while he was seeking
   (C) when he has been seeking
   (D) while he had been sought

9. Every substance, whether naturally occurring or artificially produced, ________ of one or more of the hundred-odd species of atoms that have been identified as elements.
   (A) consists
   (B) consisting
   (C) is consisted
   (D) was consisting

10. During the late 1880s, Heinrich Hertz proved the existence of radio waves and demonstrated that they ________ by objects, just as light is reflected by a mirror.
   (A) can reflect
   (B) reflection
   (C) can be reflecting
   (D) can be reflected

Error Identification

In this section, there are 15 questions. The questions have four underlined words or phrases. You will choose the one underlined word or phrase that must be changed for the sentence to be correct. During the real TOEFL test, you use your mouse to click on your answer. During this practice test, you will select the letter under the word or phrase that must be changed for the sentence to be correct.

11. Although (A) she had been exhibiting (B) since the late 1930s, sculptor Louise Nevelson will arrive (C) at a mature style only (D) in her fifties.

12. The availability of so much unoccupied land
A
required the British colonies the adoption liberal
B
land policies to attract settlers.
C D

13. Charles and Ray Eames are probably best known to design the Eames chair, constructed of two pieces
A B
of molded plywood joined by stainless steel tubing.
C D

14. During his prolific career, W. E. B. DuBois
A
publishing 19 books, edited 4 magazines, and
B C
produced scores of articles and speeches.
D

15. In the 1950s, Ealing Studios became well knowing
A
for its highly successful comedies, which dealt
B
with the exploits of unconventional, antibureau-
C
cratic individuals in realistic settings.
D

16. Two-way cable-television systems give subscribers
A
with home computers access to data banks and
B C
permitting them to interact with other online users.
D

17. Giant kelp produce algin, a complex carbohydrate
A
that is added to ice cream before freezing to
B C
prevent crystallization.
D

18. At Uffington, England, the hills reach an elevator
A
of 856 feet at Whitehorse Hill, where the turf
has been removed to reveal the gigantic figure of
B C D
a horse.

19. *The Old Farmer's Almanac* has advised generations of
A
American farmers on planting and harvesting and
B
was in continuous publication for longer than any
C D
other American journal.

20. Dramatic soprano Eileen Farrell surprised the
A
music world while she made her debut with the
B C
Metropolitan Opera in the same year she recorded
D
a best-selling album of popular music.

21. From the earlier times, Odin was a war god in
A B
Norse mythology and appeared in heroic literature
C
as the protector of heroes and a god of poetry.
D

22. Jazz has been neither an entirely composed or an
A B
entirely improvised music but has employed
both creative approaches in varying degrees and
C D
endless permutations.

23. Slide fasteners <u>were exhibited</u> (A) at the World's Columbian Exposition <u>of 1893</u> (B) in Chicago, and they <u>gave</u> (C) their modern name by B.G. Work, <u>who called</u> (D) them "zippers."

24. The <u>earliest</u> (A) historical records <u>note</u> (B) the <u>keeping</u> (C) of cattle, goats, and sheep for the production of milk, butter, and <u>cheeses</u> (D).

25. Incan history <u>is known</u> (A) <u>chiefly</u> (B) from the oral tradition <u>preserving</u> (C) through the generations by official "memorizers" and <u>from the written records</u> (D) composed from them after the Spanish conquest.

READING

In this section, you will see 3 reading passages. Each passage is followed by a series of questions about what you just read. Answer all questions based on what is *stated* or *implied* in the passage.

Questions 1–10 refer to the following passage.

Line Geothermal energy is power obtained by using heat from the earth's interior. Most geothermal resources are in regions of active volcanoes. Among the most easily exploited sources of such
5 energy are hot springs, geysers, and pools of boiling mud. Also a good source of geothermal energy are fumaroles, which are vents of volcanic gases and heated groundwater. The ancient Romans used hot springs to heat baths and homes,
10 and similar uses are still found in some geothermal regions of the world, such as Iceland, Turkey, and Japan.

The greatest potential for geothermal energy, however, lies in the generation of electricity. Geother-
15 mal energy was first used to produce electric power at Larderello, Italy, in 1904. By the late twentieth century, geothermal power plants were in operation in Italy, New Zealand, Japan, Iceland, Mexico, the United States, and elsewhere, and
20 many others were under construction in other countries.

The most useful geothermal resources are hot water and steam trapped in subsurface formations or reservoirs and having temperatures ranging
25 from 176° to 662° F. Water and steam hotter than 356° F are the most easily exploited for electric-power generation and are utilized by most existing geothermal power plants. In these plants, the hot water is converted to steam, which is then used
30 to drive a turbine, which converts the energy to electricity by a generator.

In the future, hot, dry subsurface rocks may become a source of geothermal energy once engineers solve the technical problems of circulating
35 water through them for heating and conversion to steam. The development of geothermal resources has become increasingly attractive owing to the rising cost of petroleum and the nonpolluting character of geothermal energy production.

1. What is the main idea of the passage?
   (A) Geothermal energy is an old-fashioned form of heating homes and doesn't have much potential.
   (B) Geothermal energy is used all over the world as a pollution-free means of producing electricity.
   (C) Geothermal energy is primarily used in the Eastern Hemisphere for recreation facilities.
   (D) Geothermal energy is a recent development in the search for clean ways to produce electricity.

2. Which word or phrase is closest in meaning to the word "exploited" as used in line 4?
   (A) Obtained
   (B) Rehearsed
   (C) Used
   (D) Vented

3. According to the passage, where is geothermal energy used to heat homes today?
   (A) Italy, France, and Germany
   (B) Mexico, New Zealand, and the United States
   (C) Iceland, Turkey, and Japan
   (D) Brazil, Saudi Arabia, and Nigeria

4. From the passage, it can be inferred that geothermal energy was first used to generate electricity in
   (A) North America.
   (B) Africa.
   (C) Asia.
   (D) Europe.

5. Where can the following sentence best be added to the passage?

   Many engineers from various countries visited the city to learn how it was accomplished.

   (A) After the phrase "boiling mud" in paragraph 1
   (B) After the phrase "in 1904" in paragraph 2
   (C) After the phrase "power plants" in paragraph 3
   (D) After the phrase "conversion to steam" in paragraph 4

6. According to the passage, what are most easily exploited for generating electricity?
   (A) Springs, geysers, and boiling mud
   (B) Water and steam hotter than 356° F
   (C) Fumaroles
   (D) Hot subsurface rocks

7. Which phrase is closest in meaning to the word "subsurface" as used in line 23?
   (A) Below the ground
   (B) Below the water
   (C) Below volcanoes
   (D) Below hot springs

8. From the passage, it can be inferred that hot, dry subsurface rocks are not practical sources of geothermal energy, because
   (A) not enough hot, subsurface rocks are available to make the process commercially useful.
   (B) power plants in Italy and Mexico are already in operation.
   (C) engineers have to solve technical problems of circulating water through them.
   (D) water does not efficiently conduct heat away from the rocks.

9. Which answer choice is closest in meaning to the phrase "owing to" as used in lines 37–38?
   (A) Dealing with
   (B) Borrowed from
   (C) Because of
   (D) Depending on

10. According to the passage, it can be inferred that geothermal energy is better than that produced by petroleum because geothermal energy is
   (A) non-polluting.
   (B) technologically superior.
   (C) available in Japan.
   (D) not liquid.

Questions 11–20 are based on the following passage.

Line Shelton Jackson Lee is the American filmmaker better known as Spike Lee. The son of the jazz composer Bill Lee, he was reared in a middle-class Brooklyn neighborhood. He majored in commu-
5 nications at Atlanta's Morehouse College, where he directed his first Super-8 films and met his future coproducer, Monty Ross.

In 1978, Lee entered New York University's Graduate Film School, where he met another future col-
10 laborator, cinematographer Ernest Dickerson. He gained national attention with his master's thesis, the short subject *Joe's Bed-Stuy Barbershop: We Cut Heads.* As he explained at the time, the barbershop "is second only in importance to the church
15 in the black community." The film earned him the Academy of Motion Picture Arts and Science's Student Award.

Lee's feature film debut was *She's Gotta Have It,* a prismatic character study about the love life of a
20 contemporary black woman. Establishing a careerlong pattern, Lee not only wrote, produced, directed, and edited the film, but he also played a key supporting role. Many of Lee's films can be classified as family affairs; his father, Bill, contrib-
25 uted music to *She's Gotta Have It* and *Mo' Better Blues,* among others; his sister, Joie, played major roles in several productions; and his brother David Charles Lee was the still photographer.

His next film, based on his experiences at
30 Morehouse, was *School Daze,* a satire of color prejudice, snobbery, and betrayal within the black academic community. Then, Lee was inspired by the infamous Howard Beach incident, in which a black man was chased and killed by rampaging white
35 youths. The film was his third feature, *Do the Right Thing,* an impassioned but evenhanded work that neither blamed any specific group for racial violence nor absolved any from it.

Do the Right Thing, Malcolm X, and his poignant
40 documentary *4 Little Girls* all received Academy Award nominations.

11. It is implied in the passage that Spike Lee grew up in
    (A) Atlanta.
    (B) New York City.
    (C) Chicago.
    (D) Hollywood.

12. What college did Spike Lee first attend?
    (A) New York University
    (B) American Film Institute
    (C) Morehouse College
    (D) City University of New York

13. Which answer choice is closest in meaning to the word "collaborator" as used in lines 9–10?
    (A) A person who photographs movies
    (B) A person with whom one goes to college
    (C) A person who negotiates for labor unions
    (D) A person with whom one works

14. In the passage, it is implied that the highest academic degree that Lee earned was a
    (A) bachelor's degree.
    (B) master's degree.
    (C) doctoral degree.
    (D) He received no degree.

15. Where can the following sentence best be added to the passage?

    It received a lot of attention outside the academic community of New York University.

    (A) After the word "neighborhood" in paragraph 1
    (B) After the word "community" in the paragraph 2
    (C) After the word "woman" in paragraph 3
    (D) After the end of paragraph 4

16. All of the following members of Lee's family have worked on his films EXCEPT
    (A) his mother.
    (B) his father.
    (C) his sister.
    (D) his brother.

17. Which of the following films was Lee's first feature?
    (A) *Joe's Bed-Stuy Barbershop: We Cut Heads*
    (B) *She's Gotta Have It*
    (C) *Mo' Better Blues*
    (D) *Do the Right Thing*

18. What was *School Daze* based on?
    (A) Lee's family life in Brooklyn
    (B) The life of Malcolm Little
    (C) Lee's experiences at Morehouse College
    (D) The life of a cafeteria worker

19. According to the passage, all of the following received Academy Award nominations EXCEPT
    (A) *Mo' Better Blues.*
    (B) *Malcolm X.*
    (C) *Do the Right Thing.*
    (D) *4 Little Girls.*

20. Which of the answer choices is closest in meaning to the word "poignant" as used in line 39?
    (A) Extremely funny
    (B) Extremely quiet
    (C) Extremely violent
    (D) Extremely touching

Questions 21–30 are based on the following passage.

Line Naïve art is the work of artists who live in modern, sophisticated societies but who lack or reject conventional techniques in the painting or sculpting of real objects. Naïve artists are not to be con-
5 fused with "Sunday painters," who paint for fun. The naïve artist creates with the same intensity and hard work as the trained artist but without the latter's formal knowledge of methods.

Naïve works are often extremely detailed, and they
10 usually contain brilliant, saturated colors rather than more subtle mixtures and tones. They also characteristically lack perspective, which creates the illusion that figures are anchored in space, with the result that figures in naïve paintings are often
15 "floating."

The most frequently reproduced examples of naïve art are the works of the French artist Henri Rousseau, whose portraits, jungle scenes, and exotic vegetation are widely admired. One of his
20 most popular works is *The Snake Charmer*, an oil painting he completed in 1907. It's in the Musée d'Orsay in Paris. Rousseau's paintings, like many others of this genre, convey a sense of frozen motion and deep, still space, and the figures are al-
25 ways shown either full face or in profile. As other naïve painters do, Rousseau rarely concealed much of a face and almost never portrayed a figure completely from the back. He projects his intensity and passion through his figures—especially the star-
30 ing eyes—and the precision of his line and color.

The appreciation of naïve art has been a fairly recent phenomenon: many of the artists still living never expected their work to be so eagerly collected. By the mid-twentieth century, most devel-
35 oped nations had naïve artists who had risen to some prominence. While some naïve painters consider themselves professional artists and seek public recognition of their work, others refuse to exhibit for profit and paint only for their families or
40 for religious institutions.

21. Which of the following does the phrase "the latter's" as used in lines 7–8 refer to?
    (A) Sunday painters
    (B) Naïve artists
    (C) The trained artist
    (D) Hard work

22. The passage implies that "Sunday Painters" are
    (A) well-trained artists.
    (B) confused about art.
    (C) not serious about art.
    (D) intense and hard working.

23. According to the passage, naïve paintings contain all of the following EXCEPT
    (A) brilliant colors.
    (B) details.
    (C) perspective.
    (D) floating figures.

24. Which answer choice is closest in meaning to the word "anchored" as used in line 13?
    (A) Released from constraint
    (B) Held in place
    (C) Sketched on canvas
    (D) Carved out

25. According to the passage, Henri Rousseau painted all of the following in his pictures EXCEPT
    (A) the backs of figures.
    (B) jungle scenes.
    (C) exotic vegetation.
    (D) faces in profile.

26. According to the passage, what is one of Rousseau's most popular works?
    (A) *The River Through the Jungle*
    (B) *On the Isle of Grande Jatte*
    (C) *The Quais D'Orsay*
    (D) *The Snake Charmer*

27. Which answer choice does the phrase "this genre" as used in line 23 refer to?
    (A) Naïve art
    (B) Jungle scenes
    (C) Oil paintings
    (D) Popular works

28. Where can the following sentence best be added to the passage?

    Another is *The Dream*, which depicts two lions prowling through heavy jungle grass and a woman languidly reclining on an elegant sofa.

    (A) At the end of paragraph 1
    (B) After the word "tones" in paragraph 2
    (C) After the phrase "Musée d'Orsay in Paris" in paragraph 3
    (D) At the end of paragraph 4

29. The passage implies that naïve paintings
    (A) have been in museums since the mid-1800s.
    (B) are disliked by art dealers.
    (C) have been prominent since the 1950s.
    (D) are enjoyed only by children.

30. According to the passage, what do some naïve artists refuse to do?
    (A) Paint for religious institutions
    (B) Exhibit for profit
    (C) Paint for their families
    (D) Exhibit in churches

WRITING

You have 30 minutes to complete this assignment. Make sure you time yourself during this assignment. Read the topic below and then make any notes that will help you plan your response. Then, type your response on your computer or write your answer on one side of the paper that you use.

Topic:

Do you agree or disagree with the following statement? Most bad things that happened to us seemed terrible at the time, but after we thought about them, we learned valuable things from the experiences. Give reasons and specific examples to support your answer.

ANSWER KEY FOR DAY 26—MORE STRUCTURE, READING, AND WRITING DRILLS

Structure

1. A
2. C
3. B
4. D
5. A
6. A
7. C
8. B
9. A
10. D
11. C
12. B
13. A
14. B
15. A
16. D
17. A
18. A
19. C
20. B
21. A
22. B
23. C
24. D
25. C

Reading

1. B
2. C
3. C
4. D
5. B
6. B
7. A
8. C
9. C
10. A
11. B
12. C
13. D
14. B
15. B
16. A
17. B
18. C
19. A
20. D
21. C
22. C
23. C
24. B
25. A
26. D
27. A
28. C
29. C
30. B

Writing

Check your brainstorm notes and outline. The shape of the essay should be something like the following:

I. *Introduction.* Define "bad experiences," i.e., tell specifically why they were "bad" for you, whether you were humiliated, injured, hurt emotionally, etc.

II. *Bad experience #1.* What happened and what I learned from it.

III. *Bad experience #2.* What happened and what I learned from it.

IV. *Bad experience #3.* What happened and what I learned from it.

V. *Conclusion.* These experiences helped me grow and see the world in a new way.

It was not necessary that you wrote according to this outline exactly, but you should have shaped your material in a similar fashion.

Day 27

Timed Tests

Today's Assignment

- Today, you will practice with a timed test. Find a quiet place with no distractions, and set a watch or timer to keep track of the time for each section. Try to take the test with no disturbances and all at one time to better simulate an actual testing experience. Audio for this test is provided on the CD. The answers and the script for the Listening section are printed at the end of this chapter.

Before you begin, have paper and pencils ready to answer the questions and write your essay.

The schedule for these practice test is as follows:

1. *Listening*
2. *Structure* (Set your alarm clock to sound 25 minutes after you begin working on this section.)
3. Take a 10-minute break after you have completed the Structure section.
4. *Reading* (Set your alarm clock to sound 80 minutes after you begin working on this section.)
5. *Writing your essay* (Set your alarm clock to sound 30 minutes after you begin working on this section.)

Notice that the time you will spend taking the actual test is much longer than the time you will use taking these practice tests. When you take the actual test, you may answer questions that ETS is trying out for the first time. This will take time, but you will not be scored on your answers. Also, you may be given a test that has more questions than these practice tests. And you will be taken through tutorials that show you how to use the computer during the actual tests.

Do not check your answers until you have completed this practice test.

LISTENING

Part A—Short Conversations

You may now begin listening to track 3 on the CD.

Directions: In this section, you will hear conversations between two people. After each conversation, you will be asked several questions about what you heard, and you will see the questions printed here with four answer choices. Choose an answer and mark it either in the book or on a separate sheet of scrap paper. Remember to answer the questions based on what is stated or implied by the speakers.

1. What does the woman mean?
   (A) The professor didn't let any students into the room.
   (B) The professor didn't speak the right words.
   (C) The professor didn't let anyone else speak.
   (D) The professor didn't get out of the room.

2. What does the man mean?
   (A) He hasn't made a final decision.
   (B) He thought the last exam was very difficult.
   (C) He is going to take flying lessons.
   (D) He changed his major to meteorology.

3. What does the man mean?
   (A) Patrick fell in love and will get married.
   (B) Patrick said goodbye to a famous scholar.
   (C) Patrick was only kidding about the scholarship.
   (D) Patrick will lose his scholarship for cheating.

4. What does the man mean?
   (A) He wants to tutor the equestrian team.
   (B) He doesn't want any job at all.
   (C) He wants to go horseback riding.
   (D) He doesn't like tutoring the football team.

5. What does the woman mean?
   (A) The man needs to get his eyes checked.
   (B) The man wanted more food than he could eat.
   (C) The man is gaining weight.
   (D) The man should never eat pizza.

6. What does the man mean?
   (A) The woman shouldn't eat an ice cream cone
   (B) The woman shouldn't go to the beach.
   (C) The woman shouldn't lose any weight.
   (D) The woman shouldn't go water-skiing.

7. What does the woman mean?
   (A) The time for changing topics is past.
   (B) The library is about to close.
   (C) The project is due tomorrow.
   (D) The woman would rather see a movie.

8. What does the man imply?
   (A) Sally is making a new bedspread.
   (B) Sally is involved in too many activities.
   (C) Sally is on a diet.
   (D) Sally is an excellent photographer.

9. What does the man mean?
   (A) He got a blank application form.
   (B) He was looking at a piece a paper.
   (C) He drew a picture of Abraham Lincoln.
   (D) He couldn't remember the information.

10. What does the woman mean?
    (A) The dormitory costs more than it's worth to keep.
    (B) The dormitory will be replaced by a zoo.
    (C) The dormitory is a big, clumsy building.
    (D) The dormitory isn't big enough for the university.

Part B—Long Conversations and Lectures

Directions: In this section, you will hear Long Conversations and Lectures. After each, you will be asked several questions about what you heard, and you will see the questions printed here with four answer choices. Choose an answer and mark it either in the book or on a separate sheet of scrap paper. Remember to answer the questions based on what is stated or implied by the speakers.

Questions 11–15. Listen to two students discussing graduation ceremonies.

11. What are the man and woman discussing?
    (A) Political speeches on television
    (B) Television comedy
    (C) Graduation ceremonies
    (D) Music for the President of the United States

12. What doesn't the man want to do at graduation?
    (A) Wear a cap and gown
    (B) Listen to the valedictorian
    (C) Receive a diploma
    (D) Sit next to the woman

13. Who is going to be principal speaker at the graduation ceremonies?
    (A) The President of the United States
    (B) The governor of the state
    (C) The president of the university
    (D) A television comedian

14. What will the main speaker talk about?
    (A) Television comedy
    (B) Public education
    (C) Antiques
    (D) Politics

15. What will the man and woman probably discuss next?
    (A) The valedictory address
    (B) Refreshments for parties after the graduation ceremonies
    (C) The music for the graduation ceremonies
    (D) The university president's office

Questions 16–20. Listen to a professor give a lecture about a famous film director.

On the screen, you will see the words " Film History."

16. What does the speaker mainly discuss?
    (A) The Japanese film industry
    (B) Akira Kurosawa's early work
    (C) Awards in the film industry
    (D) Art schools in Japan

17. When was Kurosawa first appointed director?
    (A) 1910
    (B) 1936
    (C) 1943
    (D) 1951

18. What movie brought Kurosawa international fame?
    (A) *Rashomon*
    (B) *Ikiru*
    (C) *Seven Samurai*
    (D) *The Bodyguard*

19. Who is the main character in *Ikuru*?
    (A) A screenwriter
    (B) An art teacher
    (C) A woodcutter
    (D) A minor government official

20. What will speaker probably discuss next?
    (A) A movie epic
    (B) A film festival
    (C) A film scenario
    (D) A government office

Questions 21–25. Listen to a lecture about Scotland's most important city.

On the screen, you will see the words "Scottish Writers" and a picture of Edinburgh Castle and Castle Rock.

21. According to the speaker, why is it important to know about the city of Edinburgh?
    (A) It is an old city filled with famous buildings, museums, and parks.
    (B) It contributed much to the lives of the writers the students will study.
    (C) It is the center of Castle Rock University.
    (D) It has many books, magazines, and newspapers in it.

22. What is the original city called now?
    (A) Margaret's Chapel
    (B) Castle Rock
    (C) New Town
    (D) Old Town

23. According to the speaker, what is location of St. Margaret's chapel?
    (A) In the center of Old Town
    (B) At the University of Edinburgh
    (C) At the highest point of Castle Rock
    (D) In James IV's castle

24. What did King James IV of Scotland later become?
    (A) King of England
    (B) Head of the University of Edinburgh
    (C) Husband of Queen Margaret
    (D) Editor of the *Edinburgh Review*

25. What will the speaker probably discuss next?
    (A) The life of Sir Walter Scott
    (B) *The Encyclopedia Britannica*
    (C) *The Edinburgh Review*
    (D) The reign of James I

STOP

DO NOT MOVE ON TO THE STRUCTURE SECTION UNTIL YOU HAVE SET YOUR ALARM CLOCK TO SOUND 25 MINUTES AFTER YOU HAVE BEGUN THE STRUCTURE SECTION.

STRUCTURE

Set your alarm clock to sound after 25 minutes. Complete both sentence completion and error identification sections before going on to the reading section. Do NOT go on to the reading section until the alarm has sounded and you have taken a 10-minute break.

Sentence Completion

During the actual test, you will see on your monitor screen an incomplete sentence with four answer choices under it. You will choose the answer that makes the sentence correct when placed in the blank. Beside each answer choice, you will see an empty oval. To mark your choice, you will move your mouse to the oval next to your answer choice. When you click the oval, it becomes black.

For these practice tests, circle the letter of the answer choice that you think makes the sentence correct.

Now, begin answering the questions.

1. John _______ the scholarship to study abroad if he had not studied so hard and gotten good grades.
   (A) will not have gotten
   (B) did not get
   (C) was not getting
   (D) would not have gotten

2. Although men in the Iroquois tribe made most decisions about war and peace, women _______ many other important decisions.
   (A) participated in the making of
   (B) are participating in the making of
   (C) will participate in the making of
   (D) have participated in the making of

3. In nineteenth-century America, monthly magazines, supported by advertisers and national circulation, _______ and created a seemingly limitless need for new material.
   (A) become the dominant literary medium
   (B) became the dominant literary medium
   (C) had become the dominant literary medium
   (D) became dominant literary medium

4. In general, a science ________ a pursuit of knowledge covering general truths or the operations of fundamental laws.
   (A) involves
   (B) is involving
   (C) is involved
   (D) involve

5. Under the practice of primogeniture, the oldest male child ________ of the family's land, which keeps estates intact and perpetuates a system of aristocracy.
   (A) inherit all
   (B) inherits all
   (C) inherited all
   (D) is inheriting all

6. There ________ crops in pre-Civil War America, but none was more important than cotton, which comprised more than half of all domestic exports.
   (A) was many important
   (B) has been many important
   (C) were many important
   (D) are many important

7. Although Samuel Morse's paintings are now recognized as some of the most accomplished of the nineteenth century, he ________ poverty during his career as an artist.
   (A) has been close to
   (B) is close to
   (C) closed to
   (D) was close to

8. The term scleroderma, which means "hard skin," indicates ________ of the skin that is the most common feature of the disease.
   (A) the hardening and thickening
   (B) hardening and thickening
   (C) the hardened and thickened
   (D) hardens and thickens

9. *Scientific American* was founded in New York City in 1845 by Rufus Porter, a New England inventor, as a weekly newspaper ________.
   (A) describes new inventions
   (B) describing new inventions
   (C) described new inventions
   (D) describe new inventions

10. By the time he arrived in America, film director William Wyler ________ the École Supérieure de Commerce in Lausanne, Switzerland, as well as the Paris Conservatory.
   (A) was already attending
   (B) will attend
   (C) had already attended
   (D) has been attending

Error Identification

In the following questions, four words or groups of words are underlined. Circle the letter under the word or group of words that need to be changed for the sentence to be correct.

11. Abandonment <u>may occur</u> (A) by throwing away the property, <u>by loses it</u> (B) and making no attempt <u>to retrieve</u> (C) it, or by vacating the property <u>with no intention</u> (D) of returning to it.

12. Xenoliths <u>are</u> (A) non-igneous <u>fragments within</u> (B) an igneous rock, and the general term <u>for</u> (C) all such fragments <u>are inclusions</u> (D).

13. The school of navigation founded by Prince Henry
A
of Portugal developed the quadrant and the cross
B
staff and designed the highly maneuverable little
C
ships known for caravels.
D

14. The city of Dallas, Texas, name for George Dallas,
A B
who was the eleventh Vice President of the United
C
States, and who was from Philadelphia,
D
Pennsylvania.

15. Yodeling, a type of singing found in every continent
A B
in the world, is also used as a mean of communi-
C
cating over moderate distances by the inhabitants of
D
mountainous regions.

16. Known by the ancient Chinese and by the Greeks,
A
the cabriole leg became fashionable in Europe in
B
the late seventeenth century, when it was incorpo-
C
rated into furniture the English, Dutch, and France.
D

17. Waffles were mentioned in French poems from as
A B
early as the twelfth century, while they were sold
C
as street food at fairs and religious festivals.
D

18. Before settling the United States in 1929, film and
A
Broadway composer, Vernon Duke, wrote music
B C
for two symphonies as well as the ballet *Zéphyr et*
D
Flore for Serge Diaghilev's Ballets Russes.

19. If ships sailing between the east and west coasts
A
of the United States did not go through the
B
Panama Canal, they have to travel an additional
C D
8,000 nautical miles.

20. Among the various demons of ancient folk tradition,
A
the vampires has enjoyed the most conspicuous and
B C
continual literary success since Bram Stoker wrote
D
Dracula.

21. The fin stabilizer is a small wing mounted on a ship
A
or aircraft to prevent unwanted rolling motions of
B
the vehicle and thus contribute to their stability.
C D

22. Beside their use in television broadcasting,
A
UHF waves are utilized in ship and aircraft
B
navigation systems and for certain types of
C
police communications.
D

23. After a great success as a stage designer and
A
director, Norman Bel Geddes formed an orga-
B
nization that eventual employed 2,000 people
C
and created skyscrapers, inkwells, yachts,
radios, and refrigerators.
D

24. Trombonist Jack Teagarden's jazz style was
A
remarkable for it's effortless flow of melodic
B
ideas, technical poise, and the tender beauty
C
of its overall effect.
D

25. Fiber optic technology has virtually replaced
A
copper wire to long-distance telephone lines, and
B
it is used in examining internal parts of the body.
C D

This is the end of the structure section. Take a 10-minute break before you begin the reading section.

READING

There are 5 reading passages. You should take no more than 80 minutes to complete the reading portion of these exercises.

In the actual test, you will click on your answers with the computer mouse. In the practice test, you will use a pencil or pen to circle your answer choices or write them on a separate sheet of paper.

Set your alarm clock to sound 80 minutes (1 hour and 20 minutes) after you begin this section. Do not check your answers until you have completed the entire practice test.

Questions 1–10 refer to the following passage.

Line The cabildo, which is Spanish for "municipal council," was the fundamental unit of local government in colonial Spanish America. Following a tradition going back to the Romans, the Spanish considered
5 the city to be of paramount importance, with the surrounding countryside directly subordinate to it.

In local affairs, each municipality in Hispanic America was governed by its cabildo, or council, in a manner reminiscent of Castilian towns in the
10 late Middle Ages. A council's members and magistrates, together with the local judge appointed by the king, enjoyed considerable prestige and power. The size of a council varied but was always small. The cabildos of important cities, such as
15 Lima and Mexico, had about 12 members.

The cabildo was in charge of all ordinary aspects of municipal government—e.g., policing, sanitation, taxation, the supervision of building, price and wage regulation, and the administration of
20 justice. To assist them in these responsibilities, the city councilors appointed various officials, such as tax collectors, inspectors of weights and measures and the markets, and peace officers. In spite of royal decrees to promote honest and efficient city
25 government, the cabildos were often corrupt and rapacious.

By the mid-sixteenth century, appointments to cabildos were ordinarily made by the Spanish crown and sometimes became hereditary. Occasionally, the propertied class in a city elected some of the councilors. Sometimes citizens were asked to attend a open town meeting on important matters. Such open meetings became very important to the movement for the independence of Hispanic America in the early nineteenth century.

30

35

1. Which choice does the word "paramount" as used in line 5 refer to?
   (A) Fundamental
   (B) Government
   (C) Tradition
   (D) Surrounding

2. Where was the cabildo used as a form of government?
   (A) In Roman colonies
   (B) In Spanish colonies
   (C) In Roman provinces
   (D) In Spanish provinces

3. Which of the following answer choices is closest in meaning to the word "reminiscent" as used in line 9?
   (A) Suggesting something in the past
   (B) Suggesting a schedule or agenda
   (C) Suggesting a small village
   (D) Suggesting an odor

4. According to the passage, how was a local judge in Hispanic America selected?
   (A) He was elected by the council.
   (B) He was appointed by the king.
   (C) He was chosen by the town's wealthy citizens.
   (D) He was the richest man in the town.

5. According to the passage, how many councilors did Lima have?
   (A) Ten
   (B) Eleven
   (C) Twelve
   (D) Thirteen

6. From the passage it can be inferred that some cabildos were
   (A) poorly educated.
   (B) important.
   (C) corrupt.
   (D) independent.

7. What word does the phrase "peace officers" as used in line 23 refer to?
   (A) Sanitation
   (B) Policing
   (C) Assist
   (D) Tax collectors

8. Which is closest in meaning to the word in the passage "responsibilities" as used in line 20?
   (A) Duties
   (B) Wages
   (C) Sanitation
   (D) Inspections

9. From the passage it can be inferred that by the mid-sixteenth century, the cabildo was all of the following EXCEPT
   (A) Elected by all registered voters
   (B) Appointed by the king
   (C) Came from the propertied class
   (D) Was an inherited office

10. Where can the following sentence best be added to the passage?

    Debates were sometimes heated, and the wealthy landowners had to defend their positions by arresting their opponents.

    (A) At the end of paragraph 1
    (B) At the end of paragraph 2
    (C) After the words "peace officers" in paragraph 3
    (D) After the words "important matters" in paragraph 2

Questions 11–20 refer to the following passage.

Line Annie Oakley, an intriguing figure in American entertainment, was a markswoman who starred in Buffalo Bill's Wild West Show, where she was often called "Little Sure Shot." She was born in
5 1860 in Darke County, Ohio, and her original name was Phoebe Ann Moses. As a child, she hunted game with such success that, according to legend, by selling it in Cincinnati, Ohio, she was able to pay off the mortgage on the family farm. When
10 she was 15 she won a shooting match in Cincinnati with Frank E. Butler, a vaudeville marksman, and they were married a year later.

For the next ten years they toured the country and performed in theaters and circuses as "Butler and
15 Oakley." In April 1885, Annie Oakley, now under her husband's management, joined "Buffalo Bill" Cody's Wild West Show. Billed as "Miss Annie Oakley, the Peerless Lady Wing-Shot," she was one of the show's star attractions for sixteen years.

20 Oakley never failed to delight her audiences, and her feats of marksmanship were truly incredible. At 30 paces she could split a playing card held edge-on, and she hit dimes tossed into the air. She shot cigarettes from her husband's lips, and, when
25 he threw a playing card into the air, she would shoot it full of holes before it touched the ground. She was a great success on the Wild West Show's European trips.

In 1887 she was presented to Queen Victoria, and
30 later in Berlin she performed her cigarette trick with, at his insistence, Crown Prince Wilhelm (later Kaiser Wilhelm II) holding the cigarette. A train wreck in 1901 left her partially paralyzed for a time, but she recovered and returned to the stage to
35 amaze audiences for many more years.

11. Which of the following is closest in meaning to the word "intriguing" as used in line 1?
    (A) Frightening
    (B) Fascinating
    (C) Fabulous
    (D) Funny

12. What was Oakley often called while performing in Buffalo Bill's Wild West Show?
    (A) Little Orphan Annie
    (B) Little Phoebe Ann
    (C) Little Sure Shot
    (D) Little Phoebe Butler

13. Which of the following is the closest in meaning to the highlighted word "mortgage" as used in line 9?
    (A) A debt left by a deceased property owner
    (B) A bank-loan contract using property as security
    (C) A measurement of debts owed
    (D) A piece of furniture loaned to a neighbor

14. What does the word "it" as used in the phrase "by selling it" in line 8 refer to?
    (A) Child
    (B) Game
    (C) Legend
    (D) Mortgage

15. The passage implies that Oakley and Butler were married in
    (A) 1873.
    (B) 1874.
    (C) 1875.
    (D) 1876.

16. According to the passage, Frank E. Butler was all of the following EXCEPT
    (A) Annie Oakley's assistant in her act
    (B) Annie Oakley's husband
    (C) Annie Oakley's teacher
    (D) Annie Oakley's manager

17. Which of the following is closest in meaning to the word "feats" as used in line 21?
    (A) Jokes
    (B) Accomplishments
    (C) Displays
    (D) Mistakes

18. Where can the following sentence best be added to the passage?

Her story was made into a Broadway musical called Annie Get Your Gun, but the real life of Annie Oakley is just as interesting.

(A) After the phrase "Little Sure Shot" in paragraph 1
(B) After the phrase "Butler and Oakley" in paragraph 2
(C) At the end of paragraph 3
(D) At the beginning of paragraph 4

19. According to the passage, who performed the cigarette trick with her in Europe?

(A) Queen Victoria
(B) Crown Prince Wilhelm
(C) Buffalo Bill Cody
(D) Princess Anne

20. Which of the following can be inferred from the passage?

(A) Annie Oakley was a talented and popular entertainer.
(B) Frank E. Butler was jealous of his wife's talent and popularity.
(C) Queen Victoria was brave when she held a cigarette for Annie Oakley.
(D) Buffalo Bill Cody was not as good a marksman as Annie Oakley.

Questions 21–30 refer to the following passage.

Line

Edward Patrick Eagan was born April 26, 1897, in Denver, Colorado, and his father died in a railroad accident when Eagan was only a year old. He and his four brothers were raised by his (5) mother, who earned a small income from teaching foreign languages.

Inspired by Frank Merriwell, the hero of a series of popular novels for boys, Eagan pursued an education for himself as well as an interest in boxing. (10) He attended the University of Denver for a year before serving in the U.S. Army as an artillery lieutenant during World War I. After the war, he entered Yale University and, while studying there, won the U.S. national amateur heavyweight boxing (15) title. He graduated from Yale in 1921, attended Harvard Law School, and received a Rhodes scholarship to the University of Oxford where he received his A. M. in 1928.

While studying at Oxford, Eagan became the first (20) American to win the British amateur boxing championship. Eagan won his first Olympic gold medal as a light heavyweight boxer at the 1920 Olympic Games in Antwerp, Belgium. Eagan also fought at the 1924 Olympics in Paris as a heavyweight (25) but failed to get a medal. Though he had taken up the sport just three weeks before the competition, he managed to win a second gold medal as a member of the four-man bobsled team at the 1932 Olympics in Lake Placid, New York. Thus he became (30) the only athlete to win gold medals at both the Summer and Winter Olympics.

Eagan was a member of the first group of athletes inducted into the U.S. Olympic Hall of Fame in 1983. Eagan became a respected attorney, serving (35) as an assistant district attorney for southern New York and as chairman of the New York State Athletic Commission (1945–51). He married soap heiress Margaret Colgate and attained the rank of lieutenant colonel during World War II.

21. What is the main idea of the passage?
    (A) Eagan's life shows how a wealthy student can achieve as much as a poor one.
    (B) Eagan's life shows that military experience makes athletes great.
    (C) Eagan's life shows that a man can be an athlete and a well-educated person.
    (D) Eagan's life shows how easy it is to win two gold medals in different Olympic sports.

22. According to the passage, who was Frank Merriwell?
    (A) A teacher at Yale
    (B) A fictional character
    (C) A student at Oxford
    (D) A bobsledder at the Olympics

23. According to the passage, how did Eagan's mother earn a living?
    (A) Renting rooms to immigrants
    (B) Teaching foreign languages
    (C) Doing laundry and cleaning
    (D) Writing fiction for women's magazines

24. Which of the following is the closest in meaning to the word "artillery" as used in line 11?
    (A) Large weapons such as cannons
    (B) Small weapons such as pistols
    (C) Shoulder weapons such as rifles
    (D) Tension weapons such as crossbows

25. According to the passage, Eagan won all of the following EXCEPT
    (A) Light heavyweight boxing, Olympic gold medal
    (B) U.S. national amateur heavyweight boxing title
    (C) British amateur boxing championship
    (D) Heavyweight boxing, Olympic gold medal

26. According to the passage, where were the 1920 Olympic Games held?
    (A) Antwerp, Belgium
    (B) Paris, France
    (C) London, England
    (D) Lake Placid, New York

27. Where can the following sentence best be added to the passage?

    He continued to be active in amateur athletics for the rest of the decade.

    (A) At the end of paragraph 1
    (B) After the word "boxing" in paragraph 2
    (C) After the phrase "get a medal" in paragraph 3
    (D) At the end of paragraph 4

28. Which word or phrase does the "competition" as used in line 26 refer to?
    (A) Sport
    (B) Gold medals
    (C) 1932 Olympics
    (D) Summer Olympics

29. According to the passage, what was Eagan's profession?
    (A) He was a boxing trainer.
    (B) He was an attorney.
    (C) He was an army officer.
    (D) He was president of Colgate.

30. According to the passage, what special honor did Eagan receive in 1983?
    (A) He was inducted into U.S. Olympic Hall of Fame.
    (B) He was promoted to lieutenant colonel in the U.S. Army.
    (C) He received a gold medal in four-man bobsledding.
    (D) He was appointed assistant district attorney for Southern New York.

Questions 31–40 refer to the following passage.

Line The first folio edition of the collected works of William Shakespeare was originally published in 1623 as *Mr. William Shakespeares Comedies, Histories & Tragedies*. This folio edition is the major
5 source for contemporary texts of his plays.

The publication of drama in the early seventeenth century was usually left to the poorer members of the Stationers' Company and to outright pirates. The would-be publisher only had to get hold of a
10 manuscript, legally or illegally, register it as his copy, and have it printed. Sometimes the publisher dispensed with the formality. Such a man was Thomas Thorpe, the publisher of Shakespeare's sonnets in 1609.

15 *Titus Andronicus* was the first play by Shakespeare to be published and was printed by a notorious literary pirate, John Danter, who also brought out, anonymously, a defective *Romeo and Juliet*, largely from shorthand notes made during performance.
20 Eighteen of Shakespeare's plays were printed in quartos (books about half the size of a modern magazine) both "good" and "bad" before the First Folio (a large-format book) was published in 1623. The bad quartos are defective editions, usually
25 with badly garbled or missing text.

For the First Folio, a formidable project of more than 900 pages, five men formed a partnership, headed by Edward Blount and William Jaggard. The actors John Heminge and Henry Condell un-
30 dertook the collection of 36 of Shakespeare's plays, and about 1,000 copies of the First Folio were printed by Isaac Jaggard, William's son. In 1632, a second folio was issued and in 1663, a third. The latter included *Pericles* and several other plays that
35 may not have been written by Shakespeare. These included *The Two Noble Kinsmen*, which is now thought to have been a collaboration of Shakespeare and John Fletcher.

31. From the passage it can be inferred that the First Folio of Shakespeare's plays is important because
    (A) It was registered at the Stationer's Office by Thomas Thorpe.
    (B) It is the major source for contemporary texts of Shakespeare's plays.
    (C) It is twice the size of the quarto editions that were badly printed by many publishers.
    (D) It was published three years after the establishment of the Plymouth Colony.

32. Which of the following is closest in meaning to the word "outright" as used in line 8?
    (A) Unfairly judged as something
    (B) Proved to be something without question
    (C) Imprisoned without a trial
    (D) Opposing the rights of an enemy

33. The passage implies that many publishers
    (A) were unsuccessful authors themselves.
    (B) printed the work of only the best writers.
    (C) used an author's work without permission.
    (D) paid the author very well for his writing.

34. Which of the following is closest in meaning to the phrase "dispensed with" as used in line 12?
    (A) Gave away to customers
    (B) Managed without something
    (C) Wrote a denial to an accusation
    (D) Compensated another's loss

35. According to the passage, when were Shakespeare's sonnets published?
    (A) 1609
    (B) 1610
    (C) 1611
    (D) 1612

36. Which word is closest in meaning to the phrase "brought out" as used in line 17?
    (A) Published
    (B) Printed
    (C) Performed
    (D) Defect

37. According to the passage, how many of Shakespeare's plays were printed in quartos?
    (A) 17
    (B) 18
    (C) 19
    (D) 20

38. The passage implies that John Danter acquired the text of *Romeo and Juliet* by
    (A) paying an actor for a copy of the script.
    (B) buying the copyright from Shakespeare.
    (C) taking notes during a performance.
    (D) hiring an actor to recite the lines to him.

39. According to the passage, all of the following were involved in the publishing of the First Folio EXCEPT
    (A) Edward Blount
    (B) Henry Condell
    (C) William Jaggard
    (D) John Danter

40. Where can the following sentence best be added to the passage?

    They sold quickly to a public anxious to have accurate copies of the master dramatist's plays.

    (A) At the end of paragraph 1
    (B) After the word "formality" in paragraph 2
    (C) After the word "performance" in paragraph 3
    (D) After the phrase "William's son" in paragraph 4

Questions 41–50 refer to the following passage.

Line
Steamboats were shallow-draft boats propelled by steam-driven paddle wheels. In the nineteenth century, they could be seen every day on rivers, particularly on the Mississippi River and its principal tributaries in the United States. (5)

The development of the steamboat as a practical means of transportation began in America in 1787, but it wasn't until 1811 that a steamboat was built specifically to travel along the lower Mississippi River. (10) The boat, called appropriately the New Orleans, was built at Pittsburgh, Pa., for Robert Fulton and Robert R. Livingston. In 1812, the two men began operating a regular steamboat service between New Orleans and Natchez, Mississippi. (15) Their vessels traveled at eight miles per hour downstream and three upstream.

In 1816 Henry Miller Shreve launched his steamboat Washington, and soon became known as the father of Mississippi navigation, because he (20) adapted steamboat design to fit the shallow waters of the river. He installed the engine high up above the water line and mounted it on a hull that was as shallow as that of a barge. He also added a tall second deck, and afterwards all Mississippi (25) steamboats copied Shreve's design. From then on and until about 1870, the steamboat dominated the economy, agriculture, and commerce of the middle area of the United States.

By 1834, there were 1,200 steamboats, carrying not (30) only cotton and sugar, but also passengers who enjoyed luxuriously appointed lounges with rich rugs, oil paintings, and chandeliers. Many steamboats were famous for their chefs, orchestras, and large staffs of maids and butlers to assist their cabin (35) passengers.

Steamboat pilots had to memorize or guess at the depths of the river and its potential obstacles along long stretches of river in order to navigate safely. The average life span of a steamboat was only four (40) to five years, because most of the vessels were poorly constructed and maintained. They sank after hitting sand bars and hidden rocks in the

river, and many of their boilers exploded, causing many deaths among their passengers. By the
45 1870s, railroads had become more efficient modes of transport and gradually caused the retirement of almost all the steamboats from the river.

41. In the passage, it is implied that steamboats were used mainly
 (A) in New Orleans.
 (B) in Washington, D.C.
 (C) along the Hudson River.
 (D) in the Mississippi River valley.

42. Which of the following is closest in meaning to the word "tributaries" as used in line 5 of the passage?
 (A) A party honoring a famous person
 (B) A stream that flows into another
 (C) A three-wheeled vehicle
 (D) A state that has a border on three other states

43. According to the passage, in what year were steamboats operating regularly on the Mississippi?
 (A) 1810
 (B) 1811
 (C) 1812
 (D) 1813

44. Which of the following does the phrase "means of transportation" as used in line 7 refer to?
 (A) Steamboat
 (B) America
 (C) Built specifically
 (D) Travel

45. According to the passage, how fast did the New Orleans travel downstream between New Orleans and Natchez?
 (A) 3 miles per hour
 (B) 8 miles per hour
 (C) 13 miles per hour
 (D) 18 miles per hour

46. According to the passage why was Henry Shreve called the "father of Mississippi navigation?"
 (A) He designed a steering mechanism that other steamboats used.
 (B) He was born and raised in a small village on the banks of the Mississippi.
 (C) He printed maps for the steamboat captains and pilots.
 (D) He adapted steamboat design to fit the shallow waters of the river.

47. Which of the following is the closest in meaning to the phrase "from then on" as used in line 25–26 in the passage?
 (A) Subsequently
 (B) Consequently
 (C) Apparently
 (D) Thoroughly

48. According to the passage, after the 1830s, steamboats had all of the following EXCEPT
 (A) Orchestras
 (B) Chefs and maids
 (C) Chandeliers
 (D) Air conditioning

49. According to the passage, how long did the average steamboat remain afloat?
 (A) Two to three years
 (B) Three to four years
 (C) Four to five years
 (D) Five to six years

50. Where can the following sentence best be added to the passage?

    Mark Twain, a steamboat pilot who became one of America's greatest writers, told about his brother's death in a steamboat explosion in his book *Life on the Mississippi*.

    (A) After the words "Mississippi River" in paragraph 2

    (B) After the phrase "Shreve's design" in paragraph 3

    (C) After the word "chandeliers" in paragraph 4

    (D) After the phrase "their passengers" in paragraph 5

WRITING SECTION

You have 30 minutes to complete this assignment. Make sure you time yourself during this assignment. Read the topic below and then make any notes that will help you plan your response. Then, type your response on your computer or write your answer on one side of the paper that you use.

Topic

Plants are important sources of food and medicine, building materials, and fiber for clothing. In your country, which plant is important to you or the people in your country? Use specific reasons and details to explain your choice.

ANSWER KEY FOR DAY 27

Listening

1.	C	14.	B
2.	A	15.	C
3.	D	16.	B
4.	D	17.	C
5.	B	18.	A
6.	C	19.	D
7.	A	20.	A
8.	B	21.	B
9.	D	22.	D
10.	A	23.	C
11.	C	24.	A
12.	A	25.	C
13.	D		

Structure

1.	D	14.	B
2.	A	15.	C
3.	B	16.	D
4.	A	17.	C
5.	B	18.	A
6.	C	19.	C
7.	D	20.	B
8.	A	21.	D
9.	B	22.	A
10.	C	23.	C
11.	B	24.	B
12.	D	25.	B
13.	D		

Reading

1.	A	26.	A
2.	B	27.	C
3.	A	28.	C
4.	B	29.	C
5.	C	30.	A
6.	C	31.	B
7.	B	32.	B
8.	A	33.	C
9.	A	34.	B
10.	D	35.	A
11.	C	36.	A
12.	C	37.	B
13.	B	38.	C
14.	B	39.	D
15.	D	40.	D
16.	C	41.	D
17.	B	42.	B
18.	A	43.	C
19.	B	44.	A
20.	A	45.	B
21.	C	46.	D
22.	B	47.	A
23.	B	48.	D
24.	A	49.	C
25.	D	50.	D

ESSAY

Your notes and outline must include the name of the plant, what it looks like, and where it grows. You have to answer the following questions:

- What affect does the plant have on people?
- How does it benefit people?
- What fruit does it produce?
- What wood or fiber does it make, etc?

DAY 27—SCRIPT

Part A—Short Conversations

(Narrator): Directions: In this section, you will hear conversations between two people. After each conversation, you will be asked several questions about what you heard, and you will see the questions printed here with four answer choices. Choose an answer and mark it either in the book or on a separate sheet of scrap paper. Remember to answer the questions based on what is stated or implied by the speakers.

1. *(Man):* That's the first time I went to a seminar and did nothing but listen to the professor lecture.

   (Woman): No one could get a word in edgewise.

   (Narrator): What does the woman mean?

2. *(Woman):* Didn't you say that you were going to drop the psychology class?

   (Man): Well, after I did so well on the last exam, everything's been up in the air.

   (Narrator): What does the man mean?

3. *(Woman):* I heard that Patrick was caught cheating on an exam.

   (Man): Yep. He can kiss his scholarship goodbye.

   (Narrator): What does the man mean?

4. *(Woman):* So how do you like tutoring the football team?

   (Man): I wish they had saddled that job on someone else.

   (Narrator): What does the man mean?

5. *(Man):* Oh. I ate too much pizza at the party.

   (Woman): I guess your eyes were bigger than your stomach.

   (Narrator): What does the woman mean?

6. *(Woman):* I've got to lose weight before I go to the beach.

   (Man): Why? You're skin and bones now.

   (Narrator): What does the man mean?

7. *(Man):* I hate the way my project is going. I think I'll find another topic to write about.

   (Woman): Isn't it rather late in the day for that?

   (Narrator): What does the woman mean?

8. *(Woman):* Sally was elected president of the photography club.

   (Man): I hope she isn't spreading herself too thin.

   (Narrator): What does the man imply?

9. *(Woman):* I was surprised that you couldn't answer Professor Parker's question about Abraham Lincoln.

   (Man): I know the answer, but when he asked, I just drew a blank.

   (Narrator): What does the man mean?

10. *(Man):* Why are they going to tear down the old woman's dormitory?

    (Woman): Well, it really is a white elephant.

    (Narrator): What does the woman mean?

Part B—Long Conversations and Lectures

(Narrator): Directions: In this section, you will hear Long Conversations and Lectures. After each, you will be asked several questions about what you heard, and you will see the questions printed here with four answer choices. Choose an answer and mark it either in the book or on a separate sheet of scrap paper. Remember to answer the questions based on what is stated or implied by the speakers.

(Narrator): Questions 11–15. Listen to two students discussing graduation ceremonies.

(Man): Look, you're the president of the senior class. Can't we do something about the way we dress at graduation? Why do we have to wear a cap and gown? I look like a nerd in this thing.

(Woman): No, you don't. Besides, everyone else will be wearing them. It's traditional.

(Man): Who is going to be the main speaker?

(Woman): We tried to get the President of the United States, but his schedule was already filled. And we asked the governor and other government officials, but they were already booked.

(Man): I think we should get someone besides a politician. What about a movie star or a writer?

(Woman): Well, we got a television star to agree to speak. Bill Cosby.

(Man): He's not going to just make a lot of jokes about his childhood, is he?

(Woman): Hey, he has a doctorate in education and has done a lot of work in early childhood education. He and his wife have given a large endowment to a University, and he's a major antique collector. He's going to speak about the future of public education, from elementary school to the university. Cosby is not just a comedian; he's a highly respected educator.

(Man): Excellent. Who is the valedictorian?

(Woman): Well, the office of the university president has not announced the name yet.

(Man): Uh huh. That means you know who it is.

(Woman): I know who it is, but I can't tell you. I can't even tell my own parents who it is.

(Man): That must mean that you are the valedictorian.

(Woman): No. I promise you, I'm not. Really.

(Man): Okay. What about the music? Let's not march in to the auditorium listening to the glee club sing "Land of Hope and Glory." Can't we have something more exciting?

(Narrator):

11. What are the man and woman discussing?
12. What doesn't the man want to do at graduation?
13. Who is going to be principal speaker at the graduation ceremonies?
14. What will the main speaker talk about?
15. What will the man and woman probably discuss next?

(Narrator): Questions 16–20. Listen to a professor give a lecture about a famous film director.

(Woman): The Japanese film director, Akira Kurosawa, was born in 1910 and died in 1998. I will concentrate on his early work today. I'll start with his early training.

After he graduated from high school, Kurosawa attended an art school and began painting in the Western style. Although he was awarded important art prizes, he gave up his ambition to become a painter and in 1936, became an assistant director in the PCL cinema studio. He also wrote scenarios, or film scripts, and they were so well received that he was promoted to director in 1943.

He gained international fame when his film *Rashomon* was shown at the Venice Film Festival, where it won the grand prize in 1951. *Rashomon* also won the American Academy Award for Best Foreign Film.

Rashomon is about a samurai, his wife, a bandit, and a woodcutter in the tenth century. A murder is recollected by the four persons in distinctly different ways. This presentation of the same event as seen by different persons caught the imagination of the audience and advanced the idea of cinema as a means of probing a metaphysical problem.

His next film, *Ikiru,* or *To Live,* is regarded by many critics, including myself, as one of the finest works in the history of the cinema. It's about a minor governmental official who learns he has cancer and will die in six months. He finds comfort only by using his position to work for the construction of a small playground in a poor section of Tokyo. Kurosawa had a strong moral message and used realism to show the collapse of the family system as well as the hypocritical aspects of officials in postwar Japanese society.

His next film was the epic *Seven Samurai.*

(Narrator):

16. What does the speaker mainly discuss?
17. When was Kurosawa first appointed director?
18. What movie brought Kurosawa international fame?
19. Who is the main character in *Ikuru*?
20. What will the speaker probably discuss next?

(Narrator): Questions 21–25. Listen to a lecture about Scotland's most important city.

(Man): Good morning. In this course, we'll read the works of novelist Sir Walter Scott, the philosopher and historian James Mill, the essayist and historian Thomas Carlyle, and the novelist Robert Louis Stevenson. I want to say a few words about the city that contributed so much to their lives. The city, of course, is Edinburgh, which was the birthplace of the *Encyclopedia Britannica* in 1768.

The original city, now called Old Town, began in the twelfth century with Edinburgh Castle as its focus. The castle was built on an immense crag of basalt that is now called Castle Rock. The medieval town of Edinburgh was built on the eastern part of Castle Rock below the castle walls. On the highest point of Castle Rock is the tiny chapel of St. Margaret, which is the oldest-surviving building and dates from the twelfth century but possibly incorporates some eleventh-century construction.

The city is the center of Scottish culture, education, and national identity. One of the principal reasons for this is the University of Edinburgh. It was founded in 1583 as the "Town's College" under a charter granted in 1582 by King James VI, who later became King James I of England. The university initially consisted of a liberal arts college and a school of divinity. In the eighteenth century, it added a school of medicine and law, and eventually, colleges of music, science, arts, social sciences, and veterinary medicine were subsequently added. The University of Edinburgh has produced a long line of eminent cultural figures, including the writers whose work we'll be studying.

We cannot finish these introductory remarks without talking about *The Edinburgh Review* and its influence on the intellectual life, not just in Scotland, but throughout the British Isles.

(Narrator):

21. According to the speaker, why is it important to know about the city of Edinburgh?
22. What is the original city called now?
23. According to the speaker, what is location of St. Margaret's chapel?
24. What did King James IV of Scotland later become?
25. What will the speaker probably discuss next?

Day 28

Timed Tests

Today's Assignment

- Today, you will continue to practice with another timed test. Find a quiet place with no distractions, and set a watch or timer to keep track of the time for each section. Try to take the test with no disturbances and all at one time to better simulate an actual testing experience. Audio for this test is provided on the CD. The answers and the script for the Listening section are printed at the end of this chapter.

Before you begin, have paper and pencils ready to answer the questions and write your essay.

The schedule for these practice test is as follows:

1. *Listening*
2. *Structure* (Set your alarm clock to sound 25 minutes after you begin working on this section.)
3. Take a 10-minute break after you have completed the Structure section.
4. *Reading.* (Set your alarm clock to sound 80 minutes after you begin working on this section.)
5. *Writing your essay.* (Set your alarm clock to sound 30 minutes after you begin working on this section)

Notice that the time you will spend taking the actual test is much longer than the time you will use taking these practice tests. When you take the actual test, you may answer questions that ETS is trying out for the first time. This will take time, but you will not be scored on your answers. Also, you may be given a test that has more questions than these practice tests. And you will be taken through tutorials that show you how to use the computer during the actual tests.

Do not check your answers until you have completed this practice test.

LISTENING

Part A—Short Conversations

You may now begin listening to track 4 on the CD.

Directions: In this section, you will hear conversations between two people. After each conversation, you will be asked several questions about what you heard, and you will see the questions printed here with four answer choices. Choose an answer and mark it either in the book or on a separate sheet of scrap paper. Remember to answer the questions based on what is stated or implied by the speakers.

1. What does the woman mean?
   (A) The man doesn't know how to treat a wound.
   (B) The man is making her unhappiness worse.
   (C) The man needs to buy salt at the supermarket.
   (D) The man's rubbing has made her wound worse.

2. What does the man mean?
   (A) The math class had a good beginning.
   (B) The man is in a math class with the track team.
   (C) The professor runs the class well.
   (D) The math class will participate in the marathon.

3. What did the woman mean?
   (A) She put her fingers in her ears so she couldn't hear Janet.
   (B) She took medicine for her earache.
   (C) She thought Janet's remarks were unimportant.
   (D) She didn't listen to the concert.

4. What does the woman mean?
   (A) What Ronnie did was not good for the team.
   (B) What Ronnie did was outstanding.
   (C) What Ronnie did was tragic.
   (D) What Ronnie did was unimportant.

5. What does the woman imply?
   (A) She wants to meet the rock group.
   (B) She doesn't want to go with the man.
   (C) She is about to come down with a cold.
   (D) She doesn't like the music by the new rock group.

6. What does the man imply?
   (A) He's been on vacation in Chicago.
   (B) He doesn't know anything about the resignation.
   (C) He is circulating a petition in favor of the dean.
   (D) He hasn't collected his scholarship money.

7. What does the man imply?
   (A) Dorian's father owns a floor covering business.
   (B) Dorian has many friends in the police department.
   (C) Dorian's parents will buy new carpets for the college.
   (D) Dorian's driving record will probably not be affected.

8. What does the woman mean?
   (A) The man has to prepare for a dangerous exam.
   (B) The man will remember what is in the book.
   (C) The man won't learn what he should about *War and Peace*.
   (D) The man will do very well on the exam.

9. What does the man imply?
   (A) He doesn't mind the student assistant.
   (B) He didn't go to the interview.
   (C) He got the job and starts tomorrow.
   (D) He slipped on the wet floor.

10. What does the woman mean?
    (A) They will eat a pizza that they make from fresh ingredients.
    (B) They will eat something other than pizza tonight.
    (C) They will scratch their names in the table at the pizza parlor.
    (D) They will not eat Italian food anymore.

Part B—Long Conversations and Lectures

***Directions:** In this section, you will hear Long Conversations and Lectures. After each, you will be asked several questions about what you heard, and you will see the questions printed here with four answer choices. Choose an answer and mark it either in the book or on a separate sheet of scrap paper. Remember to answer the questions based on what is stated or implied by the speakers.*

Questions 11–15. Listen to two students discuss the student newspaper.

On the screen, you will see the word "Journalism" and a picture of two students in the newsroom of the student paper.

11. How long have the man and woman worked on the student newspaper?
    (A) This is their first day.
    (B) This is their first week.
    (C) This is their first month.
    (D) This is their first year.

12. Where did the man and woman get their first newspaper experience?
    (A) They worked for their parents.
    (B) They don't have any experience at all.
    (C) They worked on their high school newspapers.
    (D) They watched television shows about newspapers.

13. What did the man's hometown paper let him do?
    (A) Interview important reporters
    (B) Edit some stories
    (C) Help with page layouts
    (D) Edit the paper

14. What kind of reporting does the man want to do?
    (A) Sports
    (B) Movie and theater reviews
    (C) International news
    (D) Editing his hometown paper

15. What is the probable cause of the woman's interest in sports journalism?
    (A) Her father doesn't like television reporters.
    (B) Her father lives in New York City.
    (C) Her father is a sports reporter.
    (D) Her father is a professional athlete.

Questions 16–20. Listen to an archeology professor speak to his class about Stonehenge.

On the screen, you will see the word "Archeology" and a picture of Stonehenge.

16. When was Stonehenge built?
    (A) Around 1100 B.C.E.
    (B) Around 2100 B.C.E.
    (C) Around 3100 B.C.E.
    (D) Around 4100 B.C.E.

17. Why are many of the original stones missing?
    (A) Weather eroded them.
    (B) Builders removed them.
    (C) Stonehenge was never completed.
    (D) They were destroyed by the Romans.

18. Why was Stonehenge probably built?
    (A) As a place for worship
    (B) As a place for performances
    (C) As a place for Roman banquets
    (D) As a place for mathematical computation

19. When does the northeast axis of the ring line up with the sunrise?
    (A) Autumnal Equinox
    (B) Winter Solstice
    (C) Spring Equinox
    (D) Summer Solstice

20. What is the professor probably going to discuss next?
    (A) The Roman occupation of Britain
    (B) The construction methods of 3100 B.C.E.
    (C) The influence of Druids on Celtic society
    (D) The computation of eclipses

Questions 21–25. Listen to a lecture on René Descartes.

On the screen, you will see the word "Philosophy" and a picture of the cover of the book Discourse on Method.

21. According to the speaker, what is René Descartes often called?
    (A) The embracer of wisdom
    (B) The separator of mind and body
    (C) The father of modern philosophy
    (D) The dreamer of science

22. When did Descartes describe the idea of a universal science?
    (A) 1919
    (B) 1819
    (C) 1719
    (D) 1619

23. Where did he live while he was writing his two most famous books?
    (A) Paris
    (B) Holland
    (C) London
    (D) Sweden

24. In *Discourse on Method,* how many rules did he create for the pursuit of knowledge?
    (A) Two
    (B) Three
    (C) Four
    (D) Five

25. What is the speaker probably going to discuss next?
    (A) His next work, *Meditations on First Philosophy*
    (B) His trips to Holland and Sweden
    (C) His ability to give lectures
    (D) His moves from one city to another

STOP

DO NOT MOVE ON TO THE STRUCTURE SECTION UNTIL YOU HAVE SET YOUR ALARM CLOCK TO SOUND 25 MINUTES AFTER YOU HAVE BEGUN THE STRUCTURE SECTION.

STRUCTURE

Set your alarm clock to sound after 25 minutes. Complete both sentence completion and error identification sections before going on to the reading section. Do NOT go on to the reading section until the alarm has sounded and you have taken a 10-minute break.

Sentence Completion

During the actual test, you will see on your monitor screen an incomplete sentence with four answer choices under it. You will choose the answer that makes the sentence correct when placed in the blank. Beside each answer choice, you will see an empty oval. To mark your choice, you will move your mouse to the oval next to your answer choice. When you click the oval, it becomes black.

For these practice tests, circle the letter of the answer choice that you think makes the sentence correct.

Now, begin answering the questions.

1. Numerous governments have protected colorful species of birds _______ their extinction at the hands of feather hunters.

(A) prevention
(B) to prevent
(C) prevented
(D) are preventing

2. _______ in an east–west direction, the Pacaraima Mountains mark the borders between Brazil and southeastern Venezuela.

(A) Extending for 250 miles
(B) Extended for 250 miles
(C) Extension for 250 miles
(D) To extend for 250 miles

3. Gibbons live in trees and swing from branch to branch with great agility by their arms, but on the ground, _______, holding their arms up.

(A) they will walk erect
(B) they are walking erect
(C) they walked erect
(D) they walk erect

4. Historically, the study of occupational diseases can be traced to the sixteenth-century writings of the metallurgist Georgius Agricola on the problems _______ in the metal-ore mines of Saxony.

(A) of improper ventilated
(B) of improper ventilating
(C) of improper ventilation
(D) of improper ventilate

5. Irish poet Seamus Heaney, whose work evokes events in Irish history and alludes to Irish myth, _______ for Literature in 1995.

(A) has received the Nobel Prize
(B) receives the Nobel Prize
(C) is receiving the Nobel Prize
(D) received the Nobel Prize

6. When a craftsman makes a clock pendulum that is 39 inches long, the time required for a complete swing of the pendulum _______.

(A) will be one second
(B) was one second
(C) has been one second
(D) are one second

7. According to European folk tales, if an ondine fell in love in with a man, she would die _______.

(A) if he was unfaithful to her
(B) if he were unfaithful to her
(C) if he is unfaithful to her
(D) if he has been unfaithful to her

8. Hieroglyphic symbols may represent the objects that they depict _______ particular sounds or groups of sounds.

(A) but usually stand in
(B) but usually stand up
(C) but usually stand for
(D) but usually stand out

9. If any of ________ at low pressure in a glass tube and an electrical charge is passed through it, the gas glows.
   (A) the noble gases are confined
   (B) the noble gases confine
   (C) the noble gases were confined
   (D) the noble gases is confined

10. Egyptians, who believed that fragrance indicated the presence of a god, used incense to counteract ________ odors and drive away demons.
   (A) disagreeable
   (B) disagreeing
   (C) disagreement
   (D) disagreed

Error Identification

In the following questions, four words or groups of words are underlined. Circle the letter under the word or group of words that need to be changed for the sentence to be correct.

11. Macbeth established himself on the throne of
A
Scotland after killing his cousin King Duncan I
B
in battle near Elgin, not, as Shakespeare write, by
C D
murdering Duncan in bed.

12. Playing live at the Fillmore Auditorium, the rock
A
band "Jefferson Airplane" has developed its
B
crowd-pleasing version of jamming that became
C
the hallmark of the San Francisco sound.
D

12. The Alamo was original the chapel of the Mission
A
San Antonio de Valero, which had been founded
B C
between 1716 and 1718 by the Franciscan Order.
D

13. Elihu Yale, benefactor of Yale University, was born
A
in Massachusetts, but was taken to England by
B
his family on the age of three and educated
C
at a private school in London.
D

14. The clambake is first practiced by the coastal
A
Indians, who steamed shellfish over hot stones
B
under a covering of seaweed which furnished the
C
aromatic steam in which the food cooked.
D

15. Noah Webster's dictionary contained about 70,000
A B
entries and between 30,000 and 40,000 definitions
C
that did not appear in any earlier dictionary.
D

16. One of the main type of dialects is the geographic
A B
dialect, spoken by people of the same area
C
or locality.
D

17. The summit of K2, the world's second highest
A
peak, was reached in 1954 by Achille Compagnoni
B
and Lino Lacedelli, who's guide, Mario Puchoz,
C
died of pneumonia.
D

18. After William Bligh served as captain of the HMS
A B
Bounty, he became governor of New South Wales
C
where its behavior resulted in another revolt.
D

19. As Deputy Postmaster of the American Colonies,
A
Benjamin Franklin reorganizing the postal system,
B
making it efficient, profitable, and safe.
C D

20. Ultrasound is one technique commonly used
A
during pregnancy to measure fetal heartbeat,
detects congenital defects, and ensure the proper
B C
growth of the fetus.
D

21. When the Harlem Renaissance of the 1920's, Black
A
American literature took on a more distinctive
B C
form with the works of such writers as Langston
D
Hughes and Countee Cullen.

22. Because of its color, its durability, and hardness,
A B
ebony is used for cabinetwork and inlaying, as
C
well as for piano keys and knife handles.
D

23. Tie-dyeing produces colored patterns in the fabric
A
by gathering together many small portions of
B
material and tied them tightly with string before
C
immersing the cloth in the dyebath.
D

24. Ornithologist P. V. Rogers reported that flamingos were gregarious birds, and their flocks numbering
A
hundreds may be seen in long, curving flight
B C
formations and in wading groups along the shore.
D

25. S. J. Perelman's humor mocked twentieth-century
A
clichés and used a colorful vocabulary
B
to create hilarity effects.
C D

This is the end of the structure section. Take a 10-minute break before you begin the reading section.

READING

There are 5 reading passages. You should take no more than 80 minutes to complete the reading portion of these exercises.

In the actual test, you will click on your answers with the computer mouse. In the practice test, you will use a pencil or pen to circle your answer choices or write them on a separate sheet of paper.

Set your alarm clock to sound 80 minutes (1 hour and 20 minutes) after you begin this section. Do not check your answers until you have completed the entire practice test.

Questions 1–10 refer to the following passage.

Line The "writ of habeas corpus" is used to correct violations of personal liberty by ordering a judicial inquiry into the legality of keeping someone in jail. Habeas corpus is recognized in the countries of *5* the Anglo-American legal system.

No one can say when courts began using the writ. Its modern history as a way of protecting one's personal liberty against official authority probably begins with the reign of Henry VII (1485–1509). It *10* was then that lawyers tried to free people who had been imprisoned by the king's Privy Council. By the reign of Charles I, in the seventeenth century, the writ was fully established as the appropriate process for checking the illegal imprisonment of *15* people by inferior courts or public officials. Its use was expanded during the nineteenth century to cover those put in jail under private authority.

By the time of the American Revolution, the rights to habeas corpus were popularly regarded as *20* among the basic protections of individual liberty. The U.S. Constitution guarantees that the privilege "shall not be suspended, unless when in cases of rebellion or invasion the public safety may require it." In England, such suspension had oc- *25* curred during the wars with France at the time of the French Revolution. In the United States, President Lincoln suspended the writ by executive proclamation at the outbreak of the Civil War in 1861.

Currently, habeas corpus is used in a variety of *30* ways in the United States, particularly in situations that don't involve criminal proceedings. For example, during divorce proceedings, child custody claims during a divorce may be adjudicated in habeas corpus. Also, a patient confined to a men- *35* tal hospital may in some jurisdictions bring about his release by showing at a habeas corpus hearing that he has recovered his sanity.

1. According to the passage, where is the writ of habeas corpus recognized?
   (A) In countries with an Anglo-American legal system
   (B) In countries governed by a Privy Council
   (C) In countries going through a revolution
   (D) In countries where divorce laws are strict

2. Which of the following is closest in meaning to the phrase "judicial inquiry" as used in lines 2 and 3 of the passage?
   (A) A trial of a person accused of murder
   (B) A set of questions limited to a legal issue
   (C) A legal investigation in a court run by a judge
   (D) A police department protecting a judge

3. According to the passage, when did the modern history of the writ probably begin?
   (A) During the reign of Charles I
   (B) During the American Revolution
   (C) During the American Civil War
   (D) During the reign of Henry VII

4. Which of the following is closest in meaning to the word " appropriate" as used in line 13 of the passage?
   (A) Taken as property for the state
   (B) Suitable to the conditions
   (C) Acquired funds for a government program
   (D) Supported by a wooden beam

5. The passage implies that the writ of habeas corpus is
   (A) not very important to most Americans.
   (B) recognized in France and Germany.
   (C) considered a basic protection by Americans.
   (D) used only in criminal cases.

6. According to the passage, the U.S. Constitution
   (A) allows the writ of habeas corpus only in cases involving immigrants.
   (B) allows the writ of habeas corpus to be suspended during times of war.
   (C) allows the writ of habeas corpus to apply to rebels and invaders, but not to soldiers.
   (D) allows the writ of habeas corpus to be cancelled by prisoners and mental patients.

7. Which country suspended the writ of habeas corpus during the time of the French revolution?
   (A) Italy
   (B) The United States
   (C) France
   (D) England

8. Which of the following is closest in meaning to the word "suspended" as used in line 22 of the passage?
   (A) Hung from a supporting structure
   (B) Kept out of the war temporarily
   (C) Detained for questioning by the police
   (D) Stopped for a specified period of time

9. Where can the following sentence best be added to the passage?

   A few years later, it became an important issue that was debated by delegates to the convention that organized the new American government.

   (A) After the word "jail" in paragraph 1
   (B) After the word "officials" in paragraph 2
   (C) After the word "liberty" in paragraph 3
   (D) After the word "proceedings" in paragraph 3

10. According to the passage all of the following statements about the writ of habeas corpus are true EXCEPT
   (A) it is often used by patients confined in mental hospitals.
   (B) it is often used to protect citizens from unlawful imprisonment.
   (C) it is often used in cases of rebellion and invasion.
   (D) it is often used to settle child custody claims in divorce proceedings..

Questions 11–20 refer to the following passage.

Line The world famous Abbey Theatre in Dublin, Ireland, has its roots in the Irish Literary Theatre, which was started by William Butler Yeats and Lady Isabella Augusta Gregory. That theater was *5* taken over by the Irish National Dramatic Society, led by W.G. and Frank J. Fay and formed to present Irish actors in Irish plays. In 1903, this became the Irish National Theatre Society, with which many leading figures of the Irish literary renaissance *10* were closely associated. The quality of its productions was quickly recognized, and in 1904, an Englishwoman, Annie Horniman, who was a friend of Yeats, paid for the conversion of an old theatre in Abbey Street, Dublin, into the Abbey Theatre.

15 The Abbey opened in December of that year with a bill of plays by Yeats, Lady Gregory, and John Millington Synge (who joined the other two as co-director). Founding members included the Fays, Arthur Sinclair, and Sara Allgood. The Abbey's *20* staging of Synge's satire *The Playboy of the Western World*, on January 26, 1907, stirred up so much resentment in the audience over its portrayal of the Irish peasantry that there was a riot. When the Abbey players toured the United States for the first *25* time in 1911, similar protests and disorders were provoked when the play opened in New York City and Philadelphia. The onset of World War I and the Irish Rebellion of 1916 almost caused the closing of the theatre.

30 However, in 1924, the Abbey Theatre became the first state-subsidized theatre in the English-speaking world. The emergence of the playwright Sean O' Casey also stimulated new life in the theatre, and from 1923 to 1926, the Abbey staged three of *35* his plays. In the early 1950s, the Abbey company moved to the nearby Queen's Theatre after a fire had destroyed its playhouse. A new Abbey Theatre, housing a smaller, experimental theatre, was completed in 1966 on the original site. Although *40* the Abbey has broadened its repertory, it continues to rely primarily on Irish plays.

11. What is the reading passage mainly about?
    (A) The Irish Literary Theatre
    (B) The Abbey Theatre
    (C) The Irish National Dramatic Society
    (D) The Irish National Theatre Society

12. Which word or phrase does the word "this" as used in line 7 refer to?
    (A) Irish National Dramatic Society
    (B) W.G Fay
    (C) Irish plays
    (D) Irish National Theatre Society

13. When did the theatre group move into the Abbey theatre?
    (A) 1903
    (B) 1904
    (C) 1905
    (D) 1906

14. Which of the following is closest in meaning to the phrase "bill of plays" as used in line 16?
    (A) Receipt for theatre tickets
    (B) Group of performed works
    (C) Menu in a restaurant
    (D) Planned actions of a football team

15. According to the passage, what happened when the Abbey Theatre presented *The Playboy of the Western World*?
    (A) The theatre building burned down.
    (B) The Irish Rebellion began.
    (C) The audience rioted.
    (D) The theatre was bought by Frank J. Fay.

16. Which of the following is closest in meaning to the word "peasentry" as used in line 23 of the passage?
    (A) Bird keepers at a zoo
    (B) Factory employees
    (C) Rural working class
    (D) Dramatic actors

17. It can be inferred from the passage, that two of the following American cities had a large population of Irish immigrants.
    (A) New York City and Philadelphia
    (B) Philadelphia and Chicago
    (C) New York City and Pittsburgh
    (D) Philadelphia and Detroit

18. According to the passage, when did the Irish Rebellion take place?
    (A) 1913
    (B) 1914
    (C) 1915
    (D) 1916

19. According to the passage, the following actors were associated with the Abbey Theatre EXCEPT
    (A) W.G. Fay.
    (B) Sara Allgood.
    (C) Sean Connery.
    (D) Arthur Sinclair.

20. Which of the following is closest in meaning to the word "emergence" as used in line 32 of the passage?
    (A) The exit from a cave by an animal.
    (B) The unexpected increase in value.
    (C) The rise to prominence.
    (D) The promotion to a more important job.

Questions 21–30 refer to the following passage.

Line Fairs are temporary markets where buyers and sellers gather to transact business, and they usually last several days. Historically, fairs have displayed many different kinds of products in specific commodity or industrial groupings. The older *(5)* specialty fairs evolved into the more modern trade fair, which gained in popularity during the twentieth century. Participation in trade fairs is confined to exhibitors representing one industry or even just specialized segments of an industry. *(10)*

Historically, fairs were created to solve the early problems of distribution. They provided an opportunity for the demonstration of skills and crafts, for the exchange of ideas, and for the bartering of goods. *(15)* The methods of commerce introduced at such fairs became widespread, and the rules of the fair eventually became the basis of European business law. The largest of the fairs traded products from throughout Europe and beyond, including Russian furs, Oriental drugs and spices, Flemish *(20)* cloth, and German linens.

Other fairs of historical interest were those at Kinsai in China, which flourished during Europe's Dark Ages. The great Aztec fair was found by the Spanish conquistadors on the site of present-day *(25)* Mexico City. In central Russia, there was the Nizhny Novgorod fair. All of these fairs succeeded because they were located on major trade or routes taken by religious pilgrims. Today in the United States, fairs are sometimes called "flea markets," *(30)* where merchants sell everything from antique furniture to hand-made candy. Also, the county, agricultural, and livestock fairs are still popular in the United States and in Europe.

21. From the reading passage, it can be inferred that
    (A) fairs are limited to holidays and weekends.
    (B) fairs are held all over the world.
    (C) fairs are not as popular as they once were.
    (D) fairs are good for training lawyers.

22. Which of the following is closest in meaning to the word "commodity" as used in line 5 of the passage?
    (A) A worn-out piece of clothing.
    (B) A small table used in a bed room
    (C) A transportable article of trade
    (D) A machine for the making of yarn

23. It can be implied that all of the following are trade fairs EXCEPT
    (A) the Paris Flea Market.
    (B) the New York Boat Show.
    (C) the Edinburgh Book Fair.
    (D) the Cannes Film Festival.

24. According to the passage, what did the rules of fairs eventually become?
    (A) The measurements used all over the world
    (B) The basis of European business law
    (C) The first amusement parks and recreational areas
    (D) The requirements for international trade

25. Which of the following is the closest in meaning to the word "linens" as used in line 21 of the passage?
    (A) Bedsheets and tablecloths made from flax
    (B) Underwear and other clothing that are worn next to the skin
    (C) Woolen shirts, skirts, hats, and overcoats
    (D) Slippers worn at home after getting ready for bed

26. What is the main idea of the passage?
    (A) Fairs that promote the arts, industries, and professions have been found all over the world.
    (B) Fairs are limited to exhibitors who want to make a lot of money.
    (C) Fairs are celebrations of holidays and religious observances.
    (D) Fairs bring many different cultures together an encourage violence and thievery.

27. Where can the following sentence best be added to the passage?

    Elizabethan playwright Ben Jonson wrote a comedy about the famous English fair held on St. Bartholomew's Day.

    (A) At the end of paragraph 1
    (B) At the end of paragraph 2
    (C) At the beginning of paragraph 3
    (D) At the end of paragraph 3

28. According to the passage, why did the Chinese and Aztec fairs succeed?
    (A) They were open on weekends all year.
    (B) They were the only places one could buy food.
    (C) They were located on major trade routes.
    (D) They were run by honest managers.

29. According to the passage, who were the first Europeans to see the Great Aztec Fair?
    (A) French explorers
    (B) Spanish explorers
    (C) Russian explorers
    (D) English explorers

30. According to the passage, what are fairs sometimes called in America today?
    (A) Family reunions
    (B) Professional conventions
    (C) Basketball tournaments
    (D) Flea markets

Questions 31–40 refer to the following passage.

Line The Marquis de Lafayette, who was born in France in 1757, was an aristocrat who fought with the American colonists against the British in the American Revolution. Later, by allying himself (5) with the revolutionary bourgeoisie, he became one of the most powerful men in France during the first few years of the French Revolution.

Born into an ancient noble family, Lafayette had already inherited an immense fortune by the time (10) he married the daughter of the influential Duc d'Ayen in 1774. He joined the circle of young courtiers at the court of King Louis XVI, but soon aspired to win glory as a soldier.

In July 1777, twenty-seven months after the out- (15) break of the American Revolution, he arrived in Philadelphia. Appointed a major general by the colonists, he developed a training program for the inexperienced farmers and tradesmen who made up the small American army. He also struck up a (20) lasting friendship with the American commander in chief, George Washington. Lafayette fought with distinction at the Battle of Brandywine, Pennsylvania, on September 11, 1777, and, as a division commander, he conducted a masterly retreat from (25) Barren Hill on May 28, 1778.

Returning to France early in 1779, he helped persuade the government of Louis XVI to send a 6,000-man expeditionary army to aid the colonists. Lafayette arrived back in America in April 1780 (30) and was immediately given command of an army in Virginia. After forcing the British commander Lord Charles Cornwallis to retreat across Virginia, Lafayette entrapped him at Yorktown in late July. A French fleet and several additional American (35) armies joined the siege, and on October 19, Cornwallis surrendered. The British cause was lost. Lafayette was hailed as "the Hero of Two Worlds," and on returning to France in 1782 he was promoted to the rank of brigadier general.

31. Which of the following is the closest in meaning to the word "aristocrat" as used in line 2 of the passage?
    (A) A member of a corporation's management
    (B) A member of a hereditary ruling class
    (C) A member of an exclusive club
    (D) A member of a secret society

32. According to the passage, how did Lafayette become one of the most powerful men in France?
    (A) By joining the American army during the American Revolution
    (B) By marrying the daughter of a highly influential nobleman
    (C) By becoming an ally of the revolutionary middle class in France
    (D) By training American soldiers to fight in the French Revolution

33. From the passage it can be inferred that when Lafayette got married,
    (A) he was a very rich aristocrat.
    (B) he was a major general in the American army.
    (C) he was a cadet at the French military academy.
    (D) he was a close friend of Louis XVI.

34. Which of the following is the closest in meaning to the word "aspired" as used in lines 13–14 of the passage?
    (A) To seek support from aristocrats
    (B) To sweat heavily for a long time
    (C) To have ambition for success
    (D) To look for a rich woman to marry

35. According to the passage, what did Lafayette do when he joined the American army in 1777?
    (A) He aspired to glory as a soldier.
    (B) He became a courtier at the court of Louis XVI.
    (C) He developed a training program for the army.
    (D) He married the daughter of George Washington.

36. According to the passage, where did Lafayette lead American troops as a division commander?
    (A) At the Battle of Philadelphia
    (B) At Barren Hill
    (C) At the Battle of Brandywine
    (D) At the Battle of Yorktown

37. Why did Lafayette return to France in 1779?
    (A) To develop a training program for the French Army
    (B) To become a brigadier general in the French army and fight the British
    (C) To help overthrow the king of France and organize a new government
    (D) To persuade the king to send a French Expeditionary force to America

38. Lafayette held all the following positions of responsibility EXCEPT
    (A) Brigadier General in the French army.
    (B) Army commander in Virginia.
    (C) Division commander of the American army.
    (D) Ambassador to the United States.

39. Where can the following sentence best be added to the passage?

    After a little more than 14 years since the Declaration of Independence, the Americans were free with the help of their French allies.

    (A) After the phrase "American Revolution" in paragraph 1
    (B) After "1774" in paragraph 2
    (C) After the phrase "small American army" in paragraph 3
    (D) After the phrase "The British cause was lost" in paragraph 4

40. Which of the following is the closest in meaning to the word "hailed" as used in line 37 of the passage?
    (A) Called
    (B) Saluted
    (C) Requested
    (D) Condemned

Questions 41–50 are based on the following passage.

Line George Eastman changed photography when he introduced roll film. In 1888, he introduced the Kodak camera, the first camera that was simple and portable enough to be used by large numbers *5* of amateur photographers. The camera was sold with film sealed inside and the whole unit was mailed back to Rochester for film processing and replacement. In 1900, Eastman introduced the less-expensive Brownie, a simple box camera with a *10* removable film container, so that the whole unit no longer needed to be sent back to the plant.

In following years, the company continued to produce innovations for the amateur photographer. Kodak was the first to make home-movie equip- *15* ment and an easy-to-use color slide film, Kodachrome. In 1889, Eastman introduced transparent film and in 1892, he reorganized the business as the Eastman Kodak Company. Eight years later, he introduced the Brownie camera, intended *20* for use by children. It sold for one dollar. By 1927, Eastman Kodak had a virtual monopoly of the photographic industry in the United States, and it has continued to be one of the largest American companies in its field.

25 Eastman gave away half his fortune in 1924. His gifts, which totaled more than $75,000,000, went to such beneficiaries as the University of Rochester (of which the Eastman School of Music is a part) and the Massachusetts Institute of Technology. He *30* was also one of the first owners to introduce profit sharing as an employee incentive. Eastman died in 1932, but the company continues to develop new imaging products, including digital cameras and copiers.

41. What does the passage mainly discuss?
    (A) How George Eastman promoted photography for professional portraitists
    (B) How George Eastman changed photography and business management practices
    (C) How George Eastman manufactured expensive equipment for wealthy Americans
    (D) How George Eastman created and marketed the Polaroid Camera for Europe and Asia

42. According to the passage, why was the first Kodak camera a successful product?
    (A) It was simple enough to be used by almost everyone who wanted to take pictures.
    (B) It became fashionable through excellent advertising practices.
    (C) It took color slides for projectors that were sold by Thomas Edison's company.
    (D) It didn't have to be sent back to the plant for repairs and film processing.

43. What does the word "unit" as used in line 6 of the passage refer to?
    (A) The camera
    (B) The film
    (C) The mail
    (D) The processing

44. According to the passage, what new product did Eastman introduce in 1900?
    (A) Roll film
    (B) The Brownie camera
    (C) Transparent film
    (D) Digital cameras

45. Which of the following is the closest in meaning to the word "monopoly" as used in line 21 of the passage?
    (A) Single company executive who is in charge of all aspects of the organization
    (B) Complete control of the manufacture, distribution, and sale of a product
    (C) Individual department within a multinational corporation
    (D) Unified manufacture of a product by several companies

46. According to the passage, how much of Eastman's personal fortune did he give away?
    (A) More than $10 million
    (B) More than $25 million
    (C) More than $50 million
    (D) More than $75 million

47. Which of the following is the closest in meaning to the word "beneficiaries" as used in line 27 of the passage?
    (A) Charities that are legally allowed to receive contributions
    (B) Unemployed people who receive money from charities
    (C) People or organizations that receive money as a gift from someone's estate
    (D) Universities who use the money for scholarships for poor students

48. What group was the Brownie camera intended for?
    (A) Children
    (B) University students
    (C) Professional photographers
    (D) Film directors

49. What employment benefit did George Eastman begin?
    (A) Paid vacations
    (B) Profit sharing
    (C) Employee discounts
    (D) Scholarships to universities

50. Where can the following sentence best be added to the passage?

    When families received their developed pictures from Eastman, they quickly pasted them into photograph albums that became family heirlooms.

    (A) After the word "replacement" in paragraph 1
    (B) After the word "Kodachrome" in paragraph 2
    (C) At the end of paragraph 3
    (D) After the word "Technology" in paragraph 4

WRITING SECTION

You have 30 minutes to complete this assignment. Make sure you time yourself during this assignment. Read the topic below and then make any notes that will help you plan your response. Then, type your response on your computer or write your answer on one side of the paper that you use.

Topic:

Which would you rather do, work for yourself or for an employer? Use specific reasons to explain your choice.

Answer Key for Day 28

Listening

1.	B	14.	C
2.	A	15.	D
3.	C	16.	C
4.	D	17.	B
5.	D	18.	A
6.	B	19.	D
7.	D	20.	B
8.	C	21.	C
9.	B	22.	D
10.	A	23.	B
11.	A	24.	C
12.	C	25.	A
13.	B		

Structure

1.	B	14.	A
2.	A	15.	D
3.	D	16.	A
4.	C	17.	C
5.	D	18.	D
6.	A	19.	B
7.	B	20.	B
8.	C	21.	A
9.	D	22.	B
10.	A	23.	C
11.	D	24.	B
12.	A	25.	D
13.	C		

Reading

1.	A	26.	A
2.	C	27.	B
3.	D	28.	C
4.	B	29.	B
5.	C	30.	D
6.	B	31.	B
7.	D	32.	C
8.	D	33.	A
9.	C	34.	C
10.	C	35.	C
11.	B	36.	B
12.	A	37.	D
13.	B	38.	D
14.	B	39.	D
15.	C	40.	B
16.	C	41.	B
17.	A	42.	A
18.	D	43.	A
19.	C	44.	B
20.	C	45.	B
21.	B	46.	D
22.	C	47.	C
23.	A	48.	A
24.	B	49.	B
25.	A	50.	A

ESSAY

You must choose one of the choices given in the essay topic: write about being self-employed or about working for an employer. Your notes and outline must include your ideas. Self-employment means independence, setting your own hours, deciding who your clients will be, getting all the benefits of your work, etc. Working for an employer means being part of team, being responsible only for your portion of the business process, having job security with an employer who is responsible for getting clients, designing the goods and services of which you help produce, etc.

DAY 28—SCRIPT FOR TIMED TESTS

Part A—Short Conversations

(Narrator): Directions: In this section, you will hear conversations between two people. After each conversation, you will be asked several questions about what you heard, and you will see the questions printed here with four answer choices. Choose an answer and mark it either in the book or on a separate sheet of scrap paper. Remember to answer the questions based on what is stated or implied by the speakers.

1. *(Man):* Well, how does it feel to be on the losing soccer team?

   (Woman): You really know how to rub salt in the wound.

   (Narrator): What does the woman mean?

2. *(Woman):* How's the new math class going for you?

   (Man): Oh, we're off to a running start.

   (Narrator): What does the man mean?

3. *(Man):* I hope you didn't pay any attention to those terrible things Janet said to you.

   (Woman): They went in one ear and out the other.

   (Narrator): What did the woman mean?

4. *(Man):* Did you see the way Ronnie played soccer?

   (Woman): It's only a game. Don't make a mountain out of a molehill.

   (Narrator): What does the woman mean?

5. *(Man):* That new rock group is sensational. I just bought three of their recordings.

(Woman): Well, I guess I'm just not with it.

(Narrator): What does the woman imply?

6. *(Woman):* I heard that Dean Walters is going to resign. What do you know about it?

(Man): I've been out of circulation for the last few days.

(Narrator): What does the man imply?

7. *(Woman):* Dorian was arrested for dangerous driving and is in big trouble.

(Man): Well, his wealthy parents will get the police to sweep it all under the carpet.

(Narrator): What does the man imply?

8. *(Man):* This book is only 20 pages long, and it tells me the story and all about the characters and meaning of *War and Peace*.

(Woman): Well, when you take the exam, remember, "A little learning is a dangerous thing."

(Narrator): What does the woman mean?

9. *(Woman):* How did you do in the interview for student assistant?

(Man): Oh, no! It totally slipped my mind!

(Narrator): What does the man imply?

10. *(Man):* The supermarket was completely out of frozen pizza.

(Woman): That's okay. We can make it from scratch.

(Narrator): What does the woman mean?

Part B—Long Conversations and Lectures

(Narrator): Directions: In this section, you will hear Long Conversations and Lectures. After each, you will be asked several questions about what you heard, and you will see the questions printed here with four answer choices. Choose an answer and mark it either in the book or on a separate sheet of scrap paper. Remember to answer the questions based on what is stated or implied by the speakers.

(Narrator): **Questions 11–15.** Listen to two students discuss the student newspaper.

(Man): So, Teresa, how long have you been with the paper?

(Woman): Oh, this is my first day. I'm hoping the editor will make me a reporter.

(Man): Me, too. This is my first day here. Have you done any journalism at all?

(Woman): Well, I was editor for my high school newspaper, and that was a good preparation for this. I know I have a lot to learn, but I feel confident I can become a good reporter.

(Man): Yeah. I worked on my high-school paper, too. And during the summer, I was an intern for my hometown paper. They let me edit some stories and go with reporters while they interviewed people and got information. I really like this work, but I think the editor will start both of us at the bottom. No reporting, just running errands, helping with page layout, that sort of thing.

(Woman): Yeah, you're right. This paper has won so many awards, and the Journalism Department has produced several important reporters and editors. What kind of reporter do you want to be?

(Man): I want to cover international news. I'm good with languages, and I want to see what causes all those wars. Maybe I can get a job with a big paper and run one of their offices abroad.

(Woman): I want to go into sports journalism. I know, it's not the usual thing for a woman, but women are moving into areas that used to be closed to them. I know a lot about sports. I come from a family of sports fanatics. My father was a pitcher for the New York Yankees.

(Narrator):

11. How long have the man and woman worked on the student newspaper?
12. Where did the man and woman get their first newspaper experience?
13. What did the man's hometown paper let him do?
14. What kind of reporting does the man want to do?
15. What is the probable cause of the woman's interest in sports journalism?

(Narrator): **Questions 16–20.** Listen to an archeology professor speak to his class about Stonehenge.

(Man): Stonehenge was built around 3100 B.C.E., and it is a monumental circular setting of large standing stones surrounded by an earthwork. The Stonehenge that visitors see today is a ruin, and many of its original stones were removed from the site by medieval and early modern builders. It certainly occupies a place in our imaginations. Movies have used it for a setting. Even Laurence Olivier used it as the setting of his television production of *King Lear*.

The monument is mostly circular in plan. On the outside is a circular ditch, with a bank immediately within it. On the northeast part of the ring is an entrance gap that opens to a straight path called the Avenue. At the center of the circle is a stone setting consisting of a horseshoe-shaped arrangement of tall upright stones. This horseshoe arrangement is by more tall upright stones, all originally capped by horizontal stones in a post-and-lintel arrangement.

No one knows why Stonehenge was built, though it was probably meant to be a place of worship of some kind. Popular ideas are that it was built as a temple for Druids or Romans. But this not likely, because neither were in the area until long after Stonehenge was completed. Early in the twentieth century, the English astronomer Sir Joseph Norman Lockyer demonstrated that the northeast axis of the ring lined up with the sunrise at the Summer Solstice, which caused some scholars to speculate that the builders were sun worshipers. In 1963, an American astronomer, Gerald Hawkins, suggested that Stonehenge was a complicated computer for predicting lunar and solar eclipses.

Whatever the reasons for its existence, the techniques used to construct Stonehenge give us an insight into the social structure and technology of the early Britons.

(Narrator):

16. When was Stonehenge built?
17. Why are many of the original stones missing?
18. Why was Stonehenge probably built?
19. When does the northeast axis of the ring line up with the sunrise?
20. What is the professor probably going to discuss next?

(Narrator): **Questions 21–25.** Listen to a lecture on René Descartes.

(Woman): René Descartes, born March 31, 1596, died Feb. 11, 1650, and is called the father of modern philosophy.

He completely separated the mind and the body, and his axiom "I think, therefore I am" is his most famous formulation. In March 1619, he first described the idea of a unitary universal science that linked all possible human knowledge together into an all-embracing wisdom. On November 10, according to Descartes, a visionary dream revealed the nature of this science more clearly. This dream remains controversial.

Descartes moved from place to place until 1628, when he moved to Holland, where he lived until 1649. During this period in Holland, he composed the works that made him famous in his own time and influenced succeeding ages. In 1637, he finished *Discourse on Method*, his most widely read book. In that book, Descartes sets forth four rules for the pursuit of knowledge. First, accept nothing as true unless clearly recognized as such. Second, solve problems systematically by analyzing them part by part. Third, proceed from the simple to the more complex considerations. Fourth, review everything thoroughly to make sure that you haven't missed anything.

Also, in the *Discourse*, Descartes presents some basic ideas that he later developed in his next work, *Meditations on First Philosophy*.

(Narrator):

21. According to the speaker, what is René Descartes often called?
22. When did Descartes describe the idea of a universal science?
23. Where did he live while he was writing his two most famous books?
24. In *Discourse on Method,* how many rules did he create for the pursuit of knowledge?
25. What is the speaker probably going to discuss next?

Day 29

Timed Tests

Today's Assignment

- Today, you will take your third timed test. Find a quiet place with no distractions, and set a watch or timer to keep track of the time for each section. Try to take the test with no disturbances and all at one time to better simulate an actual testing experience. Audio for this test is provided on the CD. The answers and the script for the Listening section are printed at the end of this chapter.

Before you begin, have paper and pencils ready to answer the questions and write your essay.

The schedule for these practice test is as follows:

1. *Listening*
2. *Structure* (Set your alarm clock to sound 25 minutes after you begin working on this section.)
3. Take a 10-minute break after you have completed the Structure section.
4. *Reading.* (Set your alarm clock to sound 80 minutes after you begin working on this section.)
5. *Writing your essay.* (Set your alarm clock to sound 30 minutes after you begin working on this section)

Notice that the time you will spend taking the actual test is much longer than the time you will use taking these practice tests. When you take the actual test, you may answer questions that ETS is trying out for the first time. This will take time, but you will not be scored on your answers. Also, you may be given a test that has more questions than these practice tests. And you will be taken through tutorials that show you how to use the computer during the actual tests.

Do not check your answers until you have completed this practice test.

LISTENING

Part A—Short Conversations

You may now begin listening to track 5 on the CD.

Directions: In this section, you will hear conversations between two people. After each conversation, you will be asked several questions about what you heard, and you will see the questions printed here with four answer choices. Choose an answer and mark it either in the book or on a separate sheet of scrap paper. Remember to answer the questions based on what is stated or implied by the speakers.

1. What does the woman mean?
   (A) She has no idea why the student center was closed.
   (B) She has the same number of guesses as the man does.
   (C) She has an idea but doesn't want to tell the man.
   (D) She has a friend at the student center.

2. What can be inferred from the man's statement?
   (A) The woman is going to move soon.
   (B) The woman wants to teach primary school.
   (C) The woman was the most important organizer of the club.
   (D) The woman used primary numbers at the first meeting.

3. What does the woman mean?
   (A) The man will graduate only if he takes a course in road construction.
   (B) The man will graduate regardless of the elective course he selects.
   (C) The man will graduate if he takes the course in Roman history.
   (D) The man will graduate if he takes neither elective course.

4. What does the man mean?
   (A) He is playing cards and can't talk now.
   (B) He doesn't know anything about Chicago.
   (C) He is going to give her the back of his hand.
   (D) He can tell the woman anything she needs to know.

5. What does the man mean?
   (A) Robert has personal experience in building maintenance.
   (B) Robert is nuts about working for his father.
   (C) Robert won't work for anyone but a maintenance company.
   (D) Robert didn't want the job as maintenance assistant.

6. What does the woman mean?
   (A) She got very little sleep last night.
   (B) She disagrees with the man.
   (C) She put the movies on videotape.
   (D) She is always bored in history class.

7. What does the woman mean?
   (A) The students don't like the professor.
   (B) The students enjoy the meals the professor prepares.
   (C) The students happily do everything the professor wants.
   (D) The students have meals with the professor every day.

8. What does the woman mean?
   (A) People thought Darwin's ideas insulted their beliefs.
   (B) People thought Darwin's ideas were old fashioned.
   (C) People thought Darwin's ideas would help humans learn to fly.
   (D) People thought Darwin's ideas were ahead of their time.

9. What does the man mean?
   (A) His professor read his paper again.
   (B) His professor wanted him to write about riots.
   (C) His professor liked his exam very much.
   (D) His professor severely reprimanded him.

10. What does the woman mean?
   (A) Paul McCartney spoke for only a short time.
   (B) Paul McCartney spoke to a large audience.
   (C) Paul McCartney spoke about sardines.
   (D) Paul McCartney spoke in a cannery.

Part B—Long Conversations and Lectures

Directions: In this section, you will hear Long Conversations and Lectures. After each, you will be asked several questions about what you heard, and you will see the questions printed here with four answer choices. Choose an answer and mark it either in the book or on a separate sheet of scrap paper. Remember to answer the questions based on what is stated or implied by the speakers.

Questions 11–15. Listen to two students discuss a famous British writer.

On the screen, you will see the words "British Literature."

11. What is a barrister?
   (A) A clerk in a lawyer's office
   (B) A man who serves drinks in a prison
   (C) A lawyer that represent clients in court
   (D) A factory worker in prison

12. What was Charles Dickens' first writing job?
   (A) Prison interviewer
   (B) Factory manager
   (C) Magazine editor
   (D) Newspaper reporter

13. What was his first piece of published fiction?
   (A) *The Pickwick Papers*
   (B) *Children of the Street*
   (C) *Serious Work*
   (D) *Growing Up in a Factory*

14. How was his first piece of fiction published?
   (A) As a two-volume book
   (B) As a twenty-part serial
   (C) As a magazine
   (D) As a newspaper column

15. What does the woman compare *Oliver Twist* to?
   (A) American novels about rich families
   (B) American novels about children
   (C) American novels about juvenile delinquents
   (D) American novels about lawyers and their clients

Questions 16–20. Listen to a lecture about the animals of the Serengeti Plain.

On the screen, you will see the words "Ecology and Conservation" and a picture of a map of Eastern Africa, with Serengeti Plain indicated.

16. What is the Serengeti Plain famous for?
    (A) Its forests and mountains
    (B) Its huge herds of plains animals
    (C) Its facilities for tourists
    (D) Its history of nature untouched by humans

17. How do the animals migrate to Lake Victoria?
    (A) Along the so-called "western corridor"
    (B) Inside the animal park
    (C) Next to the marshes of the Mara River
    (D) Through the acacia woodlands

18. Why have elephants moved into the Serengeti Plain?
    (A) Hyenas chase elephant herds away from their usual grazing land.
    (B) Elephants have been slaughtered for their ivory.
    (C) Humans have developed farms and settlements.
    (D) Lions have attacked herds and killed baby elephants.

19. According to the speaker, what animals have become virtually extinct?
    (A) The spotted hyenas
    (B) The alligator
    (C) The domestic dog
    (D) The black rhinoceros

20. What will the speaker probably discuss next?
    (A) Books and movies about the Serengeti Plain
    (B) Development of the Plain for farmers and factory owners
    (C) Programs to sell the ivory from slaughtered elephants
    (D) Methods to protect the animals now in the Plain

Questions 21–25. Listen to a lecture about the Taj Mahal.

On the screen, you will see the words "History of India" and a picture of the Taj Mahal.

21. Why was the Taj Mahal built?
    (A) To bring European building techniques to India
    (B) To honor the emperor's wife, Mumtaz Mahal
    (C) To unite the empires of India and Persia
    (D) To provide a mosque for the people of India

22. According to the speaker, what did the emperor's wife do that was remarkable?
    (A) She designed and constructed several minarets.
    (B) She had many children and taught them to read the Koran.
    (C) She traveled to Europe and Persia.
    (D) She accompanied her husband onto battlefields during war.

23. How many elements does the design of the Taj Mahal have?
    (A) Five
    (B) Six
    (C) Seven
    (D) Eight

24. According to the speaker, where did the construction workers come from?
    (A) China, India, and Thailand
    (B) Persia, the Ottoman Empire, and Europe
    (C) Japan, Persia, and Egypt
    (D) Persia, Thailand, and Pakistan

25. Where did Shah Jahan die?
    (A) In the Taj Mahal
    (B) In his wife's mausoleum
    (C) In prison
    (D) In a minaret

STOP

DO NOT MOVE ON TO THE STRUCTURE SECTION UNTIL YOU HAVE SET YOUR ALARM CLOCK TO SOUND 25 MINUTES AFTER YOU HAVE BEGUN THE STRUCTURE SECTION.

STRUCTURE

Set your alarm clock to sound after 25 minutes. Complete both sentence completion and error identification sections before going on to the reading section. Do NOT go on to the reading section until the alarm has sounded and you have taken a 10-minute break.

Sentence Completion

During the actual test, you will see on your monitor screen an incomplete sentence with four answer choices under it. You will choose the answer that makes the sentence correct when placed in the blank. Beside each answer choice, you will see an empty oval. To mark your choice, you will move your mouse to the oval next to your answer choice. When you click the oval, it becomes black.

For these practice tests, circle the letter of the answer choice that you think makes the sentence correct.

Now, begin answering the questions.

1. When the Moon comes between the sun and the Earth during the day, _______ because sunlight is blocked.
   (A) it has become dark
   (B) it won't become dark
   (C) it became dark
   (D) it will become dark

2. Zane Grey, the prolific writer who created the western as a literary genre, _______ in New York City from 1898 to 1904.
   (A) trained as a dentist and practices
   (B) trains as a dentist and practiced
   (C) trained as a dentist and practiced
   (D) was training as a dentist and was practicing

3. After Louis XIII began wearing a wig in 1624, the wig industry was established in France the following year _______ a wigmakers guild.
   (A) by the formation of
   (B) by the formulation of
   (C) by the forms of
   (D) by the form of

4. To avoid taxation and other conflicts with state governments, _______ the District of Columbia as the site for the Capitol of the United States in 1790.
   (A) Congress chooses
   (B) Congress choice
   (C) Congress chose
   (D) Congress has chosen

5. _______ originated with Hawaiians who wove necklaces of flowers, leaves or ferns, or sometimes strung dried shells, fruits, beads, or bright feathers for personal adornment.
   (A) The custom for wearing leis
   (B) The custom of wearing leis
   (C) The custom to wearing leis
   (D) The custom in wearing leis

6. By the time _______ from Harvard University, his first collection of poems, *Color*, had already been published to critical acclaim.
   (A) Countee Cullen received his M.(A)
   (B) Countee Cullen was receiving his M.(A)
   (C) Countee Cullen had received his M.(A)
   (D) Countee Cullen receives his M.(A)

7. Needlefish are quick moving carnivores distinguished by long, slender jaws _______.
   (A) equipment with sharp teeth.
   (B) equipped with sharp teeth.
   (C) equips with sharp teeth.
   (D) equipping with sharp teeth.

8. Drawing is often a preliminary stage before working in a more substantial medium, such as _______, sculpture, or architecture.
   (A) paint
   (B) painted
   (C) painter
   (D) painting

9. A healthy human heart contains its own electrical conducting system capable ________ and the order of cardiac contractions.
   (A) to control both the rate
   (B) of controlled both the rate
   (C) of control both the rate
   (D) of controlling both the rate

10. To defend itself and to capture prey, the electric catfish generates ________ of up to 450 volts of electricity.
    (A) the electric discharge
    (B) an electric discharge
    (C) electric discharge
    (D) a electric discharge

Error Identification

In the following questions, four words or groups of words are underlined. Circle the letter under the word or group of words that need to be changed for the sentence to be correct.

11. Aqua Regia was given its name, which meant
    A B
    "royal water," because of its ability to dissolve
    C D
    gold.

12. Upper Egypt consist of the entire Nile River valley
    A
    from Cairo south to Lake Nasser, which is
    B C
    formed by the Aswan High Dam.
    D

13. If a town or village in the nineteenth century had
    A
    not had a blacksmith, horses would not have been
    B
    shod, and farm implements were not repaired.
    C D

14. Ellery Queen was the pen name of Daniel Nathan
    A B
    and Manford Lepofsky, who were cousins
    were born in Brooklyn and wrote more than
    C D
    35 detective novels.

15. The weight of a framed building is carried by a
    A
    skeleton or framework, as opposed to supported
    B C
    by walls.
    D

16. European craftsmen in the eighteenth century used japanning, a process for finishing wood,
    A B
    leather, tin, and papier-mâché in imitating of the
    C
    celebrated lacquerwork of the Japanese.
    D

17. Relating to the raccoon, the coati has
    A
    a long, flexible snout and a slender, darkly banded
    B C
    tail that it often carries erect as it moves about.
    D

18. The Olmecs art first appeared at about 1150 B.C.E.
    A
    when their craftsmen carved colossal heads that
    B
    have characteristic flat face, thickened lips, and
    C D
    helmetlike headgear.

19. The red fox, generally considered carnivore, is
    A B
    actually omnivorous and enjoys fruits and berries.
    C D

20. Op art painters devise complex and paradoxical
    A
    optical spaces through the manipulate of simple
    B C
    repetitive forms such as parallel lines, checker-
    D
    board patterns, and concentric circles.

21. The La Brea tar pit are found in Los Angeles and
    A
    contain the fossilized skulls and bones of
    B
    prehistoric animals that became entrapped in the
    C
    sticky seepage of the pits.
    D

22. The Scottish architect and designer who transforms
    A
    Palladian Neoclassicism in England into an airy,
    B C
    light, elegant style was Robert Adam.
    D

23. Cud-chewing animals, such as cattle, sheep, and
    A
    goat, convert large quantities of grass and hay into
    B C
    meat, milk, and wool.
    D

24. A fish's gill is a branched or feathery tissue richly
    A
    supplied with blood vessels that facilitates the
    B
    exchange of oxygen and carbon dioxide with the
    C D
    surrounding water.

25. Bill Veeck, who believed that baseball's
    A
    primary function should be to entertain, became
    B
    disillusioning with what he regarded as an
    C D
    increased emphasis on baseball as a business.

This is the end of the structure section. Take a 10-minute break before you begin the reading section.

READING

There are 5 reading passages. You should take no more than 80 minutes to complete the reading portion of these exercises.

In the actual test, you will click on your answers with the computer mouse. In the practice test, you will use a pencil or pen to circle your answer choices or write them on a separate sheet of paper.

Set your alarm clock to sound 80 minutes (1 hour and 20 minutes) after you begin this section. Do not check your answers until you have completed the entire practice test.

Questions 1–10 refer to the following passage.

Line The North American porcupine is a heavy-set, quill-bearing rodent found in the woods from Canada to northern Mexico. It is about 29 inches long, with a thick, muscular tail. The quills, which (5) are modified hairs, are stiff, barbed spines about three inches long. They are white, tipped with black, and are interspersed among the dark, coarse guard hairs of the back and tail.

When approached, the North American porcupine (10) presents its rear to the enemy, and if it is attacked, it drives its powerful tail against the assailant. The quills are easily detached from its skin and remain embedded in the attacker. The animal does not throw its quills, but some may become detached (15) when the porcupine shakes itself.

The North American porcupine is a solitary, but not antisocial, animal. It shows a preference for eating the tender layer of tissue beneath the bark of trees and at times completely girdles, and thus (20) kills, trees. It may also gnaw used ax handles, canoe paddles, and other items for the salt and oil they contain. The porcupine breeds in fall or early winter, and the female bears one or two young, born with soft quills, about seven months later. In (25) forests of Mexico are found tree porcupines that have prehensile-tails that aid them while climbing through tree branches.

The African crested porcupine is found in Europe and Africa. This species is about 35 inches long (30) and weighs about 60 pounds. It has two types of quills: long, flexible, usually white, quills up to 35 cm long and shorter, stout quills banded with black or brown. The African and certain other crested porcupines have long neck and shoulder quills (35) they can erect to form a crest.

1. Which answer choice does the word "They" in line 6 refer to?
   (A) Porcupines
   (B) Tails
   (C) Quills
   (D) Guards

2. According to the passage, where do North American porcupines live?
   (A) In Mexican forests
   (B) In trees along lake shores
   (C) In woods from Canada to northern Mexico
   (D) In the Canadian Rockies

3. What is the size of a North American porcupine?
   (A) About 9 inches long
   (B) About 12 inches long
   (C) About 16 inches long
   (D) About 29 inches long

4. Which of the following is the closest in meaning to the word "interspersed" as used in line 7 of the passage?
   (A) Scattered among other things
   (B) Blocked from moving
   (C) Estimated
   (D) Traveled a long distance

5. In the passage, it can be inferred that quills remain embedded in the skin of a porcupine's enemy, because
   (A) they are modified hairs.
   (B) they are barbed.
   (C) they are three inches long.
   (D) they are white, tipped with black.

6. Which of the following is the closest in meaning to the word "antisocial" as used in line 17 of the passage?
   (A) Dislikes contact with others
   (B) Hates parties
   (C) Wants to be first in line
   (D) Avoids traps and snares

7. According to the passage, what does the porcupine prefer to eat?
   (A) The bark of hardwood trees
   (B) The layer of tissue under tree bark
   (C) The branches of Mexican trees
   (D) The leaves and roots of trees

8. According to the passage, why does the porcupine gnaw on used ax handles and canoe paddles?
   (A) For the wood they are made of
   (B) For the salt and oil they contain
   (C) For the varnish and paint on them
   (D) For the lack of other food

9. Where can the following sentence best be added to the passage?

   Although porcupines are usually spotted as they move about the forest floor, they have been seen up in trees.

   (A) After the phrase "muscular tail" in paragraph 1
   (B) After the phrase "the attacker" in paragraph 2
   (C) After the phrase "seven months later" in paragraph 3
   (D) After the phrase "60 pounds" in paragraph 4

10. From the passage, it can be inferred that the African crested porcupine
   (A) is not as vicious as the North American porcupine.
   (B) is more beautiful than the North American porcupine.
   (C) is twice as dangerous as the North American porcupine.
   (D) is much bigger than the North American porcupine.

Questions 11–20 refer to the following passage.

Line

Wagon trains are not the invention of Hollywood screenwriters but were actual caravans of wagons organized by settlers in the United States for emigration to the West during the late eighteenth and *(5)* most of the nineteenth centuries. Composed of up to 100 Conestoga wagons, which were sometimes called prairie schooners, wagon trains soon became the prevailing mode of long-distance overland transportation for both people and goods. *(10)* Wagon-train transportation moved westward with the advancing frontier.

The nineteenth century saw the development of such famous roads as the Santa Fe Trail, the Oregon Trail, the Smoky Hill Trail, and the Southern *(15)* Overland Mail route. It was, however, in transit westward over the Oregon-California Trail that the wagon trains attained their most highly organized and institutionalized character. Meeting in early spring at a rendezvous town, perhaps near the Mis- *(20)* souri River, the groups would form companies, elect officers, employ guides, and collect essential supplies while awaiting favorable weather, usually in May. The companies had to be prepared for such challenges as crossing rivers and mountains *(25)* and meeting hostile Indians. Those riding in the wagons were directed and protected by a few on horseback.

Once organized and on their way, wagon-train companies tended to follow a fairly fixed daily *(30)* routine. At about 4 a.m., people would get up, eat breakfast, check their equipment, and hitch their animals to the wagons. At 7 a.m., they would leave their temporary camp site and begin the day's trek. Nine hours later, at about 4 p.m., the wagon train *(35)* would stop and people would make camp, cook the evening meal, and take care of chores while the animals grazed. Often, there were community sings and brief dances before everyone retired for the night. Then, the routine was repeated the next *(40)* morning.

Wagon-train migrations are more widely known and written about than wagon freighting, which also played an essential role in an expanding America. Teamsters, best known as bullwhackers
45 or muleskinners, conducted commercial operations on a more or less fixed two-way schedule until replaced by the railroad and the truck.

11. What is the main idea of the passage?
    (A) A wagon train was a relaxing way to see the western part of North America.
    (B) Wagon trains were not only a way to go west, they were social and self-defense groups, too.
    (C) A wagon train would travel about 4 miles during the winter.
    (D) Wagon trains were the fictional dream of Hollywood movie makers.

12. According to the passage, what kind of wagons were used during the move west?
    (A) Conestoga Wagons
    (B) Missouri Wagons
    (C) Oregon Wagons
    (D) Santa Fe Wagons

13. Which of the following is closest in meaning to the word "rendezvous" as used in line 19 of the passage?
    (A) Village built on the French model
    (B) Site selected in advance for a meeting
    (C) Trading post for Indians and settlers
    (D) Town in a river valley

14. According to the passage, when did most wagon trains begin their journey west?
    (A) March
    (B) April
    (C) May
    (D) June

15. Who protected those riding in the wagons?
    (A) Companies with an institutional character
    (B) Friendly Indian tribes
    (C) The U.S. Cavalry
    (D) Employed guides on horseback

16. According to the passage, it can be inferred that to get ready for a day's journey, it took people
    (A) about 3 hours.
    (B) about 4 hours.
    (C) about 5 hours.
    (D) about 6 hours.

17. Which of the following is the closest in meaning to the word "grazed" as used in line 37 of the passage?
    (A) Went to sleep on the ground
    (B) Drank water from a river
    (C) Ate grass on the prairie
    (D) Stood guard over the wagon train

18. After the wagon train stopped for the day, the members of the company did all of the following EXCEPT
    (A) cook the evening meal.
    (B) elect officers.
    (C) make camp.
    (D) dance and sing.

19. Which of the following is closest in meaning to the word "migrations" as used in line 41 of the passage?
    (A) Causes of terrible headaches
    (B) Organizations for transport and travel
    (C) Expressions of gratitude for sacrifices made
    (D) Movements of groups from place to place

20. According to the passage, what, besides the wagon trains, was important to the westward expansion of the United States?
    (A) The development of trails
    (B) Treaties with Indians
    (C) Wagon freighting
    (D) Rivers and mountains

Questions 21–30 refer to the following passage.

Line The game of darts began as a training program for English archers in the Middle Ages, and the game was popular with Henry VIII. In its modern form in Britain, the game is ordinarily played (5) in the public house, or pub, or in a club, rather than in the home.

Of an estimated 5 million players in the British Isles, about 25,000 are represented by the British Darts Organization, which was founded in 1973. As an (10) indication of how popular the game has become, there is also the World Darts Federation (WDF), which represents more than 500,000 darts players in 50 countries. The major championships are the Winmau World Masters, the WDF World Cup, the (15) Embassy World Professional Darts Championship, and the News of the World Championships.

In a game, a player throws a wooden, feathered dart about six inches long at a target board. The target board is usually made of sisal but is some- (20) times made of cork or elmwood. The board is divided into 20 sectors valued at points from 1 to 20.

Players throw the darts freestyle but must stand at least 7 feet 9.25 inches from the board. The center of the board is 5 feet 8 inches above the floor. (25) These and other rules may vary slightly in countries outside the British Isles.

In the organized game, each player has three weighted and feathered darts. Before the game, a number is chosen, usually 301 or 501. All players (30) begin with this score. They subtract their scores from that number until the winner reaches zero. What makes the scoring complicated is the rule that the winner must reach exactly zero on his last throw. However, in informal pub games, players (35) usually total up their scores from the start, and the player who first reaches a predetermined number is the winner.

Beginning in the 1980s, coin-operated electronic darts machines, which feature a perforated plastic (40) board and darts made entirely from plastic, gained popularity in the United States. The number of American darts players grew to an estimated 17 million in the early 1990s, and the American Darts Organization represents more than 60,000 players.

21. What is the main idea of the passage?
    (A) Darts is a simple game that children can learn and enjoy at home.
    (B) Darts is a complex game with complex rules determined by international organizations.
    (C) Darts is used by the British army to train special combat soldiers.
    (D) Darts is a professional sport that takes years to master.

22. According to the passage, how many people does the WDF represent?
    (A) 200,000
    (B) 300,000
    (C) 400,000
    (D) 500,000

23. The following are major darts championships EXCEPT
    (A) the Winmau World Masters.
    (B) the WDF World Cup.
    (C) the Americas Cup.
    (D) the Embassy World Professional Darts Championship.

24. What is the British target board usually made of?
    (A) Sisal
    (B) Cork
    (C) Elmwood
    (D) Plastic

25. It can be inferred from the passage that outside the British Isles,
    (A) players are 7 feet 9 inches from the board.
    (B) darts are 4 inches long with plastic tips.
    (C) rules vary from country to country.
    (D) people do not play darts much.

26. According to the passage, what score does each player begin with in an organized game of darts?
    (A) 1 or 20
    (B) 101 or 301
    (C) 201 or 401
    (D) 301 or 501

27. Which of the following is the closest in meaning to the word "predetermined" as used in line 36 of the passage?
    (A) Decided in advance
    (B) Allowed to begin
    (C) Forced to quit
    (D) Created spontaneously

28. Where can the following sentence best be added to the passage?

    The rules of darts show how seriously its players take the game.

    (A) At the beginning of paragraph 2
    (B) At the beginning of paragraph 3
    (C) At the beginning of paragraph 4
    (D) At the beginning of paragraph 5

29. According to the passage, what are the darts in an electronic game made of?
    (A) Wood
    (B) Plastic
    (C) Sisal
    (D) Copper

30. Which of the following is the closest in meaning to the word "perforated" as used in line 39 of the passage?
    (A) Without flaw
    (B) Pierced with holes
    (C) Covered with a silk sheet
    (D) Untouched by hands

Questions 31–40 refer to the following passage.

Line

The decorative use of ornamental feathers has been used for adornment since prehistoric times. The Anasazi Indians of North America constructed a turkey-feather and yucca-cord fabric before they (5) began using looms. Highly advanced featherwork is also found in Hawaii, New Zealand, Tahiti, and New Guinea. The brightly colored feathers of parrots, toucans, jays, and tanagers were used on headdresses, cloaks, and other ceremonial gar- (10) ments, while more common feathers were used on mats and blankets.

The feathers were overlapped and attached like shingles to a base fabric. After the Spanish conquest, bits of feathers served as backgrounds for Chris- (15) tian symbols. The pre-Columbian Indians also used feathers in connection with stone or metal jewelry as did the Chinese, Polynesians, and Eskimos.

Feathers apparently were not used much in Europe for ornamental purposes until the close of the (20) thirteenth century. Under the early Ottoman Empire, men's turbans were decorated with feathers and jewels, and during the reign of Elizabeth I, feathers began to occupy an important place as headdress ornaments for women. In the eighteenth (25) century, housewives crafted featherwork as wall hangings. White poultry feathers were dyed various colors, although those of the pheasant, pigeon, peacock, guinea fowl, and black rooster were left natural. In the nineteenth century, craftsmen cre- (30) ated feather mosaics, often realistic pictures of birds covered with their correspondingly correct feathers. These mosaics were framed and hung like paintings. Featherwork also covered fire screens, valances, and mirror frames and to fash- (35) ion muffs, masks, hats, and dress trimmings.

In the twentieth century, commercial ostrich farms have provided plumes for feather dusters, boas, and limited millinery uses. Since the seventeenth century, fishermen have made a colorful variety (40) of fishing lures with feathers. Because the hunting of birds for feathers has almost eliminated some species, restrictions are now enforced by the conservation agencies of many governments.

31. According to the passage, by the time the Anasazi Indians started using looms,
    (A) they had already made fabric using feathers.
    (B) they were using parrots for decoration.
    (C) they made ceremonial blankets with feathers.
    (D) they used common feathers on garments.

32. Which of the following is the closest in meaning to the word "adornment" as used in line 2 of the passage?
    (A) Picturing
    (B) Making colorful
    (C) Worshipping
    (D) Making beautiful

33. According to the passage, how were the feathers applied to the fabric?
    (A) They were put on the fabric with buttons.
    (B) They were woven into the fabric.
    (C) They were overlapped and attached like shingles.
    (D) They were painted and applied while wet.

34. According to the passage, all of the following people are said to have used feathers as decoration EXCEPT
    (A) the Chinese.
    (B) the French.
    (C) the British.
    (D) the Eskimos.

35. In the passage it is inferred that feathers were not used in Europe for decoration until
    (A) the close of the thirteenth century.
    (B) the Spanish conquest.
    (C) the middle of the eighteenth century.
    (D) the beginning of the fifth century B.C.E.

36. Which of the following queens of England probably used feathers in her headdress?
    (A) Mary I
    (B) Anne I
    (C) Elizabeth I
    (D) Isabella I

37. Which of the following is closest in meaning to the word "mosaics" as used in line 30 of the passage?
    (A) Paintings of birds and small animals.
    (B) Pictures made from small colored pieces.
    (C) Reproductions of religious paintings.
    (D) Floor tiles arranged in a beautiful way.

38. When did housewives make featherwork into wall hangings?
    (A) In the twelfth century
    (B) In the fourteenth century
    (C) In the sixteenth century
    (D) In the eighteenth century

39. In the passage all of the following birds are mentioned EXCEPT
    (A) peacocks.
    (B) pheasants.
    (C) penguins.
    (D) pigeons.

40. Where can the following sentence best be added to the passage?

    Inhabitants of every part of the world have decorated their possessions and themselves with feathers.

    (A) After the phrase "prehistoric times" in paragraph 1
    (B) After the phrase "base fabric" in paragraph 2
    (C) After the phrase "Thirteenth century" in paragraph 3
    (D) After the phrase "millinery uses" in paragraph 4

Questions 41–50 refer to the following passage.

Line The American film actor Clark Gable rose to fame with his creation of a rough, masterful, romantic hero—a role epitomized in his portrayal of Rhett Butler in *Gone with the Wind* (1939). The only son
5 of an itinerant oil-field worker, Gable worked at a variety of odd jobs as a youth and then joined the Ed Lilly stock company as a callboy.

Coached by his first wife, Josephine Dillon, a former actress, he played his first Broadway lead
10 in *Machinal* in 1928. Gable had played bit parts in silent films as early as 1924. With the introduction of sound films, he returned to Hollywood in 1930 and was successful in a series of gangster roles that included *The Finger Points* and *Night Nurse.*

15 Under contract with Metro-Goldwyn-Mayer studios from 1931 to 1954, he switched gradually to the light-hearted, adventurous parts for which he became famous. During the 1930s, Gable became the American ideal of virility in such pictures as
20 *Red Dust* and *Saratoga*, two of several films made with actress Jean Harlow. In *Boom Town* and *San Francisco* he costarred with the prominent actor Spencer Tracy.

In 1934, Gable won an Academy Award for his
25 performance in the now-classic comedy, *It Happened One Night*, and he was nominated for similar awards for his work in *Mutiny on the Bounty* and *Gone with the Wind.* After the death in 1942 of his third wife, the actress Carole Lombard,
30 Gable enlisted in the U.S. Army Air Corps during World War II. He reached the rank of major and won the Air Medal. He used that experience notably as an Air Corps general in *Command Decision* and as a submarine commander in *Run Silent, Run Deep*. His final film role, completed two
35 weeks before his death in 1961, was as an aging cowboy in *The Misfits.*

41. It can be inferred from the passage that the role Clark Gable is most famous for is
    (A) Rhett Butler in *Gone With the Wind.*
    (B) the gangster in *The Finger Points.*
    (C) Fletcher Christian in *Mutiny on the Bounty.*
    (D) the Air Corps general in *Command Decision.*

42. Which of the following is closest in meaning to the word "itinerant" as used in line 5 of the passage?
    (A) Highly skilled at making tools
    (B) Moving from place to place to find work
    (C) Trained to work with tin
    (D) Making sheds and crates for storage

43. According to the passage, by what year had Gable played in movies?
    (A) 1918
    (B) 1920
    (C) 1924
    (D) 1931

44. From the passage, it can be inferred that Gable appeared in many pictures with
    (A) Carole Lombard.
    (B) Josephine Dillon.
    (C) Katherine Hepburn.
    (D) Jean Harlow.

45. Which of the following is the closest in meaning to the word "virility" as used in line 19 of the passage?
    (A) Brilliance
    (B) Muscularity
    (C) Masculinity
    (D) Durability

46. How long was Gable under contract with Metro-Goldwyn-Mayer studios?
    (A) About 13 years
    (B) About 16 years
    (C) About 19 years
    (D) About 22 years

47. According to the passage, it can be inferred that Gable received a nomination for the Academy Award
    (A) three times.
    (B) four times.
    (C) five times
    (D) six times.

48. All of the following are films that Gable appeared in EXCEPT
    (A) *Red Dust.*
    (B) *Machinal.*
    (C) *Boom Town.*
    (D) *It Happened One Night.*

49. Where can the following sentence best be added to the passage?

    Like many other movie stars, such as James Stewart and Lee Marvin, Gable was often in combat.

    (A) After "(1939) in paragraph 1
    (B) After "1924" in paragraph 2
    (C) After "became famous" in paragraph 3
    (D) After "World War II" in paragraph 4

50. According to the passage, Gable played all of the following roles EXCEPT
    (A) a gangster.
    (B) a cowboy.
    (C) a small-town doctor.
    (D) an Air Corps general.

WRITING SECTION

You have 30 minutes to complete this assignment. Make sure you time yourself during this assignment. Read the topic below and then make any notes that will help you plan your response. Then type your response on your computer or write your answer on one side of the paper that you use.

Topic:

People disagree about using land for farms, housing, and industry. Some believe that this kind of land use is more important than saving land for endangered animals. Do you agree or disagree? Why or why not? Use specific reasons and examples to support your answer.

ANSWER KEY FOR DAY 29

Listening

1. A
2. C
3. B
4. D
5. A
6. B
7. C
8. A
9. D
10. B
11. C
12. D
13. A
14. B
15. C
16. B
17. A
18. C
19. D
20. D
21. B
22. D
23. A
24. B
25. C

Structure

1. D
2. C
3. A
4. C
5. B
6. A
7. B
8. D
9. D
10. B
11. B
12. A
13. D
14. B
15. C
16. C
17. A
18. D
19. B
20. C
21. A
22. A
23. B
24. B
25. C

Reading

1. C
2. C
3. D
4. A
5. B
6. A
7. B
8. B
9. C
10. D
11. B
12. A
13. B
14. B
15. C
16. D
17. A
18. B
19. D
20. C
21. B
22. D
23. C
24. A
25. C
26. D
27. A
28. C
29. B
30. B
31. A
32. D
33. C
34. B
35. A
36. C
37. B
38. D
39. C
40. A
41. A
42. B
43. C
44. D
45. C
46. A
47. A
48. B
49. D
50. C

ESSAY

Your notes and outline should have one choice: either land for endangered animals or land for mankind's use. *Not both.* Do not be fooled by the "Why or why not?" You can give reasons for your choice, but not for both choices.

DAY 29—SCRIPT FOR TIMED TESTS

LISTENING

Part A—Short Conversations

(Narrator): Directions: In this section, you will hear conversations between two people. After each conversation, you will be asked several questions about what you heard, and you will see the questions printed here with four answer choices. Choose an answer and mark it either in the book or on a separate sheet of scrap paper. Remember to answer the questions based on what is stated or implied by the speakers.

1. *(Man):* They just closed the student center without telling anybody about it. Do you know why they did that?

   (Woman): Your guess is as good as mine.

   (Narrator): What does the woman mean?

2. *(Woman):* You did a lot of work getting the science club organized.

   (Man): Yeah, but you were the prime mover.

   (Narrator): What can be inferred from the man's statement?

3. *(Man):* I have to sign up for one more elective course before I graduate. I just can't decide which one to take.

   (Woman): Well, all roads lead to Rome.

   (Narrator): What does the woman mean?

4. *(Woman):* I'm going to visit a museum in Chicago. Do you know anything about the city?

   (Man): Oh, I know it like the back of my hand.

   (Narrator): What does the man mean?

5. *(Woman):* I don't think Robert will do a good job as maintenance assistant for the dorm.

(Man): His father runs a maintenance company, so he knows the nuts and bolts of the job.

(Narrator): What does the man mean?

6. *(Man):* Those movies about Rome really enlivened history class.

(Woman): Well, they put me to sleep.

(Narrator): What does the woman mean?

7. *(Man):* How do the students like Professor Dillingham as a teacher?

(Woman): She has all of us eating out of her hand.

(Narrator): What does the woman mean?

8. *(Man):* Why did people get angry with Charles Darwin's ideas?

(Woman): Because they flew in the face of their beliefs.

(Narrator): What does the woman mean?

9. *(Woman):* What's wrong? You're as white as a sheet, and your hands are shaking.

(Man): I didn't do well on the psychology exam, and my professor read me the riot act.

(Narrator): What does the man mean?

10. *(Man):* How many people heard Paul McCartney speak about modern music?

(Woman): We were packed in like sardines.

(Narrator): What does the woman mean?

Part B—Long Conversations and Lectures

(Narrator): Directions: In this section, you will hear Long Conversations and Lectures. After each, you will be asked several questions about what you heard, and you will see the questions printed here with four answer choices. Choose an answer and mark it either in the book or on a separate sheet of scrap paper. Remember to answer the questions based on what is stated or implied by the speakers.

(Narrator): Questions 11–15. Listen to two students discuss a famous British writer.

(Man): Dickens got his start as a solicitor's clerk.

(Woman): I don't understand.

(Man): In England, lawyers that represent their clients in court are called barristers. Lawyers that take care of contracts, wills, and that sort of thing are called solicitors.

(Woman): Oh, so Charles Dickens worked in a lawyer's office.

(Man): Right, and considering his childhood, that was a big break.

(Woman): Yeah, I read about that. His father spent some time in prison for owing his creditors too much money. And then Dickens worked as a child in a factory.

(Man): And those experiences certainly influenced his view of life and his writing.

(Woman): I wrote in my notes that he got his start as a newspaper reporter.

(Man): I think that was his first writing job.

(Woman): So, after working as a solicitor's clerk, he worked as a reporter, in the law courts, in Parliament, and on London newspapers. But his first piece of fiction was published in 1833. He wrote short stories and many essays for newspapers and magazines.

(Man): Okay. Now what was his first big success?

(Woman): Hmmm. Right. *The Pickwick Papers.*

(Man): When?

(Woman): In 1837. It was a group of comic sketches published as a serial in 20 monthly installments. And, it was so popular that it made him the most famous writer of his time in England.

(Man): You know, many people write about Charles Dickens being a comic writer, but I think his novels are very serious. *Oliver Twist* is like so many American novels about juvenile delinquents.

(Woman): And he was certainly concerned with conditions in English jails and terrible working conditions in factories and shops.

(Narrator):

11. What is a barrister?
12. What was Charles Dickens' first writing job?
13. What was his first piece of published fiction?
14. How was his first piece of fiction published?
15. What does the woman compare *Oliver Twist* to?

(Narrator): Questions 16–20. Listen to a lecture about the animals of the Serengeti Plain.

(Woman): The Serengeti Plain is in north central Tanzania and is famous for its huge herds of plains animals such as wildebeests, gazelles, and zebras. It is the only place in Africa where vast land-animal migrations still take place. The park, an international tourist attraction, was added to the UNESCO World Heritage List in 1981. The park was established in 1951 and covers 5,700 square miles of some of the best grassland in Africa, as well as extensive acacia woodland savanna.

Many of the animals migrate along the so-called "western corridor" to Lake Victoria. At any given time, there are about 1,300,000 wildebeests, 60,000 zebras, and 150,000 gazelles living there. In addition, there are about 3,000 lions and great numbers of spotted hyenas, leopards, rhinoceroses, hippopotamuses, giraffes, cheetahs, and baboons. Crocodiles inhabit the marshes near the Mara River. More than 350 species of birds, including ostriches, vultures, and flamingos, have also been recorded.

Elephants were not found in the Serengeti thirty years ago, but they have recently moved into the park because humans have developed farms along the edges of the plain. The local elephant population is estimated at some 1,360.

Elephants have been illegally killed for their ivory tusks, but they are not the only animals affected by the human population. The black rhinoceros is now virtually extinct because it was slaughtered for its horn, which is prized in many cultures for dagger handles. The last of the Serengeti's wild dogs disappeared in 1991, but there are some 30,000 domestic dogs in the area. Many scientists believe that unvaccinated domestic dogs spread rabies to the wild dogs, resulting in their local extinction. Despite these problems, there is an active campaign to protect the surviving animals.

(Narrator):

16. What is the Serengeti Plain famous for?
17. How do the animals migrate to Lake Victoria?
18. Why have elephants moved into the Serengeti Plain?
19. According to the speaker, what animals have become virtually extinct?
20. What will the speaker probably discuss next?

(Narrator): Questions 21–25. Listen to a lecture about the Taj Mahal.

(Man): The Taj Mahal is a mausoleum complex in northern India. Its near-perfect proportions and its use of graceful decorative elements make the Taj Mahal the finest example of Mughal architecture. Its design blends the styles of Indian, Persian, and Islam.

The Taj Mahal was built by the Mughal emperor Shah Jahan, who reigned from 1628 to 1658. He wanted to honor his favorite wife, Mumtaz Mahal, who died in childbirth in 1631. She was a remarkable woman and was the emperor's inseparable companion from the time they were married in 1612. She even accompanied her husband on the battlefields of several wars.

The architect Ustad Ahmad Lahawri was probably chief architect of the Taj Mahal, which comprises five main elements: the main gateway, the garden, the mosque, the mausoleum, and the *jawab*, which is a building mirroring the mosque. The mausoleum design includes four minarets, which are towers where Islamic officials, called muezzins, stood as they called the faithful to prayer.

The design of the Taj Mahal followed the rules of Mughal building practice, which allowed no subsequent addition or alteration. Building commenced around 1632, and was an international project. More than 20,000 workers were employed from India, Persia, the Ottoman Empire, and Europe. Construction of the 42-acre complex took twenty-two years and cost between 4 and 5 million rupees.

A tradition holds that Shah Jahan had intended to build another mausoleum across the river to house his own remains. The two structures would be connected by a bridge. However, the emperor was deposed by his son, who imprisoned his father in Agra Fort, where Jahan died.

(Narrator):

21. Why was the Taj Mahal built?
22. According to the speaker, what did the emperor's wife do that was remarkable?
23. How many elements does the design of the Taj Mahal have?
24. According to the speaker, where did the construction workers come from?
25. Where did Shah Jahan die?

Day 30

Review and Relax

Today's Assignment

- Review what you have accomplished so far on your road to taking the TOEFL test. Review the strategies for taking the TOEFL test, look over the *TOEFL Bulletin*, gather the materials and identification papers you will need to take with you to the testing facility, and …

RELAX!

WHAT YOU HAVE ACCOMPLISHED SO FAR

Congratulations! Give yourself a pat on the back! You should feel good about what you have done!

You have probably used computers, and you know how to write with pen, pencil, and paper. Most importantly, you have already taken standardized tests as a part of the promotion and graduation process in your country's educational system. So you know what to expect: many hours in a chair reading and answering questions.

The key to scoring high on any standardized test is knowing what kind of questions are used. You have worked for the last 29 days on learning what kinds of questions the Educational Testing Service will ask you on the TOEFL test. You have learned how to answer the questions. You have drilled with the different sections of the test, and you have practiced taking tests that are timed similarly to the actual TOEFL test.

You have filled out all the complicated application forms and gathered all the identification papers that are required for you to take the test.

What now?

Review the Testing Procedures Described in the *TOEFL Bulletin*

Make sure that you have all the necessary identification papers. If you are taking the TOEFL test outside of your country, you must present your passport to the officials at the test facility. Test center personnel will check your identification before assigning you a seat at the test center. You will be asked to sign the test center log and fill in the time. The administrator will check your signature to verify that you are the person in your photo identification, and this procedure will be repeated before and after all breaks. You must go to the center alone. Parents, other members of your family, and your friends will not be allowed into the center. Reread the bulletin for detailed instructions about being admitted to the test center.

The bulletin tells you to arrive at the test center at least 30 minutes before your test is scheduled to begin. So make sure you know different ways to arrive at the test center on time. In large urban areas, subways and commuter trains sometimes break down, and you may have to find alternate transportation quickly. Bridges, tunnels, and highways have a way of getting blocked. Test center personnel are sympathetic, but they are required to enforce rules strictly. If you arrive late, they may not admit you to the test.

Reread the sections on test center procedures and regulations. Particularly important is their ban on books, pamphlets, cell phones, print or electronic dictionaries, scratch paper, translation devices, calculators, watch calculators, lap-top computers, and other devices. Check the bulletin for the complete list. Take nothing with you that is on that list.

Dress comfortably. It is unnecessary for you to wear clothing appropriate for a school or job interview. You should dress appropriately for the climate of the city where your test center is located. Your test center may or may not be air conditioned. If it is, it may become uncomfortably chilly for you during the test. If you take the test during the winter, the test room may get too hot—or too cold. So wear clothing in layers: take a jacket or sweater that you can put on or take off as conditions in the room require.

Review All the Strategies

To review is NOT to re-read every word in every chapter. To review is to spend only about 30 minutes scanning through Days 1 through 9. Remind yourself of what you knew before you began working through this book. Remind yourself of what you have learned during the last 29 days. What about all those strategies, all that grammar and vocabulary? Well, you won't forget them, because you have used them.

Relax

After you have done all of the above, take the rest of the day off. An important part of the learning process is knowing when to stop. As important as hard work and discipline are to a student, taking a break is just as vital. During a break, your mind is still working, just not the same part that you use to acquire information. While you are relaxing, a different part of your mind is assessing, analyzing, and synthesizing what you have learned. And preparing it for your use. So, go to a movie, watch TV, stroll through the local shopping mall, eat at your favorite restaurant. You are not being lazy. You are being a good student.

The night before you take the test, go to bed knowing you are prepared. Go to bed and sleep. You need the energy that sleeps restores to you.

You are ready for the TOEFL test.